THE SOMME 1916
Crucible of a British Army

THE SOMME 1916

Crucible of a British Army

Written and illustrated by

MICHAEL CHAPPELL

WINDROW & GREENE

LONDON

Dedication

To Marilyn, for her unflagging support and encouragement.

Acknowledgements

The author wishes to express his gratitude to the following
for their assistance during the preparation of this book:
Mr Ken Dunn of Deal, Kent; Mr A.J.Rogers of Hythe, Kent;
Mr C.D.Roberts of Bunker Militaria, Kent; the late Mr Ray Westlake
of Newport, Gwent; Mr & Mrs P.Bell of West Wickham, Kent;
Mr Gerry Embleton; Mr Paul Hannon; Mr G.Nevill;
Mr Martin Pegler; The Prince Consort's Library, Aldershot,
Hampshire; The Royal Artillery Historical Trust, Woolwich,
London; and finally to my publishers,
for their help and encouragement.

This edition first published in Great Britain 1995 by
Windrow & Greene Ltd
5 Gerrard Street
London W1V 7LJ

© Michael Chappell

Design by Victor Shreeve

Printed and bound in Great Britain by
The Amadeus Press
Huddersfield, Yorkshire

A CIP catalogue record for this book
is available from the British Library

Standard edition
ISBN 1 85915 007 1

De luxe edition
ISBN 1 85915 012 8

CONTENTS

Eighty Years On: Perception and Reality

The Great War in retrospect; the tolerated deception. Unjustified dismissal of the achievements of the British armies of 1916. Background to the battles. The seeds of eventual German defeat and Allied victory sown on the battlefields of the Somme.

Prologue: Serre, 1 July 1916

The 11th East Lancashires at Serre; the crucifixion of the Accrington Pals. The French sector, 1 July 1916; the advance of XIII Corps, and the lessons learnt.

The Armies

Germany, a nation in arms; conscription, training and reserve service; mobilisation. The French Army: wagering on aggressive élan to win a short war. Great Britain: an army created overnight. The British Expeditionary Force, and the Kitchener expansion.

"One Policy, One Army, One Front"

Background to the joint Anglo-French offensive; Joffre and Haig; a battle to relieve pressure on Verdun. The terrain; German defences on the Somme. Rawlinson's appreciation of Fourth Army's task. The British build-up; the plan of battle.

Bombardment and Barrage

The mission, and resources, of the British artillery. The development of the artillery during the Great War. Shortcomings of command and control; of indirect fire; of communications; tactical confusion. The "Fuse, Graze No.100". The bombardment, 24 to 30 June.

The Infantry Battle on 1 July: VII, VIII and X Corps

Gommecourt: VII Corps, 46th and 56th Divisions. Serre and Beaumont Hamel: VIII Corps, 31st, 29th and 4th Divisions. Thiepval: X Corps, 32nd and 36th Divisions.

The Infantry Battle on 1 July: III, XV and XIII Corps

Ovillers and La Boisselle: III Corps, 34th and 8th Divisions. Fricourt and Mametz: XV Corps, 21st and 7th Divisions. Montauban: XIII Corps, 18th and 30th Divisions. The French Sector. Summary of the first day.

GLOSSARY

Battalion Unit of infantry, nominally 1,000 officers and men but in action about 20 officers and 700 men. Made up of a headquarters and usually four companies; a Lieutenant-Colonel's command.

Battery In the Royal Artillery, a unit operating four to six guns.

BEF British Expeditionary Force

Brigade (Infantry) In 1916, a headquarters, four battalions, a machine gun company and a light trench mortar battery; commanded by a Brigadier-General, with a Brigade Major as his principal staff officer. (Artillery) a Group of batteries; a Lieutenant-Colonel's command.

C-in-C Commander-in-Chief

Company An infantry company had an establishment of about 200 men divided into four platoons – in battle the strength could be anything from 100 to 150; a Captain's command.

Corps (Army Corps) A grouping of divisions under the command of a Lieutenant-General. "Corps troops" under command included heavy artillery, machine gunners, cavalry, signals and motor transport.

Division A self-contained fighting formation of three infantry brigades and supporting artillery, engineer, signals, medical and motor transport units. In 1916, about 19,000 men, 5,000 horses, 64 guns, 40 mortars, 200 machine guns, 850 vehicles, 70 motor vehicles; a Major-General's command.

Formation A group of units, for example a division.

GOC General Officer Commanding

Gun General term used to describe an artillery piece of any kind. Specifically, used to define a piece firing a shell at high velocity and low trajectory.

HE High explosive

Howitzer Artillery piece firing a shell at low velocity and high trajectory, passing over obstacles to drop steeply on its target.

Mortar (Trench-) A simple weapon, usually no more than a smooth-bore tube, designed to project its "bombs" at low velocity and high angles; of limited range but great destructive power.

NCO Non-commissioned officer

OP Observation post

Platoon Infantry sub-unit, a Lieutenant's command; 50 men "on paper", in battle about 35 or less.

RA Royal Artillery

RE Royal Engineers

RFA Royal Field Artillery (operating horse-drawn field guns).

RFC Royal Flying Corps

RGA Royal Garrison Artillery (operating tractor-drawn heavy guns).

RHA Royal Horse Artillery (operating the field guns supporting cavalry formations).

TF Territorial Force

Tommy From "Tommy Atkins" – the popular slang term for a British soldier.

Unit A battalion-sized group of soldiers.

CHAPTER ONE

Eighty Years On: Perception and Reality

"The first casualty when war comes is truth." In 1917, when these words were spoken to the Senate of the United States, the Senators had before them the example of what was happening in Europe. There the governments of the warring nations had for years used national security, political expediency, or propaganda as reasons for concealing, distorting, or contradicting the truth. The effect had been to place before their respective publics a sanitised version of the conduct of the war which played down the horror and the cost of the fighting. Patriotism and sacrifice were lauded; heroism – real and imaginary – was lavishly praised; leaders were lionised in a manner that seems obsequious by today's standards; and the sordid business of war in the trenches was dressed in the trappings of a crusade. Dissent was ruthlessly crushed, particularly if it took the form of an attempt to bring to the attention of the public a true account of anything that had been suppressed or distorted.

By the time peace was restored it was in the interest of the majority to leave the record as it stood. Families and communities mourning their fallen loved ones, or nursing the casualties who had returned, had come to terms with the horror of war as they had been given to understand it, and wanted no controversy or muck-raking to reawaken their anguish. The returning soldiers knew the truth only too well, but were content to pick up their civilian lives and to shut their minds to any discussion of contentious aspects of the war. Thus the official view of the Great War of 1914-1918 passed into history complete with – to use a modernism – most of the "spin" imposed by the wartime leadership. As far as the British Empire was concerned, the aching sense of individual loss could be assuaged to some extent by a collective consensual satisfaction regarding the official record. The British had, after all, won.

Disenchantment with the British conduct of the war took a long time to emerge, delayed as it was by another World War and by the continuing respect felt for war leaders in their lifetimes. It was perhaps the collapse of their empire and the decline of their international influence after 1945 that caused the British to examine the war of 1914-1918 more critically than before. Considered, as it was, to be the main cause of Britain's long decline, enquiry into the direction and conduct of the war took on a new significance. The coming of the television age, and the rejection of the moral codes of earlier generations bred to acceptance of all forms of social authority, furthered the debate and deepened the analysis, in the course of which many of the lies, half-truths and evasions of the 1914-1918 period were exposed.

But the revelations have done little to lift the shroud of mystery that still surrounds the great battles of the Western Front. With only specialist military historians able to fully comprehend their scope and complexity, campaigns such as Ypres, Verdun and Passchendaele have attained a misty, legendary status in the perception of the public at large to equal any of the great battles of history. For the British this is especially so in the case of the Battle of the Somme: their first great test of war, and a campaign which extracted a sacrifice from most homes in the land, the memories of which are not yet fully stilled.

Mention "the Somme" to an Englishman, Scotsman, Welshman or Ulsterman of middle or older years and it is unlikely that he will immediately think of a river meandering through the countryside of northern France; the name will almost certainly strike a morbid chord in his mind. It is synonymous with suffering and death, with the awful moonscape battlefields of the Great War and the slaughter of hundreds of thousands of his countrymen. In his reaction he will be typical of the generations of his race since 1916, when those British military operations carried out in Picardy implanted "the Battle of the Somme" in the consciousness of the British people.

The images conjured up will be little less vivid for being second-hand; by now those who fought in the battles and survived into old age have all but passed away. But in their time they passed down the folklore of the Somme to the generations who have maintained an interest sufficient to support the extensive literary outpouring which the battles continue to generate. British fascination with the Somme is not confined to the study of its literature, however. It is particularly apparent in the numbers of those who seek further contact by visits to the battlefields, and to museums preserving relics of the fighting. Societies have been formed to further the study of the battles; artefacts are traded at ever-increasing prices, and researchers delve into material of all kinds. Visual research includes the study of paintings and drawings of the time, and an almost forensic analysis of the images recorded by war photographers and – perhaps most poignant of all – of those brief moments of the battles recorded on ciné-film.

Later cinema and television offerings taking the Somme battles as their subject have tended to truncate or distort the facts in the interests of dramatic presentation or political slant. In this they follow a trend which, over the years, has been established by a succession of writers, who have picked over the historical record in a somewhat selective manner to produce a distillation of the facts to suit their themes – normally, a simple rage at the waste and the tragedy. The result of this selectivity is the current popular image of the battles of 1916, in which hundreds of thousands of eager young volunteers are seen to have been committed by their generals to the "Big Push", an irresistible offensive that was to have broken the German line, but which foundered on the enemy barbed wire under a hail of high explosive and machine gun fire.

Recounting the agony of the cost in lives and broken bodies and minds perpetuates the sense of loss felt by the

General, later Field-Marshal Sir Douglas Haig commanded the British Expeditionary Force from December 1915 until the final victory. A Lowland Scot born in 1861, he was educated at Clifton, Oxford University and the Royal Military Academy Sandhurst before receiving a commission in the 7th Hussars. Haig saw active service in the Sudan and in the South African War of 1899-1902, in which he gain promotion to Colonel. Service in India was followed by the appointment of Inspector General of Cavalry. Promoted to Lieutenant-General in 1910, he became General Officer Commanding Aldershot in 1912. Haig took I Corps to France in 1914; became commander of the First Army on its formation in December 1914; and replaced Sir John French in command of the BEF a year later.

Haig's virtues and weaknesses as a general will always be the subject of argument; but he was certainly the best the British had, and the reactionary opinions which are so often quoted against him are largely irrelevant to his actual conduct of operations. He commanded a huge army of nearly 60 divisions, and moulded it into the finest fighting machine of its time. A sound staff officer, he administered a force that had been created in an incredibly short period of time; dealt diplomatically with his allies; and showed a firm grasp when handling the professional politicians. Haig has been held responsible by historians for the terrible casualties suffered by Britain and her Empire on the Western Front. The only way these might have been avoided would have been to hold the line and avoid offensive operations – a choice that was simply not open to him. Given the actual circumstances that existed, victory could only be won by battles of attrition. Haig's keen sense of duty and unswerving single-mindedness enabled him to lead the BEF to its part in the great victory of 1918. After the war he was created 1st Earl of Bemersyde and given an award of £100,000. He died in 1928, having devoted the last ten years of his life to working for service charities. (Imperial War Museum Q3254)

British to this day, whilst the quest for those responsible for the carnage stops at the field commanders, usually labelling them and their staffs as incompetents. The 57,000 casualties sustained on the first day of the offensive, a truly grisly statistic, are frequently recalled as irrefutable proof of the senselessness of it all; while the fact that the campaign was pursued for more than four months for the gain of a few square miles of French downland, at the further cost of hundreds of thousands more casualties, is seen as a hideous act of human folly.

This perception, by now well established, makes rational analysis of the campaign difficult, and consequently does less than justice to the British Army of 1916. Whilst never denying their courage, it casts a slur on the competence of the men who fought and the officers who led them; and by ignoring, or failing to recognise the handicaps they fought under, devalues their actual achievements in the Somme battles.

The sheer scale of those battles has always made their comprehension and analysis difficult. Vast numbers of men were sent into action on the Somme, and vast quantities of high explosive were fired into a comparatively small arena of battle to produce chaotic struggles that were described by many of the participants as hell on earth. The full story of what took place suffered immediate attenuation as those who experienced the fighting became casualties. Most of the survivors did not record their experiences, and the after-action reports and official histories have tended to suppress unpalatable facts. Discouraging any attempt to evaluate the tactical performance of the armies involved has been the understandably morbid preoccupation with the enormous cost in human life and the reverence accorded the glorious dead (both of which inhibit criticism by all but the most insensitive); and the inability of the public at large to comprehend the more obscure military technicalities and tactical concepts.

In the never-ending search for scapegoats the accusation of folly is perhaps far more justly levelled at those responsible for the events which led to the war: the leaders of those European states who played that particularly dangerous game of power politics in which the threat of military action, backed by huge conscripted armies – "nations in arms" – was ever present. Few shrank from the prospect of war. On the advice of their military experts, most imagined that a European war would be a brief and inexpensive clash, a war of manoeuvre that would be settled in weeks for little expenditure of life and wealth. The naiveté of such convictions, when compared with what actually took place from 1914 to 1918, can only be seen in retrospect as criminal folly – judgement so flawed that today it beggars belief.

Great Britain was party to this deadly game by virtue of her empire, her wealth and her position as the greatest naval power in the world; but certainly not because of the size of her army. Compared to the manpower of the armies of Germany, Russia or France, the British Army deserved the sneer of "contemptibly little" thrown at it in 1914. A small, long-service force, it was well-suited to the maintenance of the British Empire; it functioned on a low budget and, to take a cynical view, its small size guaranteed that any British involvement in a European war would be limited or token.

Following the outbreak of war in August 1914 the belligerent nations were confounded by the turn events

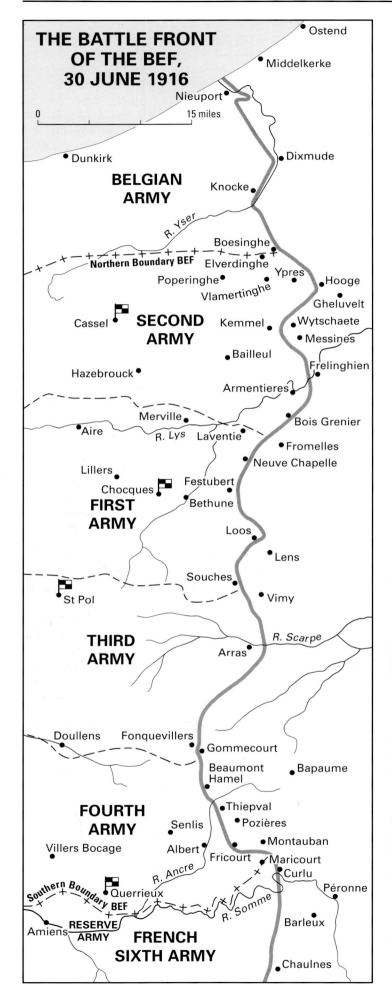

THE BATTLE FRONT
OF THE BEF,
30 JUNE 1916

0 _____ 15 miles

Ostend
Middelkerke
Nieuport
Dunkirk
Dixmude
BELGIAN
ARMY
Knocke
R. Yser
Boesinghe
Northern Boundary BEF
Elverdinghe
Ypres
Poperinghe
Hooge
Vlamertinghe
Gheluvelt
Cassel
SECOND
ARMY
Kemmel
Wytschaete
Messines
Bailleul
Hazebrouck
Frelinghien
Armentieres
Merville
Bois Grenier
Aire
R. Lys
Laventie
Fromelles
Neuve Chapelle
Lillers
Festubert
Chocques
Bethune
FIRST
ARMY
Loos
Lens
Souches
St Pol
Vimy
THIRD
ARMY
R. Scarpe
Arras
Doullens
Fonquevillers
Gommecourt
Beaumont
Hamel
Bapaume
Thiepval
FOURTH
ARMY
Senlis
Pozières
Villers Bocage
Montauban
Albert
Fricourt
Maricourt
R. Ancre
Curlu
Péronne
Southern Boundary BEF
Querrieux
R. Somme
Amiens
RESERVE
ARMY
Barleux
FRENCH
SIXTH ARMY
Chaulnes

took. There was no short, sharp clash in the West, no quick and decisive outcome. Thwarted in its advance through Belgium and into France, the German Army dug in to hold the ground it had seized, leaving the French, Belgian and British allies with the choice of either driving it from its gains or seeking an armistice under the most unfavourable terms. The decision to continue the fight left the British – whose original Expeditionary Force of pre-war regulars had suffered heavy casualties by Christmas 1914 – with the task of creating an army of continental proportions in an impossibly short time. It was to be the largest army Britain ever put into the field and, in the event, one that began its existence with almost every disadvantage that years of unpreparedness and military penny-pinching could have assured.

Manpower was the one commodity not in short supply. Hundreds of thousands of patriotic volunteers flocked to the colours in response to their nation's call. But with little in the way of weapons, ammunition, clothing and equipment, and without anything worthy of the name of a training organisation, much of their time was wasted as they waited

(IWM Q23612)

for the factories to turn out their requirements and for the military to put together the apparatus with which they might be trained, led, and generally made ready for war.

It was to be the summer of 1916 before this new British Army was seen to have surmounted these difficulties; had been transported to the seat of the war; and was judged equal to the task of mounting a major offensive on the Western Front. By this time the original four divisions of the British Expeditionary Force had grown to 55; but by this time also the German Army, while still maintaining the ground it had captured, was exerting extreme pressure on the French with an offensive at Verdun which opened in late February 1916. This burden on the French Army required relief, and affected the timing and location of the British effort and the French participation in it. Whatever plans the commander and staff of the BEF may have had to attack the German line under advantageous circumstances were put aside in the interests of their French ally. Pressure was placed upon the British to undertake offensive operations as soon as possible.

The ground chosen was that part of the front crossed by the river Somme in Picardy, where the British and French

sectors of the line met. Here the enemy was to be struck a decisive blow by a joint Anglo-French force, to effect a classic war-winning breakthrough or, failing that, to involve the Germans in a battle of "attrition" until such time as the German leadership was forced to come to the negotiating table under terms favourable to the Allies. Whatever the outcome, there was by then no alternative for the British Army on the Somme but to do its duty by fighting the battle that now confronted it. From Commander-in-Chief down to the last private soldier, it had been carried along by a tide of events that had created it, had brought it to this place, and had presented it with the orders that must now be carried out.

As the men of the formations chosen for the "Big Push" prepared for battle, few recorded any doubts that they were fully equipped or properly trained for the task ahead. Most expressed the confidence they felt on seeing the vast assembly of manpower, weapons and ammunition gathered for the assault, and at the sight and sounds of the unprecedented artillery bombardment of the enemy lines. All felt that they were ready for and equal to the task that faced them.

That task was to attack and capture ground held by the soldiers of what was then the most efficient army on earth. The German Army of 1916 was the product of a military system that had grown with the empire it served, drawing in its manpower by conscription, held in esteem by its people, and commanded by the ablest general staff in the world. It had undergone nearly two years of combat experience to place an edge on the high standard of training with which it had entered the war; and now it stood ready behind a formidable series of fortifications, dug in and wired in on ground of its own choosing. As the hours ticked away towards zero, and the British and French artillery pounded the German positions astride the Somme, the scene was set for the clash of two completely differing military systems.

Poised to strike was a British Army that had been created in a ridiculously short period of time, from a horde of patriotic volunteers and the remnants of its peacetime regulars, in a triumph of improvisation – a great, amateur enterprise in the best British tradition. Opposing it was the army of a country that had been preparing itself for this war for a very long time. Every bit as patriotic and as enterprising as the British volunteers, and better prepared, the Germans were fighting to gain for their Fatherland the position and power they felt its due. The German Army on the Somme awaited the onslaught of the Allies with the calm determination of professionals.

What took place once battle was joined is a story that has been told many times, and which is retold in the following chapters. The fighting on the Somme in 1916 went on for over four-and-a-half months at a horrendous cost in lives, with little gain in the way of ground, and failed to achieve an Allied breakthrough. It proved, like the monstrous struggle taking place simultaneously around Verdun to the south-east, to be a campaign of attrition – a competition in the infliction and endurance of pain. There were, however, two results that the popular histories sometimes undervalue or ignore.

The first is that the German Army suffered in the Somme battles to such an extent that, although able to carry on the war for another two years and to take full advantage of the Russian collapse, it was never again the effective machine of

(IWM Q37361)

early 1916. At the conclusion of the Somme fighting one German war leader stated that "The German Army had been fought to a standstill and was utterly worn out." Another said, "We must save the men from a second Somme battle." The German Army's collapse of late 1918 had its beginnings in the pounding it took on the Somme. Attrition – the cynical trade-off in lives, material and wealth – proved to be a war-winning strategy.

Secondly, it must be claimed that however bloody the means and ghastly the cost, the Somme was the training ground of the British Army. Committed to the first battles with only a rudimentary knowledge of their trade, the survivors were forced to learn in the bitterest and most unforgiving school of all. Artillerymen, infantrymen, sappers, machine gunners, fliers, and later tankmen: all gained the expertise in battle that they had not developed in their training. This expertise, particularly that of the gunners, was applied as a tactical doctrine which, as it took hold, brought professionalism to an army of amateurs, and enabled the British Army to fight its way through the war to play the major part in the victory of 1918.

The Somme 1916 was, beyond question, the greatest test of the British Army between 1914 and 1918. From a disas-trous beginning it pursued a campaign which kept the enemy under extreme pressure, eventually forcing him to abandon much of the territory for which he had fought so tenaciously, and to revise his concept of defence. As iron emerges from the flame and heat of the crucible as steel, so the British Army emerged from the battlefields of the Somme transformed into a military machine the equal of any on earth. Confident in its new-found skills, it was fully aware of the awful realities of war, yet grimly determined to fight on to victory.

★   ★   ★

There is one mental picture of the Somme fighting so harshly ingrained in our collective imagination that every reader must unconsciously be waiting to encounter it. It is perhaps as well to depart at once from a chronological sequence, and to place it at the head of this account as a reference point for what follows. Given its symbolic power, no sober attempt to understand these events can realistically be made until the scene has been faced.

CHAPTER TWO

Prologue: Serre, 1 July 1916

Crowded into the trenches from which they were to assault the German positions before Serre, Lt.Col.A.W.Rickman and his battalion – the 11th East Lancashires – endured a galling fire from enemy artillery as they waited for 7.30a.m., Zero Hour, on 1 July 1916. A New Army battalion, "Kitchener men", the 11th East Lancashires were part of the 94th Infantry Brigade, 31st Division, on the extreme left of the British line.

Overnight, gaps had been opened in the British wire and white tapes laid through them to guide the attackers. At first light these had become only too obvious to the enemy, who increased their fire on the British lines, including the machine gun concentrations which now began to fall on the trench parapets. A steady trickle of East Lancashire wounded began to make their way back from the assembly trenches to the aid posts. The harassing German batteries and machine guns should – according to the Corps artillery plan – have been destroyed or neutralised by the "counter-battery" programme that had gone on for several days; at least, that was the theory. At 6.25a.m. the East Lancashires gained relief when the British artillery began an intensive bombardment of the German positions under which, it seemed, nothing could live.

Suddenly, at 7.20a.m., the British bombardment stopped as the gunners spun their elevating wheels and ranged on to the German second line. Whistles blew, and the men of the first wave of the 11th East Lancashires climbed from their battered trenches and filed through the gaps in their own wire. Bowed under their burdens of weapons, ammunition, equipment and tools, their casualties increased as they moved into no-man's-land. The German artillery, both heavy and field, fell once more upon the British trenches, catching the follow-up waves as they strove to take up position on the first wave who were, by now, deployed forward of the British wire.

Rapid fire from the brigade Stokes mortar battery commenced at 7.22a.m., but this did not prevent the German infantry from emerging from the dug-outs in which they had endured the British barrage, to man what was left of their fire-steps. Some German riflemen stood clear of the trenches, the better to shoot, while some machine gunners ran forward towards the advancing British to set up their weapons in shellholes in no-man's-land. At 7.30a.m. the whistles shrilled again; and all four waves of the 11th (Service) Battalion, The East Lancashire Regiment – the "Accrington Pals" – rose from cover and advanced up the grassy slope towards their enemy.

To the continuing German artillery fire was now added the machine gun and rifle fire of their infantry. As if this were not enough, the unengaged German positions to the East Lancashires' left remained unobscured by a planned smokescreen, and began to fire machine gun concentrations in enfilade. In the face of this devastating fire the Accrington Pals simply marched on "until wounded or killed", as one survivor put it; and by 7.50a.m. the issue had been decided. German fire had done for most of the 11th East Lancashires. The few who got as far as the enemy wire found it mostly unbroken by the shrapnel of the British artillery, constructed as it was in impenetrable banks up to five feet high. The fewer still who got through the wire and into the German positions were either killed or made captive. None returned. The missing swelled the casualty list of 234 killed and 360 wounded. Lieutenant-Colonel Rickman, himself wounded, had witnessed the death of his fine battalion in a matter of minutes on that bright summer morning.

The Accrington Pals had been badly served by their supporting artillery, which had failed to silence the enemy guns, failed to sufficiently smash the German wire, and failed in their Corps commander's boasted intention to destroy the German trenches so that "there would not even be a rat alive". To carry out their tasks the VIII Corps artillery before Serre had deployed one heavy gun every 44 yards and one field gun every 20 yards. On 1 July their programme for the support of the assault called for six "lifts" to conform with the planned movement of the infantry, the heavy artillery lifting straight to the next objective and the field artillery "creeping" between objectives in hundred-yard steps. The 4.5in. howitzers were to engage machine guns and fortifications, and two 18-pounder batteries per division were held in readiness to move forward in support of the expected successes. In the words of the official history "The heavy artillery bombardment in this sector...had not been successful." This example of dessicated understatement may be an inadequate epitaph for the dead of the Accrington Pals – whose ill-fated choice of serving with their neighbours and workmates condemned their home town, like so many others, to an appalling collective bereavement on 1 July; but it encapsulates the reason why they died in such numbers and to so little avail.

The French sector, 1 July 1916

The dismal fate that befell the 11th East Lancashires was repeated southward all along the British line, as the infantry assaults by other battalions were bloodily repulsed for little or no gain. The exceptions were to be found in those British formations fighting alongside the French Sixth Army. Positioned astride the river Somme, the French took all their objectives, and more, on the first day of the offensive, and did so in a manner that inevitably invites invidious comparison between the Allies on 1 July. French heavy artillery concentrated south of the river outnumbered the enemy by a ratio of 85 batteries to eight, which, combined with skilful infantry tactics, enabled their I Colonial Corps to push on beyond their objective for the day.

North of the river the French XX Corps advanced with

equal success to seize their objectives. On the left of the French was the British XIII Corps, composed entirely of Kitchener "New Army" formations. Moving in alignment with the French, and sharing the secure flank provided by their success, the assaulting battalions of XIII Corps also enjoyed the support of French artillery in addition to their own. Their orders stated: "The advance of the infantry will be covered by a heavy barrage from all...guns and mortars. The heavy artillery barrage will lift directly from one line to the next. The field artillery barrage will creep back by short lifts [there were to be 35 such lifts]....The lifts have been timed so as to allow the infantry plenty of time for the advance...on the principle that it is preferable that the infantry should wait for the barrage to lift than that the latter should lift prematurely, and thus allow the enemy to man his parapets."

In their advance to their second and third objectives, the British infantry were to move behind a shrapnel barrage travelling at 50 yards every one-and-a-half minutes. Gun density was to be one heavy gun every 47 yards, and one field gun every 17 yards of front. Combined with that of the French XX Corps on its right, the artillery of XIII Corps outnumbered that of the enemy by a ratio of nearly four to one. By 1 July it had so battered the German artillery that there was, in the words of the official history, "At most a complete absence of artillery reply. Indeed, so well had it done its work that...there was little resistance except for a few of the strongpoints, and machine guns, not artillery, were responsible for the British casualties". Perhaps the official historian overstated his case; but the situation on the XIII Corps front was very different from that at Serre.

No British or French unit had an easy task on 1 July 1916, and the actions described so briefly here omit mention of the skill and tenacity demonstrated by the infantry as they fought their way forward. But what they clearly demonstrate is that only those infantry units operating with effective support had a "fighting chance" of succeeding. The Kitchener battalions of XIII Corps suffered casualties almost as severe as those of the Accrington Pals; but at least they had the satisfaction of defeating their enemy and driving him from his positions.

If the British assault on 1 July 1916 had been, overall, a failure, that failure pointed up the many lessons that had to be absorbed and adapted to – quickly. For the British Army the learning began in earnest from this date.

CHAPTER THREE

The Armies

By 1916, what had begun as a European war had widened into a world conflict. As other nations joined the quarrel fronts opened in lands far from "the cockpit of Europe", and a bitter war raged at sea. But the Western Front – the parallel of field fortifications that ran from the Channel coast to the Swiss border – remained the arena where the war would be won or lost. Here the main German Army stood at bay, conquerors of most of Belgium and a rich tract of northern France. Confronting them were the French Army; a handful of Belgian divisions resolutely clinging to a small unoccupied corner of their country; and a British Expeditionary Force steadily growing in manpower and equipment, which would gradually take over more and more of the line from the hard-pressed French, who for almost two years played the major role in containing the Germans. The great Somme battles of 1916 were to involve three distinctly different military machines; it will be worthwhile to examine each of them.

Germany: A nation in arms

The German Army of 1914 had its origins in the Napoleonic Wars, growing with the empire it served, and reaching maturity with its crushing victory over France in the Franco-Prussian war of 1870-71. Over the years it developed into a conscript army, taking the recruits it required from the reservoir of manpower provided by the entire able-bodied citizenry of the German state. Having trained them during their period of full-time service, the army discharged them to resume their civilian lives but to remain part of the military reserve system. By these means Germany was able to maintain a very large standing army backed by an enormous reserve. In time of war the active army could be expanded, reinforced and supported by virtually every able-bodied man in the German nation.

It was, however, not merely numbers that made their army so formidable. German organisation and training proved to be superior to those of any other army. On the outbreak of war in 1914 the high quality of the German reservists was immediately apparent as they mobilised into field formations to double the strength of the German Army. Going straight into action, these Reserve Divisions proved themselves the equal of the active formations. The German military system of the early 20th century was based on four basic principles: universal conscription, the localisation of units and formations (both active and reserve), periodic training for those on the reserve, and the maintenance of reserve cadres upon which reservists could mobilise.

A young German was required to register for military service at the age of seventeen. If a medical examination proved him to be fit, and if he was one of the 50 to 60 per cent of the annual class chosen for service, then at the age of 20 he would be ordered to the barracks of the active regiment with which he would undergo his training and serve

out his time with the colours – invariably, a regiment based near his family home. If drafted to the infantry he would serve for two years; if he became a cavalryman or an artilleryman he would serve for three. When his full-time service was completed he would be transferred to the reserve, to be recalled for an annual training commitment of one month. At the age of 27 he passed into the *Landwehr*, a lower grade of reserve but still liable for mobilisation in time of war, and still with a liability for periodic training. When 39 years of age he passed into the *Landsturm*, a force intended for garrison and guard duties in wartime. At the age of 45 he passed off the military register.

By 1914 the German Empire was divided into 24 military districts, each of which was the recruiting and garrison area for an active Army Corps consisting of two divisions. Each district maintained the cadres of officers and non-commissioned officers nominated to lead its reserve units after mobilisation. On mobilisation being ordered, the active units would be brought to full strength by reservists from the 23 to 24 year age group, whilst the remainder of the reserve typically formed a separate Army Corps, bearing the number of the active formation but with the title "Reserve". Surplus reservists would be formed into *Ersatz*

An anonymous German machine gun company NCO who may stand as a type for a whole proud culture of professional militarism. Photographed in 1915, wearing the ribbon of the Iron Cross, he is a "Vizefeldwebel u.Offizier-Aspirant" – a Sergeant and Officer Candidate, who would almost certainly have been a company officer by 1916.(Courtesy G.A.Embleton)

(replacement) battalions and *Landwehr* regiments for the support of the active formations (and further *Ersatz* and *Landwehr* units with other roles), to bring the totals fielded by a typical district to over 70 battalions of infantry, six artillery regiments and three cavalry regiments. In addition to the units mentioned the district controlled large numbers of uncommitted reservists, particularly of the *Landsturm* and the *Ersatz Reserve* (those men originally not called for service). Once trained, the latter would provide reinforcements and replacements for units in action.

By these means the German Empire could, on mobilisation, almost double the strength of its active field army and increase its military manpower six-fold. The peacetime establishment of 25 Army Corps (51 divisions), with a strength of 800,000 men, would be supplemented by 14 Reserve Army Corps (31 divisions), 20 *Ersatz* brigades, 30 *Landwehr* brigades, and hundreds of thousands of auxiliary troops, the total mobilised manpower being in the region of five million men. This staggering feat of organisation was kept secret by the Germans, especially the plan for the mobilisation of the reserve formations. It was hoped that their sudden and unexpected appearance on the field of battle would be a war-winning stroke.

Controlling the product of this organisational masterpiece was a corps of long-service officers and NCOs whose qualities of leadership, skill and professional knowledge were recognised to be unequalled by any other continental army. Directing them was a General Staff that was beyond dispute the best in the world; and solidly behind their army stood the German people, who had, over the years, developed a pride in their military that was unmatched elsewhere (save, perhaps, by the British affection for their Royal Navy). As the German Empire grew in power the whole ethos of militaristic fervour rose to a fever pitch, fostered by the national leaders' declared ambitions. Moving towards war and welcoming the chance to unleash its military might, Germany in 1914 was truly a nation in arms.

Amongst those arms were weapons that were to give the Germans a definite material edge in the fighting to come. Alone amongst military thinkers German planners had recognised the limitations of field guns when used against fortifications, compared to the effectiveness of the heavy howitzer firing high explosive shell; they ensured that the German Army would go to war with an adequate provision of howitzers of all calibres (some 3,500 heavy pieces to France's 300). In pre-war training and manoeuvres extensive use had been made of indirect fire techniques, indicating remarkable forethought on the part of those responsible for the German artillery's tactical doctrine. The potential of machine guns was appreciated in much the same way. These weapons and many others were supplied by an armaments industry which grew as it satisfied the demands of the German armed forces, and which made huge profits from the orders it exported to clients overseas. (The firm of Krupp, for example, exported 44 per cent of the arms they produced. German small arms manufacturers exported nearly three million rifles between 1890 and 1912.)

With the July crisis of 1914 and the declaration of war against France on 3 August, Germany mobilised a field army of 84,000 officers and 2,314,000 men; and moved to their war stations, by railway, in less than three weeks, over two million men, 400,000 tons of war material and 118,000

German infantrymen of the 268th Regt. pose with their M15 gasmasks in a well-constructed trench, 1915/16. The man at right has the canvas gasmask bag on his belt, and wears grey canvas trench waders. Three have covered the red bands of their field caps with drab cloth. (Courtesy G.Nevill)

Two "Frontschwein" in a trench shelter (not a deep dug-out), surrounded by their personal equipment, a cloth-covered Pickelhaube helmet, messtins, etc. The cheerful veteran in the foreground wears the ribbons of the Iron Cross and another decoration. (Courtesy G.Nevill)

NCO and men of a Saxon machine gun section, with their MG08 on its adjustable "sledge" mount – this allowed the gun to be mounted low above the ground for prone firing. By the outbreak of war each three-battalion infantry regiment had its own (13th) machine gun company of six guns; in 1914 further Corps troops were dispersed to some regiments as 14th companies; and there were a number of independent MG companies attached to divisions. In late 1916 a rationalisation gave each infantry battalion an MG company – 72 guns per division. (Courtesy G.Nevill)

"Handgranatentrupp" or bombing party of the 40th Fusilier Regt., 1916; note the cloth-covered Pickelhaube helmets with the spikes removed, characteristic of the early months of the Somme fighting, although the M16 steel helmet was starting to appear. Some men are festooned with stick-grenades; others carry planks, tools and empty sandbags to barricade trenches, and extra bandoliers of rifle ammunition; one has a steel "sniper's plate" with a peep-hole and prop; the NCO (centre) has a holstered Luger pistol.(Courtesy G.A.Embleton)

A German infantry section pose in a trench, probably late 1916 – several wear the M16 steel helmet, two of them with extra rein-forcing plates strapped to the front of the skull. The man standing at right has the extra-capacity 20-round Ansteckmagazin fitted to his G98 rifle; these were not widely issued. The box let into the parapet (right) is a hand grenade store.
(Courtesy G.Nevill)

horses. On 2 August Luxembourg was occupied, and on the 4th the Belgian frontier was crossed. As expected, the French were caught unawares by the appearance of the German reserve formations. By 25 August most of Belgium had been occupied; the German left had withstood the furious French attacks directed upon it in the "Battle of the Frontiers", inflicting some 300,000 casualties in two weeks; and the German right wing was surging forward towards the Marne and Paris. With their "Schlieffen Plan" apparently working the German General Staff were jubilant, antici-pating a victory as rapid and as decisive as that of 1870. On 5 September German formations were within 30 miles of Paris; but by this time their troops were close to exhaustion from the continual marching and fighting, and the offensive was faltering. Von Kluck incautiously exposed the right flank of his First Army by wheeling south-east before Paris; Gallieni and Joffre seized their opportunity; and defeat on the Marne drove the Germans back from this high point of success. After a series of costly but inconclusive battles 1914 drew to a close; both sides took to the spade, and the infa-mous trench lines were established. The "short war" of movement had not proved decisive.

In time, the German Army on the Western Front turned their positions into a formidable line of fortifications

stretching from the sea to the Swiss border, skilfully sited on ground of the greatest advantage, and covered by the maximum firepower at their disposal. Holding the tactical and strategic initiatives, and with the political initiative in

A group of French Territorials in November 1914, men in their late thirties or early forties. They wear the uniform in which the French infantry went into battle: a red-topped kepi, a grey-blue greatcoat and red trousers. (Courtesy G.A.Embleton)

Verdun, early 1916: battle-hardened French poilus clear a recently recaptured trench of German dead. The supreme test of the French infantry, the five-month battle for Verdun involved 70 of France's 96 divisions on the Western Front. Victory cost the French Army some 65,000-70,000 killed, 140,000 wounded, and 65,000 captured.

Two tired French veterans, each wearing the three sleeve chevrons marking two years' service, pose for a provincial photographer. They wear the horizon-blue uniform and Adrian helmet introduced in 1915 and 1916 respectively, the Corporal at left with the dark brown corduroy trousers which were widely worn in the mid-war years. (Courtesy G.A.Embleton)

the hands of their nation's leaders, the men of the German Army of 1915/16 stood and awaited the victory they confidently expected. They and their confederates of the Central Powers had made large gains on their Eastern Front, had driven the British and French from the Dardanelles, had defeated Serbia, and had contained the offensives against them in the West. In spring 1916 their hammer-blow at Verdun still seemed to promise the possibility of great prizes. Still strong and powerful, the German Army had grown in experience and confidence, and was at its zenith.

France: Dash and a short war

The French operated a system of military conscription which was similar to that of the Germans in many ways, particularly in the localisation of military districts; the chaos of the 1870 mobilisation, when reservists were sometimes required to travel great distances to rejoin their units, was to be avoided in future. In 1914 France was divided into 20 Army Corps districts, one of them in North Africa. Most Corps were made up of two divisions, the total available on mobilisation being 47, both "Metropolitan" and "Colonial". There were, however, fewer reserve divisions, for France possessed only 60 per cent of the manpower available to Germany. Only by extending the length of service with the colours from two to three years in 1913, and by drawing into military service a much higher proportion of the annual class, was France able to keep up with the military strength of Germany – at least in peacetime.

Young Frenchmen were called to the colours at 20, with a total military commitment to the age of 45. After their service with the colours they spent eleven years on the Army Reserve, seven years in what was termed the Territorial Army (not to be confused with the British Territorials), and the remainder on the Territorial Reserve.

This system produced for France a strength of nearly four million men on mobilisation (compared to Germany's five million), and added 25 Reserve Divisions to those of the first line. But most of these were filled by men as old as 33, instead of the upper age limit of 26 of the Germany Reserve formations. After France's Reserve came her twelve Territorial Divisions, men aged from 34 to 47, whose operational value was considered doubtful even by their countrymen.

The French General Staff had some of the ablest military thinkers in Europe; but the trauma of 1870-71 had distorted its judgement. Well aware of the shortcomings of its army in a protracted conflict, it had developed a doctrine for the conduct of a future war which betrayed a preoccupation with the morale element – the encouragement of *élan*, an aggressive attacking spirit which, it was hoped, would ensure a short war. This doctrine of "*l'attaque à outrance*" , of closing with the enemy at all costs and of counter-attacking immediately to retake any ground lost, was the creed of the powerful clique led by the pre-war chief of the Operations Bureau, Col.de Grandmaison. During the opening battles of the war, when French troops wearing bright red trousers strove to get within bayonet-reach of Germany's scientifically trained professionals, it cost France some 300,000 dead and 600,000 wounded, captured and missing by the end of 1914; the failed Artois and Champagne offensives of 1915 took several hundred thousand more. But by their heroic response to this semi-mystical appeal the French Army did contain the Germans, and then drove them back, and then held them.

Though horribly bloodied the French Army bore, among the Allies, the major burden of the first two years' fighting

without buckling. By 1916, now meeting its greatest test at Verdun, it was beginning to feel the strain; but its officers continued to give the courageous battlefield leadership which was almost all that was expected of them, and the dogged peasant soldiers continued to respond. The *poilus* of 1916 were a balanced mixture of veterans of two years' combat in their mid-twenties; of reservists in their thirties and forties whose steadiness, in basically static operations, might be thought to outweigh any physical shortcomings; and of young boys innocent of battle. The French Army of 1916 was at its peak of skill and experience.

Great Britain: An army created overnight
Great Britain's military system was wholly unlike that of the Germans and the French. Historically, the British Army had defeated Napoleon and had won and held an empire with a small army of long service volunteer regulars. The life of a common soldier was abhorrent to the British public, and when conscription had been urged by Lord Roberts in the early years of the 20th century his idea had been rejected as intolerable to the British electorate.

Britain's leaders knew that a European land war was imminent, but chose to do little in the way of preparation for it. Their best advice was that such a war would be

By 1916 the old regular battalions of the British Army had sustained grievous casualties; the bravest and the best of the BEF's "Old Contemptibles" had suffered death or wounds in the battles of 1914-15. Even in the ranks of the regular divisions and brigades on the Somme there would have been few enough of this type of soldier left. The photograph shows men of the 2nd Glosters, bayonet fighting champions of the Portsmouth garrison, 1907. (Private collection)

quickly resolved, and a token force was earmarked for this supposedly brief affair. Compared to the millions of men produced by the continental systems, the numbers of Britain's Regular Army of long service volunteers were paltry, and the reserve to this army was hardly worthy of the name. This state of affairs was well known in continental military circles, where British protestations about the quality of their troops had little effect. In the German view, Britain's army was unworthy of consideration.

The British had not contributed troops to a continental war for nearly a century. Their empire required relatively few troops to police it, and the richest nation in the world grumbled at paying for those. Where possible the security of the colonies was guarded by native troops with British officers. The bulk of what would today be called defence expenditure was allocated to the Royal Navy, an investment that had an obvious return in that it kept open the sea lanes over which flowed the commerce that made the British Empire the richest in the world. Britain was a maritime nation, comfortable in its wealth and power – but acutely aware that Germany wanted a share of it, and was not too particular about the means employed to seize it.

In the first decade of the century a reorganisation. of Britain's volunteers, militia and home based regular forces had been carried out to create – at least on paper – a Territorial Force given over to the defence of the British Isles, and an Expeditionary Force of a handful of divisions which might be deployed on the continent in time of war. (Under this scheme 14 Territorial Divisions and 14 Territorial Cavalry Brigades would be available for home defence; while six Regular Divisions and one Cavalry Division would be available to cross to the continent – a British Expeditionary Force of about 160,000 men.) On mobilisation the Territorials would recruit in order to "duplicate" their strength. No expansion of land forces beyond this point was planned for, and no provision was made for weapons and equipment other than maintenance stocks for the short war envisaged. Ammunition supplies were similarly calculated.

In August 1914 Britain mobilised her meagre army with great efficiency, and despatched her Expeditionary Force to fight under the command of the French Army. The BEF sustained a considerable battering in the 1914 fighting, its casualties necessitating reinforcement on a scale that had not been envisaged. Regular Army units drawn from imperial garrisons abroad were fed into the line, as were colonial formations and volunteer Territorial units, so that by late 1914 the original BEF had grown to five Army Corps organised into two Armies; but by early 1915 the resources of Britain's pre-war military establishment were used up. The 15 divisions then in France represented its maximum effort. A much greater British Army would be needed if the French were to be effectively assisted in the defeat of the German Army.

The Kitchener expansion
On 6 August 1914 Field-Marshal the Earl Kitchener of Khartoum became Britain's Secretary of State for War. Alone among Britain's leaders he saw that a European war would be a long and costly struggle; he also recognized that the existing British Army was totally inadequate to meet such a challenge. On the day of his appointment the Prime Minister had obtained parliamentary approval for an increase

Perhaps the most famous poster of all time: Lord Kitchener's manly gaze and accusing finger left patriotic Britons in no doubt where their duty lay.

The first clothing issued to Kitchener's New Army men was this dark blue uniform, which was universally loathed; looking at B Company of the 9th Suffolks, it is easy to see why. Note the wearing of shoulder titles as collar badges, and the two obsolete Lee-Metford rifles that were probably all the arms they had in late 1914. (Courtesy Ray Westlake)

of 500,000 men for the army; but Kitchener declared to the Cabinet that a victory could not be assured by Britain's sea power, and that the country would have to put into the field an army of millions for a war that would last – in his estimation – at least three years. Accepting the politicians' advice that conscription would not be tolerated by the British public, he realised that any new army would have to be raised by the traditional means of voluntary enlistment. His intention was to raise a series of "New Armies" that would number in all at least one million men.

Searching for a framework on which to raise his army, he decided not to use the existing Territorial organisation, and in this decision may have been guilty of prejudice. As a young man, serving as a volunteer with the French Army in the Franco-Prussian War, he had seen French reservists in action and judged them to be inferior troops. He had an equally low opinion of British Volunteers in South Africa. His New Armies were to be extensions of the Regular Army, and would be organised and trained by the regulars that Kitchener knew and trusted.

In taking this decision he condemned Britain, at a time of crisis, to a two-army system in which the New Army and the Territorials competed for manpower, equipment and weapons, with all the waste and duplication that this implied. Undoubtedly Kitchener considered the role of the Territorial Force – home defence – when he made his decision. Individual Territorials and, it was hoped, complete

units of Territorials would be permitted to volunteer for service overseas, but only a proportion did so. Until the law governing the service of Territorials could be changed their usefulness, as far as Kitchener and others were concerned, was limited. Besides, the Territorial Force was well below its establishment on the outbreak of war and now, ordered to double its strength, had recruiting problems of its own. To its ranks flocked those men whose patriotism did not extend beyond the defence of their homeland.

On 7 August 1914 the press published Kitchener's first "Call to Arms". "Your King and Country Need You", the headlines proclaimed, calling for "an addition of 100,000 men to his Majesty's Regular Army". Enlistment was to be for three years or the duration of the war, whichever was the longer. Shortly afterwards details of the organisation of the "First New Army" were made public. The six regional Military Commands into which Britain was divided were each to raise a complete division. The battalions of infantry which made up the bulk of the units were to be called "Service" battalions and numbered after the existing battalions of their county regiments. The centres on which the new formations were to form were the traditional garrisons of Aldershot, Colchester, Shorncliffe, The Curragh, Salisbury Plain and Grantham.

The response to Kitchener's call was overwhelming, as men flocked to be part of the "First Hundred Thousand". The traditionally suspicious attitude of the British towards their soldiery was put aside as men from all classes and walks of life clamoured to enlist. By 9 August recruits were being attested at the rate of 3,000 a day; by the end of the month the daily figure was 30,000. Under this flood the peacetime recruiting apparatus broke down, and local authorities were called upon to extemporise in order to process the throng.

If recruiting were a problem, handling the recruits at depots and barracks overwhelmed the resources of a Regular Army geared to the modest demands of peacetime. Accommodation was not the only thing in short supply. The available officers and NCOs were quite insufficient to train the influx, although Kitchener had issued instructions that units of the BEF were each to leave three officers and a group of NCOs to help with the formation of new battalions before proceeding to France. He had also retained in England 500 officers of the Indian Army who were on home leave at the outbreak of war. An appeal was issued for "2,000 young men of good education" to serve as officers, and casualties from the BEF's first battles were sent to New Army training camps after convalescence. Recalled to service were many retired officers – "dug-outs" – some of whom were quite elderly, but whose experience was now in demand. Non-commissioned officers were needed even more urgently, and the re-enlistment of former NCOs up to the age of 50 was authorised.

On 17 September Kitchener informed the House of Lords that his chief difficulty was "one of materiel rather than personnel". The arsenals and storehouses had been almost emptied to equip the BEF, and what little was left was rapidly absorbed by the First Hundred Thousand. The output of government arsenals and the firms accustomed to handling government contracts was regulated to the supply of the peacetime Army and the calculated requirements of the "short war" that it might have to fight. There was no way in which supplies could be accelerated. The product of many other armaments firms went to supply the Royal Navy. Rifle production was only 6,000 per month. Artillery shortages were particularly serious, in the lack not only of weapons but also of the ammunition to serve them, whose manufacture required an industry skilled in the mass production of projectiles, fuses and high explosive – an industry which simply did not exist.

Contracts for the supply of arms and equipment for the first six divisions of the New Army had been placed as early as 10 August 1914. These were spread between the government ordnance factories and the leading armaments firms; and on 30 September the government requested these firms to increase their production capabilities in order to supply the larger orders that were to be placed. A Cabinet committee on munitions was formed, one of its first acts being to issue generous subsidies to encourage the expansion of munitions firms. It also took steps to bar the enlistment of skilled workers. All of these measures were steps in the right direction, but it was to take some time before the weapons, ammunition, stores and equipment necessary found their way to the New Armies.

Whilst they waited for the means with which to fight, Kitchener's men drilled, underwent physical training, route marched and dug. Without uniforms or boots, the majority performed these duties in the civilian clothes in which they had joined up. In time these wore out to such an extent that some men were without footwear – and were ordered to practice slow marching on the grass! Blue serge was issued as a stopgap until khaki became available and the volunteers could adopt the appearance of soldiers. Much time was to pass before rifles of any sort came into the hands of the infantry, longer still before the issue of cartridges with which to practice, and even longer before modern rifles and ammunition came from the factories. It was well into 1915 and only shortly before their departure for France that the infantry of the First Hundred Thousand were properly armed and equipped; but their frustrations were as nothing compared to those of the artillery.

For months the volunteers had attempted to master the complexities of gunnery without having access to a gun. Dummy guns were constructed out of wood, and obsolete weapons were pressed into service in order to teach the rudiments; but without a full scale of weapons, sights, instruments and practice ammunition very little could be done to obtain any degree of proficiency. The 10th (Irish) Divisional Artillery trained with "Quaker" (i.e. "pacifist") guns and very few horses. That of the 15th (Scottish) Division received horses, but no harness or saddlery, and trained with a gun made from a log of wood and the Bordon garrison funeral gun-carriage. In the 18th (Eastern) Division they had one wooden gun per battery, and practised gun-laying with plywood mock-ups of dial-sights with the graduations marked in pencil. A further problem for the New Army gunners was coming to terms with the horses that were to tow their weapons and limbers – when they got them. Few of the men had experience of working with horses, and most of the horses were impressed animals, quite unused to service life; it was not a happy union. The outcome was that very little of the time available was put to best use before proceeding to France. Many gunners fired at practice camp for the first time only weeks before going to the Front. Shortages also hampered the training of other units, especially machine-gunners; they too were confined to practising with wooden dummies until their real weapons became available.

While the men of Kitchener's "First Hundred Thousand", commonly referred to as K1, underwent their nominal training, further recruits flowed into the Army through the enlistment centres in response to the call for additional men to provide the "Second Hundred Thousand" – K2 – and subsequent intakes. The Territorial Force continued to compete for enlistments; and local authorities began to raise complete units composed of neighbours, friends or workmates attracted by the promise that they would serve together, and dubbed the "Pals battalions". If shortages of trained instructors, accommodation, clothing, equipment, weapons and ammunition had hampered the training of K1, the even greater shortages suffered by K2 to K5 made the process of turning them into effective soldiers even more difficult.

Between early May and mid-July 1915 the first six divisions of Kitchener's New Army left England for active service, three proceeding to France and three to the Dardanelles. They had endured nine months of discomfort, hard work, improvisation and the most incredible muddle, but had somehow been transformed from gangs of patriotic recruits into units and formations that were considered to be fit to fight. Not all who saw them, however, agreed with that assessment – as, indeed, not all agreed with the methods employed by that great autocrat Lord Kitchener to obtain the army named after him. One general officer wrote of "K's shadow army for shadow campaigns ....Under no circumstances can these mobs take the field for two years. What we want, and what we must have, is for our little force out here to be kept to full strength." The same general declared 'Kitchener's "ridiculous and preposterous army" to be "the laughing stock of every soldier in Europe." He went on to argue that "It took the Germans forty years of incessant work to make an army of 25 Corps with the aid of conscription; it will take us all eternity to do the same by voluntary effort."

Nevertheless, from Kitchener's first call for volunteers to the disembarkation in the seats of war of the first of Kitchener's New Army divisions only ten months elapsed. This was Britain's step towards the creation of an army of continental proportions; and she was well on the way to constructing a military strength that would make those who had sneered at her "contemptibly little" army eat their words. Whatever the shortcomings of the people of Britain, their capacity for improvisation and cheerful acceptance of hard work and danger in the name of patriotism is prodigious. More than two million men had entered the British Army voluntarily within the first year of the war, and whatever mistaken directions their organisation and training had taken, that army was, by 1916, under arms and on the march.

Moving to France with the Kitchener men were Territorial divisions, Canadian divisions, and divisions back from the abortive Dardanelles campaign including regulars, Territorials, and the famous ANZACS – the Australian and New Zealand Army Corps. Problems over the terms of enlistment of the Territorials had by this time been resolved. The new-found military might of the British Empire was assembling in northern France, swelling the ranks of the BEF to 55 divisions organised into 18 Army Corps, which in turn were organised into four Armies.

The speed and measure of this expansion is even more astounding when appreciated as a volunteer effort. Moves towards conscription had started in Great Britain with the National Registration Act of July 1915, the "Derby Scheme" that followed, and – in January 1916 – with the Military Service Act; this rendered liable for service all single men (with the exception of various exempted categories) aged between 18 and 41, and was extended to married men that May. However, by July 1916 conscription had only brought in 43,000 recruits for general service, and few of these "pressed men" were present on the Somme between July and November 1916.

It is hardly possible to generalise about the character and quality of the units which would face the enemy on the Somme that summer and autumn, nor to seek to draw comparisons. At this date there was no noticeable difference between the ages of the men serving in regular, Territorial and New Army units. Regular battalions had suffered to varying degrees in the battles of 1914 and 1915, and were therefore "diluted" to varying degrees by wartime volunteers and regular reservists. Some individual units which had been particularly badly mauled would display a relative lack of resilience; others which had suffered as badly "on paper" would distinguish themselves. Generally speaking, the standards of leadership, training and efficiency were still high in 1916.

The men of the best Territorial units had volunteered en masse and gone to France piecemeal in 1914 and early 1915; battalions such as the London Scottish had suffered as severely as the regulars, and their survivors were by now as war-tempered as any troops at the front. By 1916 such battalions had rejoined their parent TF formations, which were now in France, adding a leavening of battle experience to these untried divisions. Even the newly arrived Territorial units enjoyed the benefits to morale of local recruitment and long pre-war comradeship; the knowledge that the regulars looked down upon them as amateurs added a spur to their determination. As with the regulars, relative quality usually depended in great part upon the standard of leadership.

Both regular and Territorial units had been in being for years and were composed of men who had been drawn to the military life in peacetime. The "Kitchener" battalions did not enjoy these advantages; they were fledgling units made up of men who would not have dreamed of becoming soldiers in peacetime, but were drawn to the colours on a wave of patriotic fervour. In terms of human quality they were often "the cream of the nation's manhood"; but, as discussed above, their transformation into soldiers had been a patchy affair, and their efficiency and morale would be shown to depend very much upon the quality of their leadership.

36th (ULSTER) DIVISION

In 1914 Ireland was in turmoil over the issue of Home Rule. Under the leadership of Sir Edward Carson, 80,000 men had joined the Ulster Volunteers, from which the Ulster Volunteer Force (UVF) was raised, armed, and trained to defend by force their "rights and privileges as citizens of the United Kingdom". Following the outbreak of war Lord Kitchener negotiated with Carson the raising of an infantry division from the UVF, the order for its formation being issued on 28 October 1914. The task of assembling the 36th (Ulster) Division was made much easier by drawing on the resources of the UVF, and the infantry battalions were soon raised in Belfast, Antrim, Down, Armagh, Tyrone, Londonderry, Donegal and Fermanagh. The divisional artillery was raised in England. Proudly chosen as the divisional badge was the red hand of Ulster. On 1 July 1916 the infantry of the 36th (Ulster) Division were reported to have charged the German trenches shouting "No surrender!", the battle-cry of the Derry apprentice boys and of Ulster's loyalists to this day. Four Victoria Crosses were won by Ulstermen on this anniversary of the Battle of the Boyne. The photograph shows infantry of the division marching through Belfast in May 1915.

CHAPTER FOUR

"One Policy, One Army, One Front"

The Allied Western Front offensives of 1915 made little impression on the German positions in Artois and Champagne. The enemy struck back with an offensive at Ypres in April that year, using poison gas for the first time on the Western Front, and succeeded in inflicting heavy casualties, driving both the French and the British further back in the salient. After 18 months of fighting the German Army still enjoyed the advantage of its vast pre-war preparations, unified command and interior lines of communication.

It was in 1915, at the first inter-Allied military conference to be held, that the French High Command first proposed a concerted Anglo/French offensive the following year; and in November a meeting of the Prime Ministers of France and Great Britain took place which adopted "the principle of a mixed permanent committee designed to co-ordinate the action of the Allies". A second inter-Allied military conference was convened at Chantilly in December to study a memorandum entitled "The Plan of Action proposed by France to the Coalition". This called, *inter alia*, for simultaneous attacks by France, Great Britain, Italy and Russia on the Austro-German forces, the pursuance of economic war, and the wearing down ("*usure*") of the enemy by the policy of attrition.

At this conference Sir Douglas Haig, newly appointed Commander-in-Chief of the BEF in place of Sir John French, was sent a letter by General Joffre, Chief of the French General Staff, which stated: "I have directed the General Commanding the Group of the Armies of the North (General Foch) to make a study of a powerful offensive south of the Somme in the region comprised between that river and Lassigny. This study is part of a general plan drawn up for the French Armies as a whole and will permit me to determine the points against which our principal effort will be made in the coming Spring.... Without prejudice to the area where our principal attack will be made, the French offensive would be greatly aided by a simultaneous offensive of the British forces between the Somme and Arras. Besides the interest which this last area presents on account of its close proximity to...the French Armies...I think it will be a considerable advantage to attack the enemy on a front where...activity...has been less than elsewhere."

In the exchange of views which followed Haig steadfastly resisted the French suggestion that a series of "*batailles d'usure*" be fought by the British (he considered them premature), and pressed for a simultaneous attack by the two Allied armies. In time General Joffre settled for the British proposal and agreed that a combined offensive should be carried out astride the Somme about the beginning of July. In the meantime the British took over more sectors of the line from the French.

By the time the next conference took place in March 1916 the great German offensive at Verdun was three weeks old. Many important French positions had fallen to unprecedented bombardments and relentless infantry pressure; Falkenhayn, Chief of the German General Staff, continued to commit increasing numbers of his reserves to the attempt at a breakthrough in this pivotal sector, forcing the French to do likewise (it is estimated that by the end of the battle some two-thirds of France's entire infantry would be rotated through Verdun). It was at this meeting that it was agreed that a general offensive by all the Allies, Russia and Italy included, should be mounted with the least possible delay, and with the aim of taking pressure off Verdun. The date for the offensive was to be by agreement between the commanders-in-chief. Shortly afterwards the Prime Ministers of Britain and France declared, at a meeting in Paris, that "we have to destroy the morale of the German Army and nation"; and decided to follow "common, methodical and concerted action" with "one policy, one army and one front".

Apart from the obvious aim of relieving pressure on Verdun, the decision of the French Commander-in-Chief to make the main offensive of 1916 on the Somme seems to have been based mainly on the premise that the British would then be bound to take part in it. An offensive there appeared to have no other strategic object than attrition: reduction of the German Somme position would have the effect of shortening the enemy's line, while Allied success might result in a vulnerable salient. Even a complete breakthrough would have to penetrate quite far to interrupt German communications. The notional British plan for an offensive further north, a course of action with strategic possibilities, was rejected for the time being by Joffre.

The slaughter at Verdun increased in intensity, sucking in more and more French reserves, and it began to be doubtful whether they would be able to play the part first envisioned in a Somme offensive. The British played a passive role in this fighting by taking over more of the line in order to relieve French formations for transfer to Verdun, and a less passive one by mounting a series of attacks in the Ypres area.

Gradually the planned French involvement in the Somme offensive was scaled down. As Joffre pressed him to bring forward the date for a British attack, Haig pointed out that delay would ensure the availability of more British divisions for the campaign. Joffre countered by pointing out that the French Army was being daily weakened by the battle of attrition raging at Verdun; and on 26 May he travelled to Haig's headquarters for a conference, in the course of which, after an impassioned pleading of his case, he extracted from Sir Douglas a promise that the British would be ready to attack on 1 July. Joffre pointed out that the French expected the British to make the major effort of the year. On 3 June he gave formal notice in writing to the

British that the combined Anglo-French offensive on the Somme was to begin, after a suitable artillery bombardment, on 1 July.

On 5 June the death occurred of Field-Marshal Earl Kitchener, when the warship in which he was travelling on a mission to Russia was sunk by a mine. His death removed the great autocratic bastion that had protected the British military since the outbreak of war; from this point onwards, without his stature in Cabinet, the generals were to be increasingly subject to political pressure. His mission to provide Britain with an army of continental size had been accomplished, however. The Ministry of Munitions was by now functioning and supervising the vast outpouring of war material from the factories of Britain, the United States of America and the Empire; the last of the New Army divisions was crossing to France; and the whole military machine was working with what was seen as increasing efficiency.

While the British and French Armies finalised the plans for a Somme offensive the situation at Verdun continued to create fresh crises both political and military. Quite understandably, these increasingly preoccupied the French. On 21 June their GQG (General Headquarters) issued the Commander-in-Chief of the BEF an instruction which stated: "The essential object of the operations which are about to be undertaken on the Somme is to place a mass of manoeuvre on the junctions of the enemy's lines of communications marked by Cambrai-Le Cateau-Maubeuge, etc...the road Bapaume-Cambrai will be the axis of our initial progress." It went on to discuss strategic possibilities, should the enemy front yield in a few days or should there be an immediate rupture of the front by surprise. The instruction said nothing about the action to be taken in case of complete or partial failure. In reply Sir Douglas Haig restated his immediate plans, and declared that if all went according to plan he would continue to attack, "the direction of further operations depending on whether he [the enemy] clung to his fortified positions in the north, or succeeded in concentrating a force to oppose our advance eastward". He did not mention the possibility of failure, but he had discussed this eventuality with his subordinate commanders.

And so the scene was set. The French pressure on the British to start the offensive early, at all levels from prime ministerial downwards, was irresistible. It is pointless to speculate what might have happened if Haig's arguments had prevailed and his New Army formations had benefited from further training and the support of the tanks which were on their way, or even if his attack had been mounted in the north. Whatever benefits more time might have bought for the British must always be balanced against the disasters that might have befallen the French. Verdun was proving an unprecedented test of the *poilu's* endurance, and it was claimed, with some justification, that the British Empire was not pulling its full weight in the war.

Preparations for battle

The events outlined above resulted in a succession of British plans for an offensive on the Somme. Soon after Sir Douglas Haig assumed command of the British Expeditionary Force he directed the commander of his Third Army to prepare one for an attack north of the Somme, using 15 divisions on a 24,000 yard front. In time this was amended in order to

General Joffre, the chief of the French General Staff and commander-in-chief in the field, with Sir Douglas Haig in summer 1916. An engineer by background, the unimaginative Joffre showed little strategic or tactical flair; but he was a "sound staff man", and his aura of imperturbability gave France confidence in the crisis of 1914. Haig and Joffre worked together fairly easily; they shared a phlegmatic temperament – and a distaste for the physical realities of the front line. Joffre openly declared that the sight of a busy casualty clearing station would rob him of the courage to order further attacks. (IWM Q992)

co-ordinate British and French offensives astride the Somme, in which 25 British divisions and 40 French divisions were to participate. In February 1916 the British Fourth Army began to form, and Haig directed its commander General Rawlinson to study the offensive and produce his plan.

In the reconnaissance and deliberations now undertaken the ground and the enemy came under consideration. The prospective battlefield was divided by the river Somme which cut a valley through northern France, and flowed westward across the area between Peronne and Amiens. The slopes of the valley to the south of the river were gentle while those on the opposite bank, to the north, were

steep. The river averaged a half to three-quarters of a mile in width and was edged by meadows, generally submerged in winter. In the area of the battlefield it was flanked by marshes caused by the cropping of peat, and despite the occasional causeway presented an almost impassable barrier – unfordable, and with many windings and branches. The natural obstacle of the river was enhanced by a canal, 58 feet wide, which ran roughly parallel to its course.

The slopes on the northern bank contained many small valleys, the main one being that through which flowed the Ancre, a tributary of the Somme; 20 to 30 feet wide, the Ancre was a miniature of the Somme and equally marshy. South of the Somme the plain was flat, but to the north were hills, and a main ridge rising more than 300 feet above the level of the river on which stood the villages of Guillemont, Longueval, Bazentin le Petit, Pozières and Thiepval, where the ridge, running east to west, dipped to the Ancre. Beyond the stream the ground rose again in a northerly direction through a line including the villages of Beaucourt, Hébuterne, Gommecourt and Fonquevillers.

The area contained a few large woods, but practically no isolated farms, the bulk of the population dwelling in the villages which dotted the area. The largest town in the region was Albert with a population of some 7,000. The subsoil consisted of chalk, and the whole area was richly

An American 75hp petrol-engined Holt track-laying tractor towing an 8in. howitzer into position. Such vehicles had been used by the British Army for some years; they were to be the inspiration for the tanks which first saw action on the Somme in 1916. (IWM D363)

cultivated, making for free movement of troops and horses everywhere but in the woods – which contained thick undergrowth – and across the water obstacles. A main road ran from Amiens through Albert to Bapaume. A railway ran from Albert along the valley of the Ancre in the direction of Arras away to the north. A light railway ran from Albert through Fricourt to Combles, and other light railways radiated from Bapaume.

★   ★   ★

The German front line defence system, running south to north, crossed the Somme in the area Frise-Curlu, turned west around Maricourt and then resumed its northerly course at Fricourt, crossing the Ancre between Thiepval and Beaumont Hamel and running onwards to Gommecourt. Behind their front line the Germans had constructed a second position set back 2,000 to 5,000 yards from the first. This second position generally followed the Guillemont-Pozières ridge to the Ancre and then from

An ammunition dump on the Somme; high explosive 8in. howitzer shells, with their boxed fuses in the foreground, wait beside a light railway along which they will be conveyed to the battery positions.(IWM Q29974)

Grandcourt northwards by Puisieux. Between the first and second lines a number of defended localities had been constructed, including Montauban, Mametz Wood, Contalmaison, Pozières and Serre. All positions were heavily wired and featured deep shelters (dug-outs), which the well-drained chalk permitted. The German front system could be observed and shot at all along the Allied line that confronted it; but their second position, although within range of Allied artillery, could only be observed from the air.

Manning these formidable defences was the German Second Army of General Fritz von Below, which consisted of three Army Corps which had been considerably weakened by the withdrawal of formations for the Verdun battle. Von Below lacked any appreciable Army reserve. By May 1916 he had become convinced that an Allied attack was imminent. From Hébuterne south to the Ancre the German positions, though skilfully sited in woods and re-entrants, were on ground mostly overlooked by the British; south of the Ancre the Germans held all the high ground. It is not surprising, therefore, that German appreciations concluded that the main Allied effort would be against their right flank, and that their left, although vulnerable, was less threatened.

The German High Command had warned its Army commanders that one of the consequences of the Verdun battle would be Allied relief attacks elsewhere. In the case of such attacks they were not to expect reinforcements. Orders were issued that strength was to be concentrated as far forward as possible, and positions were to be held to the last man and the last round. There was nothing for them to fall back on. This order placed most German troops within the range of Allied artillery, forcing them to dig extensive fortifications and to stock them with ammunition, rations and water sufficient for a protracted fight. It also led to the construction of the redoubts, or strongpoints, which backed up the German front line. In these were placed the many machine guns that covered no-man's-land with their crossfire. Some of the positions were interconnected by tunnels to allow their garrisons safe deployment. General von Below's warning of an expected Allied attack resulted in his being sent some artillery reinforcements and some labour units to speed the construction of a third line of defence five miles to the rear of the first. From March onwards the

Typical of the aircraft operated over the Somme by the RFC in 1916 was the flimsy-looking 100hp "pusher"-engined De Havilland DH2 single-seater scout, which for operations mounted a Lewis gun in the nose of the pilot's nacelle, with an unobstructed forward view and field of fire. In the hands of such aggressive units as No.24 Squadron, led by Major Lanoe Hawker VC, DSO – whose squadron standing orders read simply "Attack everything" – it dominated the skies over the Western Front from early spring to autumn 1916. The introduction of new scouts such as the DH2, FE2b and Nieuport 11 made the skies relatively safe for Allied reconnaissance aircraft until the appearance, from September 1916, of the Jagdstaffeln equipped with the new Albatros D-series scouts. (IWM Q67534)

German wire in front of their defensive positions was progressively thickened.

On 6 June von Below reported that "The preparations of the British in the area of Serre-Gommecourt...lead to the conclusion that the enemy thinks first and foremost of attacking the projecting angles of Fricourt and Gommecourt....It is quite conceivable that he will attempt only to pin the front [south of the Ancre] by artillery fire, but he will not make a serious attack." He went on to say that his forces opposing the French south of the Somme were weak.

★ ★ ★

Shortly after taking over command of the Fourth Army front, which ran from the Somme to Fonquevillers, General Rawlinson warned his Corps commanders of the coming offensive, outlined the troops and firepower he hoped would be available, and gave them a planning date for the initial operations of June or July. He instructed them to get on with such preparations as they could, including the selection of battery positions and observation posts and the laying of field telephone cable. In late March Rawlinson received confirmation of the troops, artillery and ammunition which he would have for the offensive, should this have to be mounted earlier than anticipated (15 to 17 divisions).

On 3 April Rawlinson sent details of his plan to GHQ. This envisaged operations on a ten-mile front between Maricourt and Serre, and called for the capture of the enemy's first position, followed by extensive consolidation before the German second line was tackled. He stated: "It does not appear to me that the gain of two or three kilometres of ground is of much consequence, or that the existing situation is so urgent as to demand that we should incur very heavy losses in order to draw a large number of German reserves against this portion of our front. Our object rather seems to be to kill as many Germans as possible with the least loss to ourselves, and the best way to do this appears to me to be to seize points of tactical impor-

tance which will provide us with good observation and which we may feel certain the Germans will counterattack under disadvantages likely to conduce heavy losses."

General Rawlinson had pondered the value of a short, intensive bombardment in support of the attacking infantry as opposed to a prolonged one. It was the profusion of German wire which decided the issue, as this had to be destroyed by the guns before the infantry could get to the German positions. He wrote: "The intense bombardment must take place by daylight; therefore the whole of the assaulting troops would have to be at, or near, their assembly trenches during the whole time and would undoubtedly suffer casualties and lose morale. This would be avoided in a more prolonged bombardment, as the attack could take place in the early morning, and the attacking troops get into position under cover of darkness." He further considered that such a bombardment would also destroy the machine guns which guarded the approaches to the German wire, and felt that if the artillery did its work well the rest would be easy.

It was after the receipt of this plan that Sir Douglas Haig's artillery advisor at GHQ, Major-General Birch, told his chief that he felt the plan was "stretching" the artillery too much. Sir Douglas, a cavalryman, disagreed with his head gunner, pointing out the ample ammunition promised for the offensive. He decreed an increase in the scope of the initial operations, and argued in favour of the short, sharp bombardment. The issue of artillery wire-cutting was avoided.

On being informed of Sir Douglas's thoughts and criticisms, which rebuked him for his limited view, General Rawlinson assured Haig that he would loyally carry out his instructions, though it is recorded that he privately felt them to be based on false premises, and too optimistic. Those instructions stated that the Fourth Army attack would form part of a general offensive in close co-operation with the French, and continued: "Your principle effort in the first instance will be directed to establishing a strong defensive flank on the spur from Serre to Miraumont and to capturing and securing the high ground above Pozières and the spurs running thence Beaucourt-sur-Ancre and Grandcourt and towards Fricourt. A simultaneous attack should be made on the enemy's trenches from Fricourt eastward to the point of junction with the French. In this area Montauban and the ridge running thence to Mametz, as well as the Briqueterie

south-east of Montauban, are very important features, which should be captured as early in the operation as you find possible with the means at your disposal. Their possession will be of considerable tactical value to us in the second stage of the operations.

"After the gaining of the ground described above, your next efforts must be directed to capturing, by attacks from the west and south, the Ginchy-Bazentin le Grand ridge, and then pushing eastward along the high ground towards Combles, in order to co-operate with and assist the French Army on your right in effecting the passage of the river Somme.

"Operations subsequent [to those] outlined above must depend on the degree of success gained and on developments which cannot be foreseen. But the object will be to continue to prevent the enemy from re-establishing his line of defence and to exploit to the full all opportunities opened up for defeating his forces within reach, always, however,

GERMAN DEFENCES

Throughout the war the German attitude to entrenchment contrasted with that of the Allies, who never intended to hold any given line for long and therefore did not dig in or wire on the scale of the enemy. The German Army, having captured a large area of enemy territory, also seized the tactical initiative by the skillful siting of positions extensively dug-in and wired to withstand the inevitable Allied onslaughts.

On the Somme they dug deep into the chalk to construct shelters designed to withstand Allied bombardment. So well equipped were some of these dug-outs – more properly, bunkers – that after their capture the Tommies were astonished to find electric light, piped water, and even linoleum floors in these dormitories, command posts, aid posts and communications centres. All were linked by interconnecting tunnels; as these rose towards the forward trenches they were protected by traversed

stairs and anti-gas curtains. The German Army saw no point in sitting out enemy shelling in open trenches; leaving sentries to raise the alarm, whole units went deep underground when bombardments began, rushing up the stairways to man the wreckage of their trenches once the shelling lifted.

In the villages they had an on-site source of defence stores in the timber and masonry of the houses, a series of ready-made bunkers in the cellars, and water from the wells; they used these resources to fashion the redoubts which anchored their trench lines. To the rear, equally skillfully sited and dug, were the positions of the supporting machine gun and artillery units. Machine gun crews could vanish underground with their weapons to escape shellfire; this was not possible for the artillery, but they used alternative positions to evade counter-battery fire.

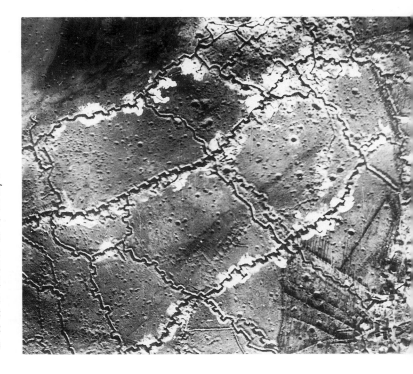

Aerial photograph of German first position trenches north of the Ancre. They show the classic pattern of three lines, "crenellated" by the regularly-spaced traverses to limit casualties from shellfire and to prevent enemy infantry who got into a trench firing straight down it for any distance. The three lines are linked by less regularly traversed communication trenches coming up from the rear; and are complicated at various points by local defensive schemes. Note the bright chalk spoil thrown up by digging, and the pocked evidence of Allied bombardment. (IWM Q61479)

with due regard to the need to assist the French Army."

Briefly, this meant an advance on a 25,000 yard (14 mile) front and the capture of the enemy position to a depth of about one and a half miles. General Rawlinson's original idea for a limited offensive had been overruled by Sir Douglas in favour of an optimistic plan aimed eventually at a complete breakthrough, followed by cavalry exploitation of the enemy rear – a plan that echoed the ideas proposed by General Joffre. The step-by-step, seize-and-hold proposals of the Commander of the Fourth Army had been shelved in favour of a much grander strategy based in part on Haig's belief of French reports of the tremendous effect of German artillery at Verdun, and the conclusion that this could be repeated by the Allied artillery on the Somme.

The British build-up

The unprecedented build-up of British land forces since the outbreak of war had served to swell the ranks of the BEF, in less than two years, to 18 Army Corps (55 divisions) organised into four Armies. There had been a corresponding expansion to provide the command and administration for the enlarged force, as well as the creation of a number of new arms and services. These included such exotica as the "special brigade" (gas), special works parks (camouflage), anti-aircraft searchlight companies, field survey companies, electrical and mechanical companies, a meteorological section, a printing company, kite balloon sections, and medical laboratories. Many schools had been organised to meet the need for men trained in a huge range of specialist skills.

Army Troops now included heavy and anti-aircraft artillery, tunnelling companies, pontoon parks, Royal Flying Corps aeroplane squadrons and balloon sections, workshops, remount units, omnibus companies, casualty clearing stations, medical stores units, mobile X-ray units, ordnance units and sanitary sections. Corps Troops, originally limited to a signals unit, now included a Corps cavalry regiment, a cyclist battalion, a motor machine gun battery (motorcycle), a Corps ammunition park, three supply columns, two mobile ordnance workshops, two or more heavy artillery groups and a detachment of the Royal Flying Corps. In addition to their twelve infantry battalions the establishment of divisions now included 16 batteries of field artillery, three batteries of trench mortars, three field companies Royal Engineers, a signal company, a pioneer battalion, a divisional train, three field ambulances, a sanitary section and a mobile veterinary section. Divisional artillery was actually weaker than before, with 64 guns as opposed to 76. Each of the division's three infantry brigades now had a machine gun company and trench mortar battery.

The sheer scale of the British build-up, a masterpiece of enterprise, was astounding. But the vast majority of the manpower had had no connection with soldiering until recently, and their commanders had much to learn in the handling of large formations. Communications were primitive, and those that were available were extremely vulnerable in battle. At an intermediate level many of the commanders and their staffs either lacked experience or were entirely new to their jobs. Throughout the Army there was a dearth of "trainers" – those officers with an intellectual grasp of how a modern battle was best fought, and the ability and determination to teach their troops the necessary skills to fight efficiently. It should be remembered that this "modern battle" and the skills it demanded had only confronted these officers in the past two years; most of them were the products of a wholly different military environment.

There were many new weapons to be mastered. In 1914 the British Army did not possess a single trench mortar; these had been introduced gradually in a variety of calibres. By July 1916 four Stokes 3in. mortars equipped each infantry trench mortar battery, and the others were in the hands of Royal Artillery trench mortar batteries. A Machine Gun Corps had come into existence on 27 October 1915, bringing under its command all existing machine gun companies and taking over responsibility for the training and organisation of further machine gun units. The Vickers or Maxim machine guns – heavy, tripod-mounted, belt-fed weapons for sustained fire – were thus taken out of the hands of the infantry, to be replaced by an issue, at an initial scale of two per company, of Lewis guns – light, shoulder-fired, bipod-mounted weapons fed by magazines and portable by one man. This scale increased as more guns became available, and by the time of the Somme battles each battalion had 16 guns. The "special brigade" responsible for the discharge or projection of gas into enemy positions also contained a unit trained to handle the crude flamethrowers of the time (this dreadful weapon had been introduced to the battlefield by the Germans at Verdun that February).

By July 1916 the strength of the Royal Flying Corps in France was 27 squadrons. The aircraft with which they were equipped were a great improvement, both in perfor-

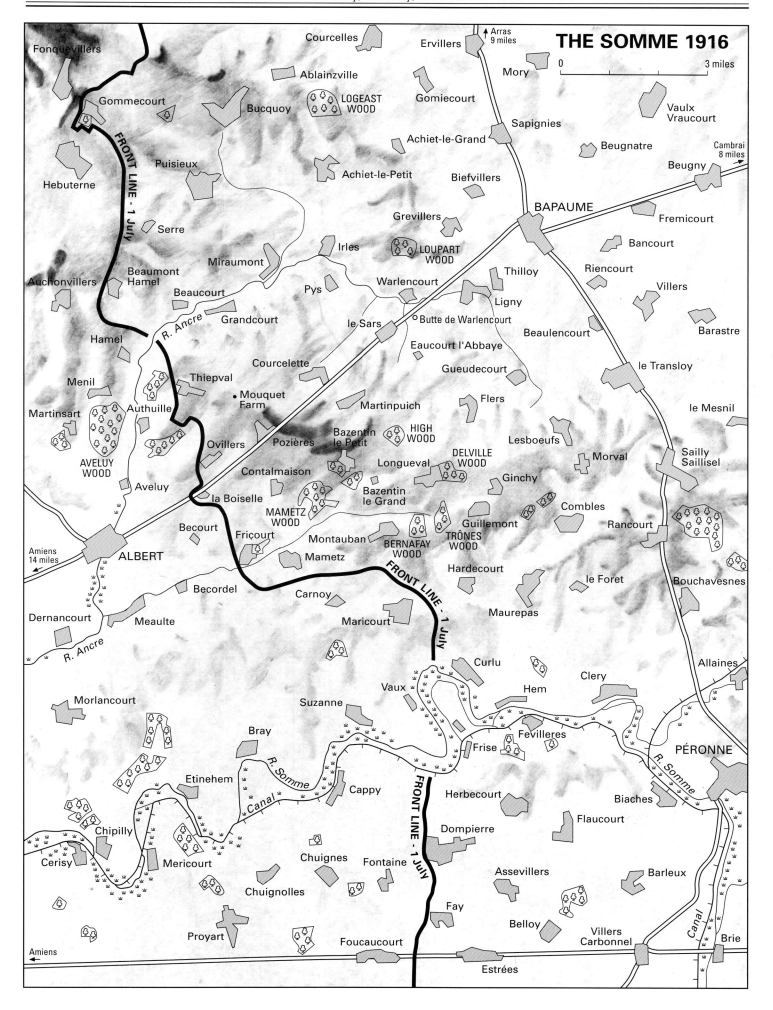

THE SOMME 1916

0 _____ 3 miles

Fonquevillers
Courcelles
Ervillers
Arras 9 miles
Mory
Ablainzville
Gommecourt
Bucquoy
LOGEAST WOOD
Gomiecourt
Sapignies
Vaulx Vraucourt
Puisieux
Achiet-le-Grand
Beugnatre
Hebuterne
Achiet-le-Petit
Biefvillers
Cambrai 8 miles
Serre
Grevillers
Beugny
Miraumont
Irles
BAPAUME
Fremicourt
Beaumont Hamel
LOUPART WOOD
Thilloy
Bancourt
Pys
Warlencourt
Ligny
Riencourt
Villers
Auchonvillers
Beaucourt
le Sars
Butte de Warlencourt
Beaulencourt
Barastre
R. Ancre
Grandcourt
Eaucourt l'Abbaye
le Transloy
Hamel
Courcelette
Gueudecourt
Menil
Thiepval
Mouquet Farm
Martinpuich
Flers
le Mesnil
Martinsart
Authuille
Pozières
HIGH WOOD
Lesboeufs
Sailly Saillisel
Aveluy
Ovillers
Bazentin le Petit
Longueval
DELVILLE WOOD
Morval
AVELUY WOOD
Contalmaison
Bazentin le Grand
Ginchy
Combles
Rancourt
Amiens 14 miles
la Boiselle
MAMETZ WOOD
Guillemont
Becourt
Fricourt
Montauban
BERNAFAY WOOD
TRÔNES WOOD
ALBERT
Mametz
Bouchavesnes
Becordel
Hardecourt
le Foret
Dernancourt
Carnoy
FRONT LINE - 1 July
Meaulte
Maricourt
Maurepas
R. Ancre
Curlu
Allaines
Morlancourt
Suzanne
Vaux
Hem
Clery
Bray
Frise
Fevilleres
PÉRONNE
Etinehem
R. Somme
Cappy
Herbecourt
Biaches
Canal
Dompierre
Flaucourt
R. Somme
Chipilly
Chuignes
Fontaine
Cerisy
Mericourt
Assevillers
Barleux
Chuignolles
Belloy
Canal
Proyart
Fay
Villers Carbonnel
Brie
Amiens
Foucaucourt
Estrées
FRONT LINE - 1 July

31

mance and in armament, on the types of 1914 and 1915. The official establishment of a squadron had been raised from twelve to 18 aeroplanes in March 1916, and by the opening of the Somme battles more than half the squadrons had received this increase. The deployment of the RFC in early 1916 was one brigade to each Army, each brigade consisting of headquarters and two wings, an aircraft park and a kite balloon squadron (two or more balloons). One wing had the tasks of reconnaissance, photography and artillery observation, while the other operated under the Army Commander's directions on aerial fighting, long-range reconnaissance and photography missions. A special wing was allotted to GHQ for strategical work.

The appearance, in late 1915, of the German Fokker *Eindekker* single-seat monoplane, with the interrupter gear which allowed its machine gun to fire forward through the arc of its revolving propeller, had drastically curtailed freedom of reconnaissance by single British aircraft over the German lines. To meet this threat new tactics were devised, involving flying in formations in which a reconnaissance aircraft was escorted by at least three "scouts" (fighters). Aircraft flying bombing sorties also adopted formations for mutual defence.

By early 1916 the war in the air was becoming specialised. In order to win freedom of action for reconnaissance, artillery observation and bombing while denying such freedom to the enemy, a relentless fighter offensive was waged in the air. All available fighters were gathered into Army squadrons the better to concentrate their striking power; and with such types as the DH2, FE2b, the French Nieuport Scout, and the appearance in May of Sopwith two-seaters fitted with interrupter gear, dominance was established over the German flying service. The first crude wireless transmitters fitted in aircraft greatly enhanced artillery fire control, as did the aerial photographs by which

the results of bombardment could be studied and maps updated. Otherwise air-to-ground signalling was by lamp, message drops or Very lights. In the build-up to the Somme offensive GHQ brought into the battle area additional RFC squadrons and balloon sections, until the concentration totalled 185 aeroplanes. This build-up considerably outnumbered the German air service in this sector, committed as that service was to a maximum effort over Verdun.

The fledgling Tank Corps, which was to make its dramatic appearance later in the Somme battles, was at this time a closely guarded secret and masqueraded under the title of the Heavy Branch, Machine Gun Corps.

The area for the offensive having been settled, its communications had to be extended and improved to provide facilities, including water, for the long-term accommodation of over 400,000 men and 100,000 horses. The railways were inadequate, the roads few and poorly

An MG08 section pose during training, which concentrated on weapon handling, range practice, signalling, entrenching, and sustained fire practice. Like the British Vickers, whose ancestry in the Maxim design it shared, the MG08 was deadly not merely as a direct fire weapon, but could also lay down a murderous volume of indirect "barrage" fire from positions behind the front trenches. It fired the standard 7.92mm round out to a maximum range of 4,400 yards at a cyclic rate of fire of between 400 and 500 rounds per minute. Though its integral sights were limited to 2,200 yards a 2½-power optical sight could also be fitted, as well as a variety of indirect fire instruments.

The six guns of a machine gun company were usually positioned in three two-gun sections, the flank sections interlocking their fire with that of the centre section to produce a total coverage of the company's front. (Courtesy M.Pegler)

A group of veteran German NCOs off duty behind the lines, supposedly photographed on the Somme front. (Courtesy M.Pegler)

surfaced, and the available accomodation required massive expansion by the construction of camps of huts and tentage, with the attendant need for thousands of latrine boreholes. Work began on laying railway lines sufficient for the 31 trains each day that the Fourth Army would need for its minimum requirements. Light railways, or tramway systems, were constructed to push railheads forward to within reach of divisional horse transport. A great deal of work had to be done repairing and widening bridges and providing passing places on roads. After the first fortnight of the battle the thin crust of road metal began to deteriorate, and the periodic rain combined with heavy traffic turned the surface of roads into a mass of liquid mud, seriously hampering transport communications. A shortage of crushed stone made the creation of roads difficult, and the heavy burden of military traffic was to create difficulties and to keep labour units busy for the whole campaign.

Various labour units were employed in the building and repair of roads, the construction of camps, timber cutting, quarrying, sanitary work, dock labour, and the digging of rear defensive works. Their manpower came from medically down-graded infantrymen, conscientious objectors called up after the passing of the Military Service Act, and the personnel of the original labour battalions Royal Engineers, formed from elderly navvies and tradesmen who had volunteered for service. Another form of heavy manual work, with its own psycholigal pressures, was performed by the men of the tunnelling companies who dug the shafts out under no-man's-land below enemy positions, in which were placed the huge quantities of high explosive for what were then called "mines".

Boxed ammunition of all descriptions was built up in the open in dumps with only tarpaulin covers. From these were drawn the quantities of ammunition held in readiness when the artillery took position (e.g. in the case of 18-pounders, 354 rounds per gun; for 6in. howitzers, 200 rounds; and for 8in. howitzers, 90 rounds per gun), and the interim dumps at unit, division and Corps. Similar dumps for rations and other stores were established in much the same way.

Traffic control was carefully organised and regulated by military police; control posts were established and mounted military police constantly patrolled roads. A "forward examining line" was established and civilian inhabitants living east of this were encouraged to evacuate. As work progressed and men and materials poured into the area, the Fourth Army had reason to be thankful for the work of the 3rd Wing, Royal Flying Corps. During the whole build-up period not a single enemy aircraft came over their area, either to bomb, direct artillery fire, or observe the preparations for attack. The only bombs which fell were dropped by an aircraft of the Royal Naval Air Service by mistake.

The Plan

In its broadest terms, the British plan was to make a belt of the German defences 2,000 yards deep untenable by means of gunfire, and then to occupy it. Montauban, Contalmaison, Pozières, Miraumont spur and Serre were to be the objectives during the first day's operations by the Fourth Army, while to the north divisions of the Third Army would carry out simultaneous attacks on the Gommecourt salient. The three Corps on the Fourth Army left had as their objectives the German second position, requiring an infantry advance of over 4,000 yards in some cases and the splitting of the artillery effort between the German first and second lines. Strategic surprise was impossible under the circumstances, but it was hoped that tactical

Canadian motorcyclist taking a pannier of homing pigeons out to a forward unit; later they will be released to "home" with their messages to the mobile loft in the background. In 1916 radio communications were primitive, and had serious limitations for field use. Great dependence had to be placed upon field cables for telephone and key communication; visual signalling by flag, mirror and lamp; runners and despatch riders; and pigeons. All these means were vulnerable in battle: field cables were constantly being cut by shellfire, which also disoriented pigeons; visual signalling stations were often destroyed or obscured; and runners and depatch riders often became casualties.

Later chapters of this book offer many instances of the tragic results of unreliable communications; it has even been argued that the invention of a reliable man-portable radio would have saved more lives in the Great War than any other technical innovation. Once an attack was launched commanders in the rear often received no prompter or more accurate reports of progress than enjoyed by their great-grandfathers at Waterloo. Simple ignorance of what was happening, to whom, and where, caused both failure to exploit local success and costly perseverance in hopeless attacks.(IWM CO2171)

surprise might be achieved if the enemy could be deceived as to the timing of the assault. The precise objectives for the Corps of the Fourth Army were issued by General Rawlinson to their commanders at a conference on 17 May. Rawlinson pointed out that his intention was to gain possession of the line Montauban–Pozières–Serre, and for the Corps on the left to establish a defensive flank while the rest of the Army pushed on to gain the high ground in the neighbourhood of Guillemont and Ginchy towards Combles. He stated that he had twice as many guns for the bombardment than for that at Loos in 1915, and that there was practically unlimited artillery ammunition. He admitted that wire-cutting by the artillery was not, in some cases, going to be easy; the more distant wire could only be dealt with by 60-pounder guns. Success in the later phases of operations would depend on the rapidity with which the

artillery could be got forward in the support of the infantry. Brigades were to be constantly practised in passing through others for the attack, and training areas similar to the ground over which units were to advance should be sought. General Rawlinson concluded by issuing his Corps commanders a pamphlet entitled "Tactical Notes".

On 11 June a request was received from General Joffre that the assault might be brought forward to 25 June. After some revision a provisional plan based on the new date was issued and the programme for the dumping of ammunition speeded up. It was finally settled that the assault should begin on 29 June, with the preparatory bombardment beginning on the 24th.

On 16 June Sir Douglas Haig issued a directive for the action to be taken after the capture of the first objective. The advance was to be "pressed eastward far enough to enable our cavalry to push through into the open country beyond the enemy's prepared lines of defence. Our object then will be to turn northwards, taking the enemy's lines in flank and reverse, the bulk of the cavalry operating on the outer flank of this movement, whilst suitable detachments (of all arms) should be detailed to cover the movement from any offensive of the enemy from the east." For this venture the 1st, 3rd and 2nd Indian Cavalry Divisions were assembled in the area of Albert. Four infantry divisions were also deployed for the exploitation.

General Rawlinson held a final orders group on 22 June, during which he discussed the courses open to the enemy and the possible reactions to them. He concluded by reminding his commanders that they would be working with troops of the New Army who lacked the discipline, training and tradition of the old Regular Army; it was therefore most important to impress upon them that reorganisation must be undertaken as soon as a position was captured.

By now the theory of the assault had been well disseminated and was understood. A preliminary artillery bombardment – with the object of cutting the enemy's wire and destroying his trenches, machine gun emplacements and gun positions – would be fired over a period of days. Folowing this phase the infantry assault would be launched after a short, intense barrage on the enemy front trenches. At the time of the assault, Zero Hour, this barrage would be lifted and dropped on the enemy's second position. Great emphasis had been placed on the effectiveness of the artillery programme, by both Sir Douglas Haig and General Rawlinson, who stated that "nothing could exist at the conclusion of the bombardment in the area covered by it".

Amongst the orders issued was one stating that the front line trenches from which the attack was to be delivered should be within 200 yards of the enemy's front line (an order that few chose to obey). It was definitely ordered that the attack was to be carried out "in successive waves or lines, each line adding fresh impetus to the preceding one when this is checked, and carrying the whole forward to the objective...a single line of men has usually failed, two lines have generally failed, but sometimes succeeded, three lines have generally succeeded, but sometimes failed, and four or more lines have generally succeeded". Infiltration was to be discouraged; "mopping up", flank protection and consolidation were to be left to the follow-up waves. "Troops once launched to the attack must push on at all costs till the final objective is reached...All must be prepared for heavy casualties."

CHAPTER FIVE

Bombardment and Barrage

The programme for the preliminary artillery bombardment was issued on 5 June. It spread the fire tasks to be undertaken over a period of five days – nominally U, V, W, X, and Y Days – prior to Z Day, on which the infantry were to assault. The tasks and the stages were many but, briefly stated, the first two days were to be given over completely to registration and wire-cutting, and the third, fourth and fifth days to the destruction of defences and the continuation of wire-cutting. Tasks included the destruction of barbed wire obstacles, in which the trench mortars were to assist; bombardment of trenches, fortified localities, strongpoints, observation posts, machine gun emplacements and rear areas; counter-battery work; bombardment by trench mortars; smoke barrages; the discharge of phosphorus bombs and candles, and the discharge of gas. In order to deceive the enemy, bombardments of a definite length of time at particular hours of the day were to be fired to accustom him to take cover. This would be varied somewhat on Zero Day in the hope of achieving surprise.

The bulk of the destructive tasks fell to the heavy artillery. To the 18-pounders of the field artillery were assigned the tasks of wire-cutting, searching trenches, villages, woods and hollows, while the field artillery 4.5in. howitzers were ordered to destroy communication trenches and machine gun emplacements and to assist in the bombardment of villages and woods. A joint task for the field artillery was the interruption of communications, especially at night, and the prevention of the enemy from repairing damage. Many of the heavy batteries arrived late in position, and until their observation officers became familiar with the area their shooting was not entirely accurate. The RFC photographed the enemy lines when weather permitted, however, and greatly assisted the artillery in judging the results of their work.

The total number of guns available to the Fourth Army included the following: 18-pounder guns, 808; 4.7in. guns, 32; 60-pounder guns, 128; 6in. guns, 20; 9.2in. guns, 1; 12in. guns, 1; 4.5in. howitzers, 202; 6in. howitzers, 104; 8in. howitzers, 64; 9.2in. howitzers, 60; 12in. howitzers, 11; 15in. howitzers, 6; French 220mm howitzers, 16; French 75mm guns, 60; and French 120mm guns, 24. There were 288 medium and 28 heavy trench mortars, three gas-cylinder companies, three smoke companies and one flame-projector company.

Roughly half the assembled pieces were 18-pounders, weapons designed for open warfare where their mobility, fixed shrapnel ammunition and high rate of fire were highly desirable. They were, however, less than efficient for the conditions of siege warfare prevailing in 1916. The pole trail of the 18-pounder limited its maximum elevation to 16 degrees and consequently its maximum range to 6,525 yards (almost 6,000 metres). Its shrapnel round burst in the air

above a target and, acting like a gigantic shotgun, showered it with lead/antimony bullets, which had a lethal effect against troops in the open but were relatively ineffective against trenches and ineffective against fortifications. The high explosive round for the 18-pounder, produced from 1915, carried a paltry 13oz. (368g) of Amatol – a "payload" of only four-and-a-half per cent of the total shell weight. (The flat trajectory of the 18-pounder, coupled with the small explosive content of its HE rounds, made it the equivalent of the German 77mm "whizzbang".) The stress of repeated firing brought about malfunction in the hydro-spring recoil system, the springs losing their resilience or, in some cases, breaking; as early as 1915 work was undertaken to modify the fault, resulting in the design and fitting of a hydro-pneumatic recoil system and a variety of other improvements, but these were not available for the Somme battles.

Regarding ammunition, the Fourth Army was allotted 2.6 million rounds of 18-pounder, 260,000 4.5in. howitzer, 100,000 6in. howitzer, and a decreasing scale with the rise in calibre to 15in. howitzer at 3,000 rounds. Many problems plagued the fuses for British HE ammunition. Development and modification of fuses progressed through 1915 and 1916, resulting in an effective fuse being introduced in 1917; but British gunners fought the Somme battles with fuses that were sometimes defective, and always inefficient in that they allowed the round to partially bury itself before detonation. (This had the effects of limiting the destructive power of the shell splinters, and creating the craters which covered the battlefield, filling with water and hampering the movement of men, horses and vehicles.) Mortar ammunition amounted to 800,000 rounds and 35,000 smoke bombs. There were 100,000 smoke grenades and 100,000 smoke candles.

★   ★   ★

In 1916 the artillery arm of the British Army was in a state of transition. The field artillery that crossed to France with the BEF had begun the war as a small, highly trained force wedded to the tactical doctrines of manoeuvre and direct fire. Most of its ammunition was the shrapnel which was so effective against an enemy in the open. Left behind was the garrison artillery, the branch of the Royal Regiment whose job it was to operate the big guns in Britain's fortresses at home and abroad, and to provide the modern equivalent of a "siege train" when required. By 1918 the artillery of the BEF had developed into a powerful and homogeneous force adapted to the conditions of the Western Front, and was by then so effective that it had mastered the enemy artillery and had taken gunnery to the limits of its possibilities. The journey had been a long and hard one, and there had been much to learn along the way. In June 1916 that journey had just begun.

The early problems for Britain's gunners had been those shared with the rest of an army coping with a rapid expansion in manpower: training difficulties, and shortages of weapons and equipment. By the time of the Somme battles the problems of manpower and materiel appeared to be solved. Industry had supplied the guns and a sufficiency of ammunition. The resources of the garrison artillery had been mobilised to bring to France the heavy ordnance that the new warfare demanded (from a handful of 60-pounder batteries in 1914 this branch had grown to 191 heavy batteries of all types by July 1916). The chopping and changing of artillery establishments seemed to have produced the right balance of guns to units. All seemed to augur well for the forthcoming battles.

There were, however, indicators of problems to come, the first being that of command. Long-established staff procedures laid down that orders were to be issued by commanders of Armies, Corps or divisions through their respective General Staffs. Under these rules Royal Artillery generals at Corps and Army headquarters occupied the roles of advisors – possessing no staffs of their own, nor means of communication with the artillery of their formations. This system worked in the early days of mobile warfare, when field gunnery was a comparatively uncomplicated business and could be understood by officers of all arms. But with the advent of trench warfare, which was, to all intents and purposes, a vast linear siege, gunnery had become increasingly technical, requiring experienced artillerymen to appre-

A British 9.2in. gun on a Mark I railway truck mounting at Moricourt, September 1916. These weapons could send a shell weighing 380lbs. out to a range of 21,000 yards – nearly twelve miles. "The Big Push" was the name given by the popular press to the British offensive on the Somme.

June 1916: one of the 64 British 8in. howitzers which took part in the bombardment on the Somme, sending a 200lb. high explosive shell out to a range of up to 10,500 yards. (IWM Q569)

ciate its possibilities and to exercise control over its direction. This could not be done above divisional level, or that of the heavy artillery group.

For years there had been an ongoing struggle with the General Staff for the appointment of artillery commanders with real powers of command. The argument seemed to have been won when, in October 1915, the status of artillery generals attached to headquarters staffs of Army Corps had been changed. Instead of being advisors they became General Officers Commanding, Royal Artillery of the Corps, "charged with the co-ordination of the action of the artillery of the Corps and the executive command of such portion of it as the Corps commander may direct from time to time". No longer, it seemed, would the General Staffs exercise total control over the artillery. But when a redeployment of heavy artillery took place in March 1916, ambiguity arose as to the powers of command of the officers now designated as "Brigadiers RA of the Corps". These were later defined as being "available to take executive command of any concentration of the Corps and divisional artillery". This had the effect of limiting their powers to the command of concentrations only, resulting in a reversion to the previous situation in all other cases.

On the Somme the Major-General Royal Artillery of the Fourth Army had no powers to compel Corps artillery to follow his plan for 1 July 1916; and only the artillery of XIII Corps did so – with conspicuous success. It was not until December 1916, after the conclusion of the fighting on the Somme, that the powers of GOCs RA of Corps were positively resolved, as were those of the senior artillery officers at Army level, who were given the title "Major-Generals Royal Artillery, attached to Army Headquarters".

Organisational problems in 1916 centred on the best use to be made of the limited number of experienced battery officers; and obtaining the maximum effect from the available gun power. Battles were increasingly becoming artillery contests, and the tying up of most of the field artillery with divisions created difficulties. Infantry needed resting more frequently than artillery; so the divisional field artillery were disrupted in their effective engagement of the enemy by frequent trekking in and out of the line. Heavy artillery, organised into mixed groups and operating at Corps or Army level, did not suffer this disruption, and it was realised that a greater proportion of the field artillery should be used in this way. After the Somme battles one field artillery brigade was removed from each division to become an Army brigade, but those battles were fought with less than perfect use being made of the available field gun power.

The shuffling of gun establishments that led to four-gun field batteries was completed in May 1916, but it became increasingly difficult, especially when casualties began to be sustained, to find sufficient experienced battery comman-

June 1916: a British 15in. howitzer is prepared for action. Its high explosive shell weighed 1,400lbs. – more than half a ton – and could be fired nearly 11,000 yards. The Royal Garrison Artillery brought more than their hard-hitting guns to France after the establishment of the trench lines; they also brought the skills and techniques of long-range gunnery that were to be so much in demand in the linear-siege conditions that developed. Long sneered at as "slide-rule" gunners by their brethren of the Royal Field Artillery and the Royal Horse Artillery, the RGA found a war ideally suited to their training. The remainder of the artillery dug in their guns, led their horses to the rear, and set about the business of applying the skills of the RGA. (IWM Q35)

ders. Eventually, in early 1917, a reversion was made to the six-gun battery establishment.

Over the course of the war the British artillery arm was constantly developing the technical equipment and skills necessary for accurate application of indirect fire, especially against enemy batteries. Sound-ranging, flash-spotting, the calibration of guns, application of meteorological data, accurate field survey and observation of all kinds were developed in order to locate unseen targets and to shoot at them with effect. These methods were perfected in 1917, but in mid-1916 British artillerymen were only beginning to develop these skills. As a consequence many enemy batteries went unlocated or undamaged.

Difficulties over communication were a handicap which the gunners shared with the rest of the Army; but poor or non-existent communications affected gunnery to a greater extent than any other arm. It limited or prevented contact between observers and gun positions, and this prevented the flexibility of fire control so essential if infantry in battle were to be given effective close support. This lack of reliable means of communication generally committed the artillery to "timetable" bombardments and barrages which used up enormous quantities of ammunition.

There were difficulties with the guns. There were too few heavy howitzers and a preponderance of field artillery, mostly the 18-pounders whose limitations in range, shell power and mechanical reliability have been discussed above. The deterioration or failure of buffer springs in the recuperator systems required guns to be taken out of action for repair or repositioned after each shot. Wartime manufacture may have resulted in some springs of doubtful quality, but this inherent design fault caused great difficulties which were only resolved by the fitting of a modified recoil system after the Somme battles. The gun situation is well summed up in the official history:

"The hurried expansion of the munitions industry involved considerable sacrifice of quality to quantity. Even so, at various times during the [Somme] offensive the reserves of guns and howitzers of all calibres were not sufficient to replace casualties without some delay; and a lack of spare parts prevented the Armies from keeping all units up to strength. Only by the constant husbanding of ammunition could the operations be kept going, and on 31st October the War Office was asked to double the estimates of requirements previously made. There were many defects both in guns and ammunition. Early in the operations the 4.5 inch howitzer had frequent prematures, and when in September this trouble seemed over it recurred with the 18-pounders."

Perhaps the greatest problems of all were those concerned with ammunition. A lack of gas shells necessitated the "borrowing" of French 75mm batteries and, although the tried-and-tested shrapnel ammunition continued to serve safely and well, there were difficulties with high explosive. Britain had been late in developing high explosive projectiles, and those in the hands of the British artillery in 1916 suffered from a variety of faults caused by poor materials, poor design, and rushed production. The "shell scandal" of the previous year had served to bring ammunition shortages to public attention, and in the haste to overcome these a number of mistakes in design and manufacture were made which had serious consequences in the battles of 1916. (Even so, as Sir Douglas Haig later put it, "Throughout the

Somme battle the expenditure of artillery ammunition had to be watched with the greatest care".)

At various times during 1916 many types of artillery ammunition were undergoing examination, repair, or reconditioning due to some flaw or defect. There was general agreement that the quality of ammunition was below that used in the battles of the previous year, and throughout 1916 there was a steady increase in the number of "prematures" in proportion to the rounds fired (a premature being a shell which detonated before its fuse activated, most seriously in the barrel of the gun or a few feet from its muzzle — in either event it put the gun out of action and caused casualties, usually fatal, to the crew and anyone else in the immediate vicinity). Some of the prematures were traced to defective shells where minute cracks in the shell-casing caused the filling to detonate on firing. But a great many of the prematures were due to defective fuses, particular the "Fuse, Graze No.100".

The 100 fuse was used in British HE shells generally. It went from drawing board to production in ten days in 1914, and began to give trouble right from the start. Even today it is hard to say with certainty whether its lethal qualities were due to an inherently unsafe design, sloppy manufacture, bad reaction to mishandling, or a combination of all three. What is obvious is that the 100 fuse lacked any external indication as to whether its mechanism was "safe" or "armed"; its smooth exterior had no safety pin to be drawn before firing, nor any aperture through which its safety could be checked. A "pre-cocked pellet" carried the detonator, which was armed by the shock of firing, and then driven onto a firing pin when the shell "grazed" an obstruction. Unfortunately, rough handling could arm the fuse before it was fitted to a shell — with horribly obvious consequences when firing provided the second shock. Among the first users of the 100 fuse were the 4.5in. howitzer batteries, who suffered so many premature detonations that for a time they were known as "suicide clubs". When, in 1915, high explosive shell was manufactured for the 18-pounders, their crews also suffered from sporadic outbreaks of prematures; in fact, it is recorded that all guns using this fuse suffered in this way.

In time the 100 fuse was replaced by safer designs, or modified to ensure proper functioning. Even so, at one time it was expected that one gun must "burst" for every one thousand rounds fired — a horrifying statistic when it is remembered that 1.7 million rounds were fired during the bombardment prior to 1 July. Such was the concern of the authorities that special programmes were set up to examine consignments of the 100 fuse in an attempt to identify those faulty. An enquiry traced the factory that had made the batches proved faulty, and little by little this menace was overcome. But its effect had been such that for many months gun crews were forced to play Russian roulette on a gigantic scale.

The morale of the gunners condemned to use this risky equipment is not difficult to imagine, and nor are the steps they took to shield themselves from its dangers. To what extent their possible action accounted for the quantities of unexploded British HE shells which littered battlefields from 1915 onwards is unknown; human nature being what it is, any tampering with the 100 fuse to render it permanently "safe" would not have been a matter for general discussion. "Duds" were put down to faulty manufacture,

1 July 1916: the crew of this British 6in. howitzer, "The Vimy Queen", seem extraordinarily cheerful as they load yet another 100lb. round, given the evil reputation of the Fuse, Graze, No.100. Note cleats fastened to the wheels and the dial-sight clamped to the carriage. (IWM Q3)

even sabotage on the part of unsympathetic munitions workers in Britain and America. To this day, thousands of unexploded British shells are regularly ploughed up by French farmers on the Somme.

Overriding all problems and limitations was the question of how to make the best tactical use of what was to hand, a conundrum made more difficult for the gunners by the inability of the rest of the army to settle on a common tactical doctrine. The Commander-in-Chief apparently saw no conflict of purpose between a battle fought to effect a breakthrough and one planned to wear down the enemy's strength. Rupture and attrition, however, did not mean the same thing to the commander of the Fourth Army, who thought that one required separate tactics from the other. A battle with breakthrough as its aim tied field artillery to the divisions it must support in the "open" warfare that followed, as well as requiring large numbers of cavalrymen and their horses to wait in anticipation, consuming resources and forage at an alarming rate. In 1916 an effective tactical doctrine for the attrition battle was some way off, as were the means and methods for the most efficient artillery support of such a battle. The theory of artillery tactics such as creeping barrages and neutralising fire were being discussed, but had yet to be tested in practice.

In time the technical problems would be solved, as would the dilemmas over the tactics. But in 1916 there was little time to seek solutions in the context of the ongoing battle. What was at fault was not always clear, but that all was not well with the British artillery was obvious to all.

A German HE shell bursts forward of the British wire: a "still" from the film The Battle of the Somme. *This shot clearly indicates the burrowing effect of this type of ammunition. Until more efficient fuses became available, or time-fuses were used to burst HE in the air, these shells continued to crater the landscape, which reduced their lethal effect. (IWM Q79487)*

On 24 June, U Day, the bombardment opened. Under conditions of rain and low cloud the British batteries began the task of wire-cutting. This had been judged best done with shrapnel, detonated by time fuse above the entanglements so that the shrapnel balls were fired into them to break and scatter the wire. (In the case of 18-pounder shrapnel, there were 375 balls per round, each weighing three-eigths of an ounce or about 11 grammes.) Very little counter-battery work was possible until the weather cleared to allow aircraft and balloon observers to correct the fall of shots. There was some bombardment of trenches and redoubts. After nightfall the systematic shelling of communications began. What little enemy artillery retaliation there was received a fourfold reply, and if that was not sufficient larger guns and howitzers were directed on to the enemy batteries. A release of gas at one point on the British front incurred very heavy enemy artillery fire.

On the 25th the weather was bright and clear, and the programme continued with wire-cutting all day and concentrations of fire on rear areas. At night there was intermittent fire on defences and a continuous fire on communications. Fires and large explosions indicated that concentrations on enemy batteries had been effective. Enemy artillery retaliation enabled observers to fix the posi-

tions of 102 hostile batteries, mainly on the enemy right. Night shoots were co-ordinated with a series of infantry trench raids, which reported varying degrees of damage to the enemy wire and fortifications.

On 26 June the weather deteriorated, bright intervals alternating with heavy showers and low cloud for most of the day. The destructive bombardment began, with concentrated shelling from 9a.m. to 10.20a.m., resulting in more fires and explosions. Gas and smoke discharged from various points along the British front over the course of the day and night was answered by enemy artillery fire. An aerial photography mission flown at 3.30p.m. brought back

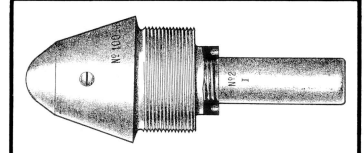

The "Fuse, Graze, No.100" with "Gaine No.2" – an attempt at a simple design that could be mass-produced by factories with no experience of the manufacture of ammunition. It contained a "cocked" pellet holding a detonator, which was driven on to a needle when the shell "grazed" its target; there was no safety pin to lock the pellet in transit, nor any external indication of its arming status. Shortly after its introduction enquiries were instituted into the rash of dangerous premature shell bursts, but these were conducted in the teeth of the "shell scandal" which put extreme pressure on industry to step up production of ammunition. In late 1915 responsibility for designs and inventions was taken from the military and assumed by the Ministry of Munitions; this had the effect of disrupting investigations into the malfunctioning of the 100 fuse, which continued to be supplied right through the period of the Battle of the Somme. In 1917 the French Army's HE percussion fuse was copied and issued to British gunners as the "Fuse, Percussion, Direct Action, No.106". This had not one, but eventually five safety devices – one internal and four external. Not only was the fuse totally safe to use, but it detonated its shell before it buried itself in the earth.

evidence of the effect of the bombardment so far, and showed satisfactory deterioration of enemy positions and wire. It was decided that the howitzers and mortars were not showing good progress, however, and 18-pounders were ordered to supplement their fire resulting, in some divisions, in 400 to 500 rounds per gun being fired every 24 hours. Night raids were again carried out by the infantry, seizing prisoners and reporting on the state of the enemy's wire and trenches.

The weather was bad again on 27 and 28 June, with morning mist followed by heavy showers on both days. Low cloud continued to hamper the work of the RFC in the direction of fire. However, the full programme of bombardment went ahead whether the fall of rounds could be observed or not. The usual infantry raids reported varying damage to the enemy wire. At 11a.m. on 28 June, as a consequence of the bad weather and its limiting effect on the accuracy of the bombardment, the British and French headquarters agreed to postpone Zero Day for 48 hours, from 29 June to 1 July. The two extra days were fitted into the artillery programme as Y1 and Y2, the fire tasks due for day Y to be fired on both days except for some

July 1916: an 18-pdr. gun in action on the Somme (though this scene was probably posed for the camera – the gun position officer was unlikely to order the gun fired while the horses and limbers were to his front). The ammunition laying ready is all high explosive, fused with the "Fuse, Graze, No. 100"; its tiny explosive payload of less than a pound gave unimpressive results. Note the central "pole trail" – as opposed to a split trail – which limited the gun's elevation, and therefore its range. The 18-pdr. represented about half the total number of British guns on the Somme during the preparation for the infantry offensive. (IWM Q4066)

economies of heavy artillery ammunition. Even so, the extra demands resulted in "thinner" barrages on 1 July. The artillery was ordered to make the most of the two extra days especially in the completion of wire-cutting and the destruction of enemy batteries. On the night of 28/29 June raiding parties reported the enemy to be more vigilant and their trenches more strongly held than before.

On 29 June the weather improved, enabling aerial observation and the location of 57 enemy batteries in action. British retaliatory shoots started fires in Martinpuich, Miraumont and Gommecourt. Raids that night reported some of the enemy positions unmanned, and his wire severely damaged. The 30th was a day of cloud and high wind, but some aerial observation was possible and counter-battery fire was directed on some of the 171 enemy batteries observed. The infantry raids that night were ordered to make a special examination of the enemy's wire, and in places to cut it.

Reports varied, two patrols from one division reporting it "very much damaged", whilst two others claimed it to be "not much damaged". It appeared to be more effectively damaged on the British right, in front of XIII and XV Corps. In front of Thiepval and Gommecourt it appeared to be intact and very dense. Opposite the 8th Division it was reported to be "not properly cut". In the 31st Division two units reported that on their front there was at no point a clear gap, a third reported their wire to be not a serious obstacle, whilst a fourth claimed there were gaps every 20 yards. Certainly the assaulting infantry were going to have to bunch in order to pass through some of the gaps. During the bombardment period no infantry raid on the VIII Corps front had got through the wire and into the German position. Sir Douglas Haig demanded an explanation from the Corps commander, and on the night before the infantry assault wrote: "The only doubt I have is with regards to the VIII Corps staff, which has no experience of the fighting in France and has not carried out one successful raid".

While the gunners completed the fire tasks of Y Day, 30 June, the infantry made their last minute preparations for the morrow. Equipment was inspected and checked and the plan for the assault gone over again and again. Messages of encouragement from commanders were read out, some units indulged in a final burst of ceremonial, and as dusk approached the battalions formed up for the march to the assembly trenches. Medical officers and orderlies laid out their instruments and dressings; military police took post at their "battle stops" a mile and a half behind the front to arrest or turn back stragglers; and the personnel in charge of the prisoner-of-war "cages" waited in anticipation.

For the gunners the period of the bombardment had been a time of unremitting toil as they strove to keep their guns in action, to clean and service them during the lulls, to bring up more ammunition, and to snatch food and sleep when they could. The assault infantry, filing down the communication trenches to their jump-off points, endured a different kind of stress as the minutes to Zero Hour ticked away. Physically burdened with helmets, weapons and ammunition, entrenching tools, gas helmets and "fighting order" equipment, they picked up extra ammunition, grenades, wire cutters, and empty sandbags, picks and shovels (for use in repairing captured positions) from the dumps of trench stores as they moved along. The total weight carried by each man was reckoned at 66lbs., a burden which made it difficult to climb out of a trench or move faster than a walk; but many men were carrying even heavier loads, especially those with machine guns, machine gun magazines, and signal equipment.

The mental burden of men going into battle is not so easy to compute, whether they were veterans of many actions or, like most of the British infantrymen moving forward that night, men facing the test of their first battle. Whatever their thoughts or fears, they trudged and stumbled on through the clear summer night in hundreds of columns, guided by tapes and shaded lanterns until they reached the assembly trenches from which they would attack on the following morning. By 5.15a.m. all were in position, with the British wire cleared to allow their passage. Enemy shelling and gas discharge was spasmodic, raising hopes that the Allied bombardment had done its job. Deep beneath the earth at several points along the German line many tons of high explosive waited packed in the chambers of the mines which had been dug over the preceding months, and sapper officers stood ready to detonate these awful weapons.

From 6.25a.m. on the morning of 1 July there was an unending roar from the gun positions, followed by a cacophony of screams and shrieks as the shells of all calibres passed over the heads of the waiting infantry to burst in a deluge on the German positions. Eight minutes before Zero Hour the Stokes mortars joined in with a hurricane bombardment during which their crews fired at the rate of 30 rounds each minute.

At 7.30a.m. the roar ceased as the gunners realigned their weapons on their secondary targets. Now was the time for the British infantry to surge up the ladders and "over the top", to advance across no-man's-land and take possession of the German front line in the manner described at their briefings. But, ominously, as the British gunners elevated and directed their weapons on to their more distant targets, so the German gunners facing them ceased their counter-battery shoots and trained their weapons upon no-man's-land.

Salvage: a dump of 18-pdr. shell cases on the Somme. The British artillery fired about 1.7 million rounds during the bombardment prior to 1 July; and it was reckoned that one in every thousand rounds detonated prematurely in the gun. (IWM Q113)

Shrapnel shells required accurate placing and careful fuse-timing if they were to cut or sweep away belts of German wire. Where the effect of such fire could not be observed and corrected, the wire remained intact to greet those infantrymen who survived no-man's-land to reach it. (IWM Q2548)

June 1916: men of a Royal Engineers tunnelling company (probably former coal or tin miners) at work in a mine chamber while an officer listens for sounds of enemy counter-mining with a "geophone" — essentially, a giant stethoscope; counter-mining could lead to desperate underground encounters. A flaring lamp hangs on the chalkface just behind the central man's face. The chalk subsoil of the Somme allowed cleaner cutting and much less shoring-up than the waterlogged clay of the Ypres Salient. (IWM Q115)

CHAPTER SIX

The Infantry Battle on 1 July: VII, VIII and X Corps

During the brief lull in the barrage the soldiers in the Allied trenches could hear birdsong. It was a perfect, cloudless summer day, marred only by the patches of mist that hung over the German lines. At 7.30a.m. the whistles of the officers shrilled; and out of the trenches, along 25 miles of the Allied front, clambered the assault infantry of three Armies – two British and one French – to advance on the German positions. (The French XVII Corps south of the Somme had orders to delay its advance until later in the morning.) On the front of the British Fourth Army battalions from eleven divisions moved forward, seven of which were New Army formations – Kitchener's men, in their first major battle.

Their fortunes were to vary on this day. The artillery of the British Army had fired the greatest bombardment in its long history, and now the British infantry was about to fight its greatest battle, the first day of which was so momentous that several volumes would not do justice to what took place. In order to best describe the events of 1 July 1916 in broad outline, a description of what took place in each Corps sector follows, from the north to the south of the front.

Gommecourt: VII Corps, Third Army

Sir Douglas Haig, in an attempt to lengthen the front of the offensive, had ordered the Third Army to attack Gommecourt. VII Corps was chosen for the operation; and the 46th and 56th Divisions, both composed of Territorials, were ordered to mount the attack. Gommecourt was a strongly defended salient which had resisted all previous attempts at its capture. It projected like the beak of a bird of prey into the Allied line, with the point of the beak a tangled mass of partially destroyed forest that masked the main defence, a strongpoint known to the British as "the Maze" and to the Germans as Kern Redoubt. For additional security the Germans had covered the salient by three retrenchments, the 1st and 2nd Switch Line and the Intermediate Line. The area was criss-crossed with numerous communication trenches, which combined to provide a series of defence lines from which attackers could be blocked and encircled, from whatever direction they penetrated. On 1 July the garrison consisted of three regiments (nine battalions) with one in reserve.

The British plan was to "pinch out" the salient with convergent attacks against its north and south faces, the 46th (North Midland) Division attacking in the north and the 56th (London) Division from the south. A battalion from each division was to keep busy the defenders of the intervening gap. The width of no-man's-land varied from 800 yards in front of the 56th Division to 400-500 yards in front of the 46th, requiring the pushing forward of trenches in order to shorten the distance to be covered, especially on the front of the 56th Division. Masses of barbed wire in front of the 46th Division were tunnelled under with "Russian saps" (communication trenches with overhead cover), and the digging of new assembly trenches had proceeded despite the constant flooding of these new works. All this activity was observed by the Germans. Four days before the assault the Corps commander told Haig that "they know we are coming, all right".

During their bombardment the British artillery on the VII Corps front had been unable to deal effectively with the German artillery, whose heavy batteries were beyond the range of all but a few super-heavy British weapons. This meant that on 1 July, including the fire from batteries north and south of the salient, the German barrage put down on no-man's-land was more severe than in any other sector. It was the German artillery which proved to be the main factor in their successful defence of Gommecourt.

The imminent attack of the British infantry was obvious to the Germans, who reported that "the new British assault trenches, the pushing forward of saps, the frequent bombardment of important points, the appearance of heavy trench mortars, and the increasing artillery fire, which from time to time rose to 'drum-fire', left no doubt as to the intention of the enemy". At 4a.m. on 1 July the German artillery began to shell the British assault positions, and continued to do so until the British assault barrage caused them to switch to the British battery positions; but some German guns again shelled the British trenches so consistently that the infantry of the 46th and 56th Divisions were glad when the order was given to advance and they could momentarily move away from the German fire.

The 56th Division assaulted with two brigades in line and one in reserve. At 7.20a.m. smoke was discharged to mask the attack, and at 7.25a.m. the infantry left their trenches and began to deploy under its cover. At 7.30a.m. they began their advance in the face of an intensifying enemy barrage that began to fall on the British trenches. Despite problems with the German wire the Londoners moved rapidly and entered the enemy trenches before meeting serious opposition. The ruins of the front three German trenches were occupied, the last after gathering enemy opposition and a fire-fight. At 9.30a.m. tactical sign boards were seen by observers in the rear which marked the gains of the 56th Division, and indicated that consolidation was taking place. Nearly 300 German prisoners were escorted back across no-man's-land, but after losing 80 of them to their own shellfire hundreds of others were confined in their own dug-outs.

German artillery fire had by now become so severe that the digging of flank protection positions could not go ahead, and reinforcements for the next stage of the British advance could not get forward. In time the assaulting battalions became entirely cut off by the enemy barrage falling on no-man's-land and the lost German trenches and, with grenades and ammunition running short, they began to yield to the pressure of German counter-attacks. As long as grenades (both British and captured German) were available the Londoners stood their ground, but when these ran short they were forced out of the German third line. Little help could be got from the British artillery, which was now firing, according to programme, on the enemy rear. Later, five field batteries were directed on to the communication trenches down which the Germans were attacking.

At 2p.m. the assault brigades were still clinging to the first

"The Battle of Albert", 1 July 1916: these British infantrymen, waiting in a support trench for the order to go forward, seem pretty tired already. They probably passed the night in these uncomfortable quarters; and it is certain that their last hot meal was many hours ago. In the last hour before they have to go forward they will be buoyed up by the furious crescendo of the British artillery bombardment, and may climb from the trenches convinced that no enemy could survive in the German first position.(IWM Q64)

and second lines, but processions of men, mostly wounded, were drifting back across no-man's-land. By 4p.m. the Germans had retaken their second trench and had entered the first. Plans were drawn up to renew the attack with fresh troops at nightfall, but before this could take place the British lodgement in the German front line had been reduced to five officers and 70 men holding a bare 200-yard section. They were finally driven from this; and at 9.30p.m., their ammunition gone, the last survivors returned. They left behind them the bodies of over 1,300 of their comrades killed in the attempt to take Gommecourt.

The 46th Division, assaulting from the north, also had two brigades forward. Their objectives were to set up a defensive flank north of Gommecourt, then to join hands with the 56th Division. Smoke was again used to obscure the assembly and advance of the North Midlanders, but it caused many of them to lose their way over ground that was a confused maze of old trenches and wire. Their deployment was neither uniform nor simultaneous. Half way across no-man's-land the smoke dispersed and at the same time the German infantry came up from their dug-outs. On reaching the German wire the attackers found that it was either still intact or, if damaged, had been repaired. As the German infantry manned their parapets their artillery opened a barrage on the British infantry, increasing in intensity as batteries to the north of the salient joined in. Machine gun fire from a projecting German position swept in enfilade down the German wire and through the companies of British infantry struggling with it. Grenades with smoking fuses fizzed over the wire to explode among them, and rifle fire shot down those determined enough to attempt its passage.

Despite opposition, the men of two battalions of the Sherwood Foresters (139th Brigade) succeeded in getting through and breaking into the German first trench. Some pushed on to the second trench, only to be attacked from the rear by the German infantry they had failed to "mop up" and who now emerged from their deep underground shelters. With the intense German barrage making movement in no-man's-land all but impossible, and pinning the Sherwood Foresters to their gains, confused attempts were made to reinforce them. Smoke was sought to cover movement across no-mans-land, but this could not be obtained until 3.20p.m. Even then it was not enough for the purpose, and the operation was called off. Few of the trapped Sherwood Foresters survived, those who did making their way back under cover of darkness. The remainder met their fate; in the words of a German report, "though they fought stoutly [they] were, except for a few prisoners, annihilated". Eighty per cent of the two battalions perished, including both commanding officers; the enemy reported only one officer and 30 men as prisoners.

Carrying out its orders to divert against itself forces which might otherwise be directed against the left flank of the main attack near Serre had cost VII Corps nearly 7,000 casualties. There was great difficulty in evacuating the wounded; but early on the morning of 2 July the Germans, who had suffered only 621 casualties, put up a large Geneva flag and both sides attended to their wounded unhindered. When all were gathered in salutes and the exchange of courtesies marked a return to the business of war as usual. Lists of prisoners were later exchanged by aeroplane message drops.

Panoramic view of part of the Somme battlefield in July 1916. Note the chalk-spoil scars of the trench systems; the strike of the British artillery shells bombarding the German positions; and the absolutely featureless terrain of no-man's-land. (IWM Q137-140)

Serre and Beaumont Hamel: VIII Corps, Fourth Army

Three miles south of the Gommecourt salient, the fortified village of Serre sat atop a small knoll on the Grandcourt spur, completely overlooking the British line. Forming up to assault Serre was the left hand division of VIII Corps (and of the Fourth Army), the 31st (New Army) Division. The 31st was one of the later Kitchener divisions, its infantry being mostly "Pals" units from towns such as Hull, Leeds, Bradford, Accrington, Sheffield, Barnsley and Durham. Their task was to form the left defensive flank of the main British effort, entailing the capture of ground on some parts of the divisional front to a depth of 3,000 yards.

As elsewhere, the infantry of the division began to emerge from their trenches to deploy in assault formation at 7.20a.m. They filed through narrow passages in their own wire to lie out in no-man's-land and await the signal to advance; and it was while this was being done that fire from German artillery and machine guns was directed upon them, including an accurate barrage that fell on the British front trench, bracketing it by 50 yards to the front and to the rear. British counter-battery fire and a Stokes mortar barrage did nothing to reduce the intensity of the German fire. At 7.30a.m., when the infantry of the 31st Division stood up to advance, the enemy shelling increased, while German infantry began to man their front line (the British barrage having passed on, this threat went unchecked).

Under the concentrations of fire now directed against them only isolated groups of the 31st Division were able to get to the German front trench, where they were overwhelmed by the defenders. The remainder, still bravely marching forward, had dropped in their tracks as they were hit by bullets, shell splinters or shrapnel. None wavered or ran away, most becoming casualties in the first hundred yards of their advance. In a few minutes the assaulting infantry of this fine division had been cut down by a fire so well directed and concentrated that it went on record that the cones of the enemy shell explosions gave the impression of a thick belt of poplar trees.

On the left of the division a company of the 11th East Lancashires managed to break into the German front line, and were later seen advancing into Serre village. (They were identified by observers in the British front line from the patches stitched to their jackets – red discs on their sleeves and red-and-white patches on their collars.) A number of men from the 12th York and Lancasters also succeeded in getting to Serre, where they suffered the same fate as the East Lancashires. Their bodies were found in the village when it was taken in November.

With the assault broken the fighting died down until, by noon, fire had almost ceased. On the left, continuing reports that some of the division's infantry had made it into Serre led to the organisation of a series of attempts to reinforce them. In the prevailing chaos of the British trenches all came to nothing; and at 6p.m. the Corps commander, aware that his troops were unfit to pursue the offensive, ordered a reorganisation in the British front trenches. As darkness fell the wounded and unwounded began to crawl in from no-man's-land, enabling a picture to be built up as to the degree of failure. The awful task of bringing in and evacuating the wounded began, followed by the burial of the dead. It was to last for 48 hours. Rolls were called and casualty lists compiled, and these showed that the division had sustained a loss of 3,600 men killed, wounded and missing.

South of Serre the fortunes of the other two assaulting divisions of VIII Corps, the 4th and 29th – both Regular Army – were similar to those of the 31st Division. A mine containing 40,000lbs. of Ammonal had been placed under the Hawthorn Redoubt, a German strongpoint opposite Beaumont Hamel village, and differing opinions as to the time it should be detonated were to have dire consequences. VIII Corps wanted it blown, and the crater occupied, four hours before Zero. GHQ had issued orders that all mines were to be fired between Zero and eight minutes before Zero; but reached a compromise with VIII Corps by agreeing to let them fire the Hawthorn Redoubt mine at ten minutes before Zero. As British infantry were then to

rush the resulting crater the British barrage was ordered to be switched from its vicinity at 7.20a.m.; but by some mischance the order was passed to the whole VIII Corps heavy artillery. As a consequence "the howitzers firing on the first line lifted to the reserve trenches, and at 7.25a.m. were joined there by the howitzers which had been firing on the support trench".

This left only an 18-pounder shrapnel barrage, due to lift off the front line at Zero Hour. However, the field batteries supporting the 29th Division had decided to avoid a pause by lifting half their effort at Zero minus three minutes. This meant that on the front of the division the German front line received no heavy barrage for the ten minutes preceding Zero Hour, and for the last three minutes only half the 18-pounder fire.

At 7.20a.m. the mine was fired, the heavy artillery barrage lifted off the German front trenches, and the Stokes mortars commenced their barrage. Two platoons of the 2nd Royal Fusiliers dashed forward to occupy the crater. They found the Germans, who had been completely alerted by the detonation, in possession of the far lip of the crater, from which they directed a heavy fire on the Fusiliers. While this battle in miniature was fought out the infantry of the rest of the division were attempting to form up for the assault under the full force of the German artillery and infantry defensive fire. In the words of a German report: "This explosion [the mine] was a signal for the infantry attack, and everyone got ready and stood on the lower steps of the dug-outs, rifles in hand, waiting for the bombardment to lift. In a few minutes the shelling ceased, and we rushed up the steps and out into the crater positions. Ahead of us wave after wave of British troops were crawling out of their trenches, and coming forward towards us at a walk, their bayonets glistening in the sun".

The Germans took up whatever positions they chose, standing up or prone in shellholes, and shot at the advancing infantry with rifles, machine guns and mortars as their artillery fell upon the British trenches. In the few places where men of the 29th Division managed to get through the enemy wire and enter the German trenches they were either killed or driven back. Without being able to summon artillery support the British infantry were unable to get

forward, and fell back under the severity of the German fire. At 9.15a.m. a confused attempt was made to reinforce the attack and the 1st Newfoundland Regiment were ordered forward. Pressing on without faltering over open ground swept by German fire, they fell in their hundreds. Some managed to reach the German wire and a few got into the German front line before being killed, thus completing the annihilation of a battalion which suffered over 700 casualties including every one of its officers. At 10.05a.m. news of the disaster reached the divisional commander, who called off the assault.

The 4th Division had an equally disastrous experience, but not before elements of its infantry had fought their way into the German trenches, a few even penetrating to the support line. But with their flanks endangered by the failure of the divisions on their right and left, they fell back or were cut off by the Germans, who killed or captured them as their ammunition ran out. Attempting to rally those who began to drift back was a drummer of the 2nd Seaforth Highlanders. Walter Ritchie stood upon the parapet of a German trench and sounded the urgent, ascending notes of the "Charge" again and again. His conduct was to gain him one of the eight Victoria Crosses awarded for gallantry that day.

The full measure of the failure of British bombardment now became evident. Counter-battery work had been unsuccessful in suppressing the German batteries, which had shelled the assembly of the 31st Division, had struck a water main which flooded the trenches of the 4th Division, and had lashed the 29th Division. Intelligence had informed VIII Corps that only 55 enemy heavy guns opposed it; but at Zero Hour 66 batteries engaged the divisions of the Corps, and the volume and accuracy of their fire had broken the British attack at its outset.

Attempts made by commanders over the course of the day to direct reinforcement or support on the VIII Corps front met with scant success. Very little coherent intelligence filtered back and confusion was everywhere. Initiative everywhere seemed to be with the Germans, who were soon counter-attacking through familiar ground, driving back the troops of the 4th Division who had made the only significant gains, and compounding British disorganisation.

Frames from the film The Battle of the Somme *showing the 40,000lb. mine beneath the German positions in the Hawthorn Redoubt being detonated at 7.20a.m. on 1 July. (IWM Q79492-79494)*

At the end of the day VIII Corps had nothing to show for their heavy losses other than a footing on the front of the 4th Division, and this had to be abandoned the following morning. Once again, the British infantry who had broken into the German positions had failed to "mop up", with the result that they themselves were cut off and "mopped up". To VIII Corps went the dubious distinction of having suffered more casualties than any other Corps – over 14,000 men. The Germans facing them lost just 1,214.

FILMING ON THE SOMME

On the Somme, ready to record the "Big Push", were the cinematographers Geoffrey Malins and J.B.McDowell. The footage which they shot of the preparations and the battles was edited into a film, *The Battle of the Somme*, which was a sensation when shown in cinemas in Britain; at one time it was being screened simultaneously in 30 London cinemas. Possibly the first true war film, its dramatic impact can still be felt today (although several sequences purporting to show troops in action are now known to be bogus). Just prior to Z Day Malins began filming in the VIII Corps sector, particularly in the "White City" area opposite Beaumont Hamel. He filmed the explosion of the great mine under the Hawthorn Redoubt, and various sequences of British infantry advancing and then falling back. One unknown cameraman went forward of the British trenches and took a sequence of the 1st Lancashire Fusiliers, 29th Division, waiting in their assault positions for the signal to advance; this was as close to the German positions as any cameraman got on 1 July. Various "stills" from *The Battle of the Somme* have been used to illustrate this book.

Thiepval: X Corps, Third Army

The German positions opposite X Corps were constructed on the Thiepval plateau, the western end of the Pozières ridge, which dominated the valley of the Ancre and overlooked the British positions. The German fortifications here had been sited and built to present a formidable line of defence, and dominating all stood the fortified village of Thiepval. Once a cluster of over 60 buildings, it had been bombarded to rubble – or so it appeared from the British lines. In its cellars, now covered by a mass of fallen masonry that gave protection from all but the heaviest shells, lurked the German infantry and their machine guns. At a signal they could man a number of positions to the west of the village and set up a series of interconnected machine gun emplacements forming what was known as Fortress Thiepval. From here they could enfilade no-man's-land to the north, out to the limit of their weapons' range.

Further south stood the Leipzig Redoubt, an equally formidable strongpoint with numerous machine guns which commanded no-man's-land to the west and to the south, in places varying from 100 to 600 yards wide. Backing up these positions were four equally strong self-contained works: the "Wonder Work", the rear of Thiepval village, the Schwaben Redoubt and, guarding the river flank, St.Pierre Divion. As if the position were not strong enough, it enjoyed crossfire support from the positions north and south.

Far from being subdued by the British bombardment, the German artillery on this front had frequently shelled the British front positions. Battalions of X Corps reporting that the enemy machine guns had not been silenced were told by the staff that they were "windy". One infantry brigadier reassured his men by telling them, "I'm convinced that the German lines are full of men, but they will be in their dugouts".

X Corps was ordered to capture the whole of the

Thiepval spur and plateau in its first attack. On the Corps right the 32nd Division, a New Army formation with a stiffening of regular battalions, was to attack the Thiepval spur between the Leipzig Redoubt and Thiepval village. On the left the 36th (Ulster) Division, another New Army formation, was to assault along the valley of the Ancre to take St.Pierre Divion. From here both divisions were to press on to the line Grandcourt-Mouquet Farm, which according to plan would be taken three hours after Zero. Once again the British barrage was to lift off the German front line at Zero Hour. Two 9.2in. howitzers were specially detailed to shoot at any machine guns in or around Thiepval which might hold up the assaulting infantry; unfortunately, one had a "premature" which not only destroyed it but also put its companion out of action. Shortly before 7a.m. gas was released to drift across the Thiepval position.

The 32nd Division was one of those which chose to ignore the orders to stay put until the barrage lifted, and at 7.23a.m. some of the assaulting infantry had begun to creep forwards to within 30 or 40 yards of the German front line. When the bombardment lifted at 7.30a.m. they dashed through the gaps in the German wire and seized part of the Leipzig Redoubt salient, taking prisoner its defenders as they emerged from their dug-outs. But success was short-lived, for as the attack went forward across the open slope machine gun fire from the "Wonder Work" caused such heavy casualties that the attack was brought to a halt.

It is interesting to note that this event was reported by telephone to the brigadier-general whose troops had been halted, by the commanding officer of his supporting field artillery brigade. The gunner had observed it all from his observation post, but could do nothing to bring fire on the machine guns responsible for the check as the barrage was still going forward. The general ordered him to take two batteries out of the barrage and direct them on to the

German positions. This was done, and the British infantry were able to withdraw to the Leipzig Redoubt.

Renewed efforts to get forward failed. Unaware of what had taken place, the reserve battalions set off according to programme, and immediately came under fire from enemy machine guns. The small parties which succeeded in crossing no-man's-land reinforced those already in the Leipzig Redoubt. Subsequent attempts to develop the lodgement met with a similar fate.

Elsewhere on the divisional front the assaulting infantry were beaten back, after suffering massive casualties, by heavy German machine gun fire. On the extreme left the survivors of one battalion did manage to break into the defences of Fortress Thiepval, about a hundred of them penetrating to the north side of the village where their wanderings eventually led them to link up with troops of the 36th Division. Their adventures gave rise to a series of optimistic air reports which led to the belief that part of Thiepval was in British hands. One of the consequences of this muddle was that British artillery left the village alone for the rest of the day; another was that further attempts were made to reinforce the suspected British holdings, which led to more casualties as troops attempted to cross no-man's-land.

The assault of the 36th (Ulster) Division was carried out with great dash and impetuosity, and overran a great part of the German line. The anniversary of the Battle of the Boyne, 1 July was an auspicious day for the Ulstermen, who were determined to do well in their first major battle. Unfortunately the lack of success of the divisions on the flanks left them in an extremely vulnerable position, from which they were eventually beaten back with great loss. The day had started for them as they crept forward under cover of the British barrage, contrary to instructions, to within a hundred yards of the German position. At 7.30a.m., with their buglers sounding the advance, they rose

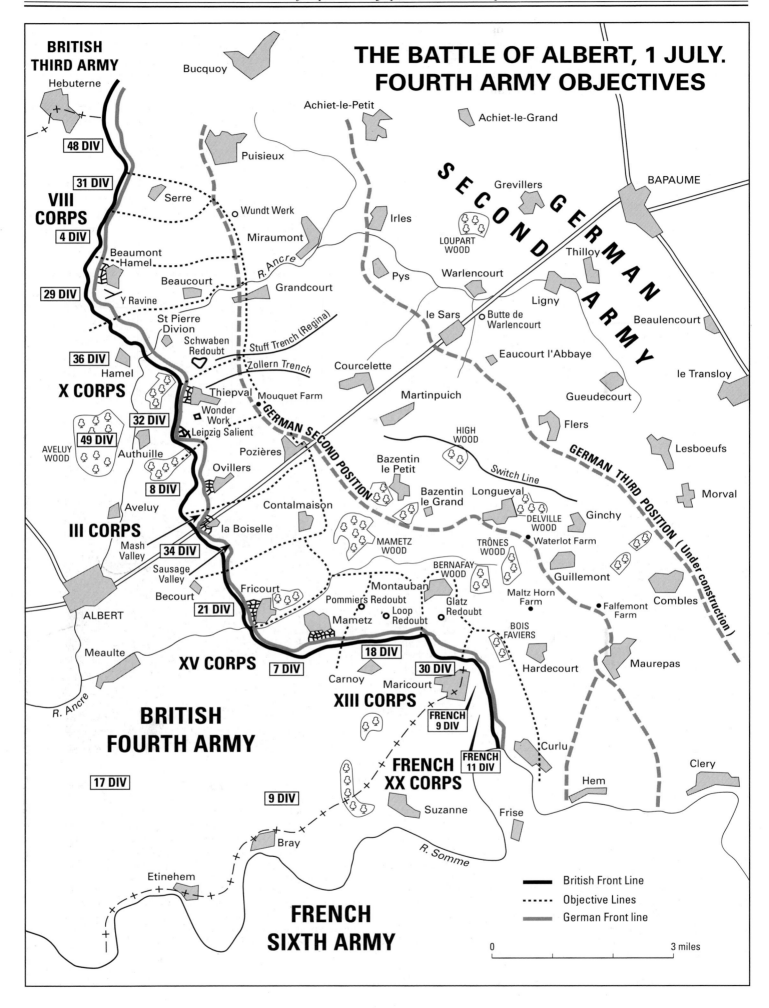

THE BATTLE OF ALBERT, 1 JULY.
FOURTH ARMY OBJECTIVES

and moved forward through the morning mist to spring upon the German infantry just as they were emerging from their dug-outs. On the right the enemy front and support trenches were taken with hardly any loss; but at the German reserve trench, 500 yards further on, machine gun fire from Thiepval began to plunge amongst them causing heavy casualties. The advance was not checked, however, and by 8a.m. the German reserve trench and part of the Schwaben Redoubt had been entered and over 400 prisoners taken. In spite of increasing flanking machine gun fire from Thiepval and St.Pierre Divion the attack was continued until the Mouquet Switch line was reached at 8.30a.m.

On the left, battalions of the division with the task of advancing up the right bank of the Ancre in conjunction with the 29th Division on their left met with less success. They had sustained considerable casualties in crossing the 600 yards of no-man's-land that separated the lines at this point, and were halted before taking the German front trench.

Shortly before 9a.m., despite attempts to secure a delay, three battalions of the reserve brigade of the 36th Division advanced according to plan. They sustained heavy losses while deploying and crossing no-man's-land, and continued to do so as they followed the course of the first two brigades. By 9.15a.m. they had reached the Mouquet Switch line and reorganised; and shortly afterwards they set off to secure their objective, the Grandcourt line some 600 yards ahead. They got to within a hundred yards of their

THE LANCASHIRE FUSILIERS

The unit most featured in the film *The Battle of the Somme* was the 1st Bn., Lancashire Fusiliers. At Gallipoli on 25 April 1915 the battalion had won three (later increased to six) Victoria Crosses "before breakfast" for their conduct during the landings at Cape Helles. This had attracted enormous publicity, and the legend of "Lancashire Landing" hung about the battalion. But the 1st Lancashire Fusiliers of 1916 were a different unit to that which had stormed ashore in Gallipoli. More than 600 of the old-time regulars lay dead there, and their places had been taken by reservists and volunteers. The media of the time, however, hoped for a repeat performance, and focused ciné and still cameras on the unit during their preparation and in the initial stages of their attack. There was, alas, no glorious episode on 1

July. The 1st Lancashire Fusiliers suffered 486 casualties without even getting through the German wire.

Almost certainly posed for the camera on 30 June 1916, the photograph shows Company Sergeant Major Nelson and others of C Company, 1st Lancashire Fusiliers fixing bayonets ostensibly for the attack of 1 July. C Company followed the first attacking waves of their battalion and came under fire as they attempted to get out of their trenches. The company commander and CSM Nelson were among those shot before the order was given to get forward through the trenches and tunnels that had been dug for the first waves. Note the triangular red divisional signs worn on the sleeves by all members of the 29th Division; and the yellow fusilier "hackle" painted on this battalion's steel helmets. (IWM Q744)

Drummer Walter Ritchie, VC, 2nd Seaforth Highlanders, photographed while convalescing from wounds in 1917; he wears the blue armband, white shirt and red necktie worn with uniform by soldiers recovering from wounds. Note the ribbons of the VC which he won on 1 July 1916, and the French Croix de Guerre; and the gold wound stripes below the good conduct chevrons on his left sleeve. (Courtesy Ray Westlake)

AT THE THIEPVAL SPUR

Ernest Shephard, a pre-war regular who was CSM of B Coy., 1st Dorsets, 14th Inf.Bde., left in his diaries a vivid account of his experience on 32nd Division's front on 1 July:

"Place already nearly crammed, only 4 dug-outs for company, 2/3 of us slept outside, enemy sending heavy shell and shrapnel all round us....I got no sleep, it was bitterly cold. Had a limited walk round at 4a.m., roused troops as all breakfast to be finished by 6.30....At 6.30a.m. our artillery were bombarding intensely, a most awful din. At 7.30a.m. we moved to 'the attack' by companies at 200 yds intervals in the order C, D, A, B. We took the track...into the Authuille Wood....A battery of artillery was in action half way in wood, enemy sending heavy shrapnel all over the place....We had a terrible dose of machine gun fire sweeping us through wood, could not understand why....Had to wait nearly 2 hours on the track waiting for the brigade ahead of us to get forward...had a rough time from enemy artillery. Finally we got to Wood Post...across the opening I saw the last platoon of A Coy. going over the open ground in front of wood...about 120 yds. Half of this platoon were killed and almost all of remainder wounded in the crossing, and I at once realised that some part of the attack had gone radically wrong, as we were being enfiladed by batteries of enemy machine guns from the ridge on our right front...

"We were told to cross as quick as possible. I went on ahead, Gray the Company Orderly behind, and No.5 platoon behind him. How I got over I cannot imagine, the bullets were cracking and whizzing all round me. I got bullet holes through my clothing and equipment in several places and was hit in left side. The ground was covered with our dead and wounded....Gray was shot dead beside me, and very few of No.5 platoon left....I got to a communicating trench...it was simply crammed with troops of all units in utter confusion, some badly wounded and a number of dead...."

CSM Shephard spent most of 1 July holding a badly shelled section of trench with his battalion Adjutant and a mixed party of 1st Dorsets and 11th Border Regiment, under direct enemy observation and intense artillery fire which caused continuing heavy casualties; it was impossible to evacuate the wounded. Relieved by troops of 15th HLI at midnight, he led his ten remaining NCOs and men of B and C Coys., 1st Dorsets to the rear. He later learned that a strong party from the other companies, led by Captain Lancaster, had penetrated the enemy positions and fought Prussian Guard troops with some success, returning with many souvenirs of their "luxuriously fitted dug-outs".A rollcall held the next morning, after many stragglers had come in, recorded that B Coy. had lost 111, including all platoon sergeants and three platoon officers, of 201 all ranks; and the battalion, 20 officers and 490 other ranks. (From *A Sergeant-Major's War*, ed.Bruce Rossor, Crowood Press, 1987)

objective, and then ran into the British barrage, which was not due to lift from that line until 10.10a.m. Heavy casualties resulted, and the delay was fatal, as it allowed the enemy to direct heavy rifle and machine gun fire on the Ulstermen from their left rear. Nevertheless, when the British barrage lifted several groups of the reserve brigade got on to their objective, while the remainder lay pinned by the enemy fire. By now the position of the Ulstermen was untenable. Rather like the courageous cavalrymen of the Light Brigade in a previous war, they had driven deeply into the enemy's defences and now, unsupported, they were shot at from all sides. It was not yet noon.

By now the situation in the X Corps area was one of confusion. Communications were poor and intermittent,

many spurious reports were filtering back, and it was almost impossible for commanders to obtain information on the dispositions and situations of their forward troops. Elements of the division in Corps reserve, the 49th (West Riding – Territorials) were brought forward to resume the attack, while commanders attempted to resolve the disorder that confronted them and arrange for the reserve infantry to get forward with supporting artillery fire. None of the schemes, which went on into the night, met with any success. In trenches packed with infantry trying to get forward and with wounded, stretcher bearers and runners trying to get to the rear, it was almost impossible to issue orders and to have them effectively carried out.

Little by little the infantry of the 36th Division were

1 July: bringing in a wounded man after the attack on the German positions near Beaumont Hamel. Both men may be wounded in the legs; they have dumped their web equipment, but both keep their gas helmet haversacks. (IWM Q752)

driven back from their gains, losing heavily as they went, until by nightfall they held only a portion of the German front line which they had taken so easily that morning. When darkness fell and the German machine gunners could no longer see targets, the survivors of the British attack made their way back to their own lines, and attempts began to recover and evacuate the wounded – a long and painful process that was not completed in this sector until 3 July. The total casualties of the divisions in X Corps on 1 July had been over 9,000, more than half of this total being Ulstermen of the 36th Division.

German reports of the day congratulate "the wonderful effects of the machine guns, which without exception, thanks to the well built machine gun emplacements, were all able to go into action when the attack began". They referred to the British attack coming on in "solid lines without gaps, in faultless order, led by its officers carrying little flags and sticks. Wave after wave were shot down by well aimed fire...a wall of dead British was piled up on the front".

MISSILE EFFECT

Into the advancing ranks of the British infantry the Germans fired musketry, machine gun bursts and artillery high explosive shell. Massed riflemen shooting at a rapid rate were capable of producing a lethal fire effect, as anyone who has witnessed a demonstration of such firepower can attest. The volume of fire from belt-fed, tripod-mounted machine guns was even more murderous, covering the ground to be crossed with streams of bullets that linked in skillfully sited crossfire, or took the lines of advancing men from a flank – "in enfilade".

Bullets at the limit of their range buzzed and droned like angry bees, but rifle shots from closer up cracked like whips as they passed their intended targets, while machine gun bursts made a hideous crackling. When they found their mark, bullets struck flesh and bone with a sickening thud. The detonation of high explosive shell was preceeded by a high-pitched shriek, and was followed by the buzz, whine and moan of the shell splinters driven outward from the core of the explosion. These fragments might be of any size, and could inflict injuries ranging from superficial cuts and punctures to the most ghastly dismemberment.

Under such a hail of fire a great measure of safety could be obtained immediately by simply lying down. But the orders were to march forward and to keep formation; and the British infantryman obeyed, all too often until a German bullet or shell fragment released him from his duty to do so.

Some German weapons captured by the British on 1 July 1916. As well as the standard German machine gun – the Maxim MG08 at bottom centre, with pieces of armour plate to protect the water jacket and firer – there is a "Muskete" (Danish M1902 Madsen automatic rifle) at left, a Russian Maxim machine gun on a wheeled carriage at centre, and a German trench mortar at right. The Madsen design was used by "Musketen Battalions", of which three were formed in 1915; their place was behind the first positions, to cover any breach which might be made.(IWM Q132)

1 July: after their reverse at Beaumont Hamel the CSM of B Coy., 1st Lancashire Fusiliers calls the roll of the unwounded survivors. His company would have started out with between 180 and 200 men; about 35 men are visible in this photograph, taken in a reserve trench during the afternoon.
(IWM Q734)

CHAPTER SEVEN

The Infantry Battle on 1 July:
III, XV and XIII Corps

Ovillers and La Boisselle: III Corps, Fourth Army

The enemy positions confronting III Corps had been constructed on three spurs projecting from the main Ginchy-Pozières ridge. In the centre was the La Boisselle spur with the village of that name, alongside which ran the main Albert-Bapaume road as it crossed the opposing lines. To the British left was the Ovillers spur and to the right the western slopes of the long Fricourt spur. The valleys between these features had been christened "Sausage" to the south and "Mash" to the north. They were bare and open, and any advance up them would be met by fire from both sides. The high ground of the spurs was covered with a network of trenches including four strongpoints south of the main road: Sausage Redoubt (Heligoland), Scots Redoubt, Schwaben Höhe and La Boisselle village. Across the road to the north Ovillers had also been fortified as a strongpoint. All were dominated by the great Thiepval spur to the north. The width of no-man's-land varied from 50 to 800 yards in places, and the whole area was ideally suited for defence.

The Albert-Bapaume road became the boundary for the two assaulting divisions of III Corps, the 34th (New Army) Division on the right and the 8th (Regular) Division on the left. Their daunting task was to capture the two fortified villages of La Boisselle and Ovillers and six lines of trenches, and to pushing on through the enemy defences to a depth of two miles.

The Corps artillery, positioned west of Albert and on both sides of the Bapaume road, consisted of 98 heavy guns and howitzers in addition to the field brigades of the three divisions of the Corps; there was also a *groupe* of French 75mm guns. Over the course of the bombardment preceding the assault infantry commanders are recorded as having expressed dissatisfaction with the damage to La Boisselle and Ovillers, a bad omen for the coming attack. The barrage programme for 1 July called for eight lifts of the heavy artillery, and decreed that "after the assault the subsequent movement of the infantry will be assisted and regulated by a system of barrages which will move back slowly" (two miles in 1 hour 47 minutes). The divisional element of the barrage, by contrast, was to go back "very slowly" (a series of short lifts of 50, 100 or 150 yards) but "faster than the infantry can advance". There were many problems with ammunition during the bombardment, with numerous prematures and casualties amongst the gunners. Many heavy howitzer shells "dropped short" and many failed to burst, one observer reporting "a dud shell every two or three yards over several acres of ground".

On 1 July two mines positioned beneath the German trenches at La Boisselle were fired at Zero minus two minutes. The southern mine, known as "Lochnagar", contained 60,000lbs. of Ammonal; the other, "Y Sap", 40,600 pounds. At Zero Hour all twelve battalions of the 34th Division climbed from their trenches and advanced in successive waves in four columns, each column three battalions deep on a frontage of 400 yards. Their plan was to encircle and cut off La Boisselle while pushing on to their objectives, leaving behind storming parties to attack the redoubt from its flanks.

The battalions were in plain view of the German machine gunners and artillery observers, who opened such effective fire that within ten minutes 80 per cent of the men in the leading battalions had fallen. An ever increasing number of machine guns were traversed, elevated and depressed to cover the area on which the infantry of the 34th Division were now pinned. As the leading battalions were held up in this way, those following telescoped on them to add to the confusion and carnage.

On the right elements of two battalions broke into Sausage Redoubt and got to the top of the Fricourt spur, where they made contact with the troops of the left hand division of XV Corps. After various skirmishes they established a position around Scots Redoubt. A party attempting to follow them up through Sausage Redoubt was burned by a flame-thrower which the Germans had brought up. Elsewhere, parties managed to enter the German trenches before La Boisselle but were unable to make progress towards the village. In various places small groups of men infiltrated considerable distances into the German defences before they were killed or taken prisoner.

By 10a.m. the 34th Division situation was that a lodgement had been consolidated on the extreme right, a small section of German trench had been taken in the Lochnagar mine area, and the infantry of the rest of the division were lying dead, wounded, or pinned down in no-man's-land, where a pall of dust and smoke raised by the German shells and bullet strike obscured the scene and left divisional headquarters in confusion. At 11.25a.m. the divisional commander asked III Corps for reinforcements, and was sent a battalion of the 19th (New Army) Division. It was then decided that no further action should be carried out until after nightfall, and then by the 19th Division. Attempts to improve what gains the division had made came to nothing; but by nightfall two communication trenches had been dug across no-man's-land to link up with the trenches which had been captured, and when darkness fell the survivors who had lain out in the open all day were able to make their way back to the British trenches, now manned by infantry of the 19th Division.

The 8th Division attacked with elements of all three of its infantry brigades, into a hail of machine gun and rifle fire which grew in volume. Despite this the advance was carried

One of the best-known images of the Great War: detail from a photograph of a ration party of a regular battalion of the Royal Irish Rifles resting in a communication trench on 1 July. (IWM Q1)

out in excellent order up to within 80 yards or so from the German trench, when the fire rose to such a pitch that the British infantry tried to charge across the intervening space, breaking ranks and bunching into groups into which the enemy fire plunged. Only isolated parties reached the German lines, where they worked their way forward in some places to the German second trench; but once again, after confused fighting, they were driven back or overpowered by the enemy, who by the afternoon were in complete possession of the defences before Ovillers. Subsequent attempts to launch British attacks met with little success in the chaotic situation prevailing.

Between them, the losses of the 8th and 34th Divisions on 1 July were over 11,000, for which III Corps had nothing to show except for the two small lodgements on the front of the 34th Division. The task of recovering the wounded was made easier by the conduct of the Germans, who offered no opposition to their evacuation. A graphic German report of the British attack is worth quoting at some length:

"Looking towards the British trenches...there could be seen a mass of steel helmets above the parapet showing that the storm-troops were ready for the assault. At 7.30a.m. the hurricane of shells ceased...our men at once clambered up the steep shafts leading from the dug-outs to daylight and ran...to the nearest shell craters...a rough firing line was thus rapidly established. As soon as the men were in position, a series of extended lines of infantry were seen moving forward from the British trenches. The first line appeared to continue without end to right and left. It was quickly followed by a second line, then a third and a fourth. They came on at a steady easy pace as if expecting to find nothing alive in our front trenches....A few moments later, when the leading British line was within a hundred yards, the rattle of machine gun and rifle fire broke out along the whole line of trenches...red rockets sped up into the blue sky as a signal to the artillery, and immediately afterwards a mass of shell from the German batteries in rear tore through the air and burst among the advancing lines.

"Whole sections seemed to fall...the advance rapidly crumpled under this hail of shell and bullets. All along the line men could be seen throwing up their arms and collapsing, never to move again....The British soldier, however, has no lack of courage....The extended lines, though badly shaken and with many gaps, now came on all the faster...they covered the ground in short rushes at the double. Within a few minutes the leading troops had advanced to within a stone's throw of our front trench, and while some of us continued to fire at point blank range, others threw hand grenades among them. The British bombers answered back while the infantry rushed forward with fixed bayonets.

"The noise of battle became indescribable. The shouting of orders and the shrill cheers...could be heard above the violent and intense fusillade of machine guns and rifles and the bursting bombs, and above the deep thunderings of the artillery and shell explosions. With all this were mingled the moans and groans of the wounded, the cries for help, and the last screams of death. Again and again the extended lines of British infantry broke against the German defences like waves against a cliff, only to be beaten back. It was an amazing spectacle of unexampled gallantry."

Fricourt and Mametz: XV Corps, Fourth Army

The Fricourt salient represented the keystone of the German positions between the Ancre and the Somme, and Fricourt and Mametz spurs were its principal features. Between them ran the Willow stream. The German defences around the villages of Fricourt and Mametz were exceptionally strong, with a maze of trenches 1,200 yards deep and forward positions that provided many salients from which the wire could be swept with enfilade fire. The ruins of the villages had been turned into fortresses, with deep dug-outs, some of which were on two levels and lighted by electricity. There were numerous machine gun emplacements, two intermediate lines, and second and third positions three and six miles behind the forward one. The position was garrisoned by six battalions. By 1 July the German artillery in this area had been effectively dealt with, and the attacking British infantry were subjected only to intermittent German shelling, not at all comparable to that further north. Enemy resistance was almost entirely from the machine gunners who emerged unscathed after the British barrage.

The Willow stream formed the boundary between the two attacking divisions of XV Corps, the 21st (New Army) Division on the left opposite Fricourt and the 7th (Regular) Division on the right attacking Mametz. The British plan was not to attack the Fricourt position frontally but to encircle and cut if off prior to capturing it at a later stage. The 7th Division was to capture Mametz and form a defensive flank along the Willow stream, while two brigades of the 21st Division were to outflank Fricourt to the left and link up with the 7th. The inner brigades of both divisions were to await a favourable opportunity to attack Fricourt.

At 6.25a.m. the British assault barrage began, and at 7.15a.m. gas was released over the German centre. At 7.22a.m. a Stokes mortar barrage commenced, and at 7.26a.m. smoke screens were set off. At 7.28a.m. three mines of 25,000, 15,000 and 9,000lbs. of high explosive were detonated under the German "Tambour" position in front of Fricourt; several lesser mines were also detonated, and an 18-pounder battery which had been brought up and dug in close behind the British front line opened fire at close range at an enemy strongpoint before Fricourt.

The orders for the artillery of XV Corps required that "When lifting, 18-pounders should search back by increasing their range, but howitzers and heavy guns must lift directly onto the next objectives ....During the advance of the infantry a barrage of artillery fire will be formed in front of the infantry according to the timings shown...The divisional artillery will move their fire progressively at the rate of 50 yards a minute. Should the infantry arrive at any

point before the time fixed for the barrage to lift, they will wait...to assault directly the lift takes place." This plan was not the complete "creeping barrage" developed later. As it started at the enemy front trench it did not assist the infantry in crossing no-man's-land; it employed few guns to "drift forward"; and on the day it moved too fast for the infantry to keep up with it.

Some companies of the attacking battalions of the 21st Division managed to get across no-man's-land and into the German front trenches with little loss before the enemy machine gunners took post, but once these were in position they inflicted serious casualties on the units following up. During a morning of confused fighting parties of those who managed to cross no-man's-land got into the German position and fought their way through it to establish a lodgement north of Fricourt to a depth of 1,000 yards. A link was established with troops of the 34th Division on the left, and consolidation of the British gains took place.

On the front of the 7th Division four Russian saps had been dug right up to the German front line, and when these were opened soon after Zero Hour the assault waves managed to get into the German position with little loss, although heavy casualties were inflicted upon them once they began an advance across the open. Nevertheless, by 7.45a.m. the leading troops of the 7th Division were 700 yards inside the German position and entering the ruins of Mametz. German resistance at this stage was patchy, some machine gun detachments fighting fiercely while elsewhere the enemy surrendered freely. In time the opposition hardened as the enemy rallied, but the British infantry pressed on, securing their first objective on the right by 1p.m. Progress on the left was slower against a more determined

---

INTO THE ENEMY TRENCHES

In October 1916 an NCO of the 22nd Manchesters, 7th Division, wrote the following description of his experiences on 1 July for the *Westminster Gazette*:

"...All the time one was intent on practical details, wiping the trench dirt off the bolt of ones rifle, reminding the men of what each was to do, and when the message came round, "five minutes to go", seeing that all bayonets were fixed. At 0730 hours we went up the ladders, doubled through the gaps in the wire, and lay down, waiting for the line to form up on each side of us. When it was ready, we went forward, not doubling, but at a walk. For we had 900 yards of rough ground to the trench which was our first objective, and about 1,500 yards to a further trench where we were to wait for orders. There was a bright light in the air, and the tufts of coarse grass were grey with dew....

"All the time...one was shouting the sort of thing that NCOs do shout and no one attends to: "Keep your extension", "Don't bunch", "Keep up on the left"....We crossed three lines that had once been trenches, and tumbled into the fourth, our final objective....While the men dug furiously to make a firestep I looked about me. On the parados lay a wounded man of another battalion, shot, to judge by the blood on his clothes, through the loins or stomach....I tried, without much success, to ease his equipment, and then thought of getting him into the trench. But it was crowded with men and there was no place to put him....

"Far away, a thousand yards or so half-left, we could see tiny kilted figures running and leaping in front of a dazzling white Stonehenge, mannikins moving jerkily on a bright green cloth. 'The Jocks bombing them out of Mametz', said someone....It was time to advance again, and we scrambled out of the trench."

An extraordinary evocation of the infantry attacks early on the morning of 1 July, the first day of the "Battle of Albert". Heavily laden infantry of the Tyneside Irish Brigade, 34th (New Army) Division, are photographed advancing to attack the German positions at La Boisselle. They have just clambered out of a trench and have started forward into the German fire. (IWM Q52)

The same spot a few minutes later: survivors hug the ground to escape German machine gun fire while, further off, two men try to recover casualties. (IWM Q50)

Barbed wire around captured German positions at La Boisselle. Wire-cutting by the British artillery prior to 1 July 1916 was patchy; in some parts of the line it was hardly touched, leaving the attacking infantry more or less trapped in full view of the defending riflemen and machine gunners. (IWM Q890)

34th DIVISION

Nine of the 13 infantry units of this New Army division were raised on Tyneside as "pals" battalions of the Northumberland Fusiliers. Four had the subsidiary title of Tyneside Scottish, four Tyneside Irish, and one Tyneside Pioneers. All were raised in the city of Newcastle; and the effect on that community of the casualties suffered before La Boisselle can be imagined. The 6,380 casualties incurred in a single day represented a catastrophe on a scale that dwarfed the pit disasters and shipyard accidents to which the people of Newcastle were hardened. Their shocked grief was echoed throughout Britain in the home towns of Kitchener's "pals" units. Fine though it may have been to allow friends and workmates to serve together, the concentration of suffering when heavy casualties were taken struck a hammer blow to morale on the home front.

The chequerboard divisional sign of the 34th Division was a crude representation of the "Shepherd's" tartan of the Tyneside Scottish.

---

opposition, but by just after 4p.m. the whole of the Mametz position was in British hands and their first objective along its north-west edge was consolidated. Enemy resistance on the front of the 7th Division appeared to be completely broken.

On the front of the 21st Division reserve battalions were sent forward to relieve those who had suffered the heaviest losses in the attack, and the 17th (New Army) Division was summoned from Corps reserve. As night fell an eerie silence prevailed over the battlefield, broken only by an occasional shot. XV Corps had done well: on its right its troops had advanced 2,500 yards and captured Mametz, and on its left they had driven in a salient that threatened the rear of Fricourt. Over 1,600 prisoners had been taken. Nearly all of the Corps' more than 8,000 casualties had been caused by the fire of the German machine guns.

Montauban: XIII Corps, Fourth Army

At the southern end of the British line, adjoining the French, the British XIII Corps faced the German positions on the Montauban ridge. The Corps had in prospect just as daunting a task as the rest of the Fourth Army, but it was to enjoy two distinct advantages not shared by them. Firstly, the artillery bombardment in this area had been much more effective. Secondly, the Germans were not anticipating an infantry attack here; in fact, they were planning to relieve one of the regiments holding this part of the line on 1 July. These were not the only factors which enabled the XIII Corps attack to go according to plan, but surprise and artillery domination certainly helped.

The German positions on the Montauban ridge were garrisoned by about nine battalions who were holding a network of front trenches, a reserve line 700 to 1,000 yards in rear, a second position some 3,000 yards from the first, and a third position that was in the course of construction. The front position was constructed in the usual German manner with a number of self-contained strongpoints, including the Glatz and Powders Redoubts, and another

1 July: a distant view of British infantry going forward to attack the German positions near Mametz, horribly exposed on open ground and against the white chalk spoil of the trenches. Yet here, the right wing of the 7th (Regular) Division broke into the German front and pushed on to capture Mametz. From this point to the right all went well; but from here to the left, northwards, the Germans beat back the British infantry and inflicted massive casualties. (IWM Q86)

A Tommy of the 7th Division killed in the attack on the German positions before Mametz, 1 July: a frame from the film The Battle of the Somme. *Still with his bag of grenades slung around him, this "bomber" probably served with the 21st or 22nd Manchesters. (IWM Q79520)*

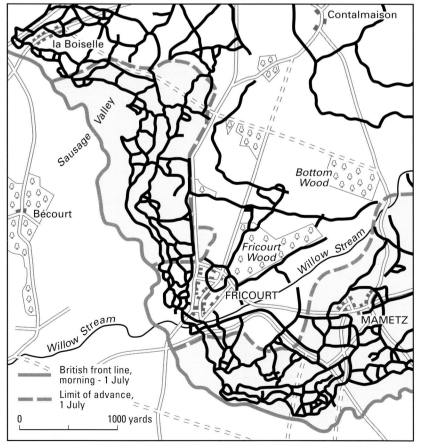

Minden Post, 1 July: German prisoners supervised by a guard of the 1st Royal Welsh Fusiliers, 22nd Infantry Brigade, 7th (Regular) Division – note the white grenade device on his sleeve. Another frame from the film footage later edited into The Battle of the Somme. *(IWM Q29509)*

Most maps, for reasons of scale, inevitably show the German front position as a single line – and are, inevitably, misleading. This sketch map shows an approximation of the actual first line trench system between La Boiselle and Mametz, giving a better idea of the task facing the assaulting infantry.

nicknamed "The Castle". Montauban village had been fortified, and the whole area was a maze of barbed wire perimeters and trench blocks.

XIII Corps had under command the 9th (Scottish) Division, the 18th (Eastern) Division and the 30th Division – all New Army formations. The 9th was to be held in reserve while the others made the attack, in which the 30th was to capture the German second line at "Dublin" trench and then move on to capture Montauban. On the left the 18th Division was also to go for the second line, before pushing on to capture a German trench called "Montauban Alley" which ran to the rear of the village. The Corps barrage plan laid down that "The field artillery barrage will creep back by short lifts..."- the first use of this word in connection with an artillery barrage; fully developed, the creeping barrage was to become a battle winner, but this was a tactic for the future. The Corps heavy artillery, combined with that of the French Corps on the right, was greatly superior to that of the Germans in this sector, by a ratio of nearly four to one. It had already obtained domination by Z Day, and in the course of the barrage fired on that day would practically destroy the German artillery.

No smoke was laid down to cover the advance of the British infantry, and six Russian saps had been dug across no-man's-land. On the morning of 1 July the leading battalions of the 30th Division advanced across no-man's-land, the commanding officers of the British and French battalions at the juncture of the Allied line arm-in-arm; finding that the German wire had been well cut, they got into the German front trenches and captured them with little resistance. While follow-up battalions "mopped up", taking many prisoners, the leading battalions pressed on, following the barrage, to Dublin trench and Glatz Redoubt, the first objectives. These were reached at or just after 8.30a.m., despite some resistance on the division's left. Dublin trench had been so heavily shelled that it was in places unrecognisable, some units passing beyond it and consolidating in lines of shellholes.

On the front of the 18th Division two mines below the enemy's front trench were fired at 7.27a.m., while a flamethrower had been set up to assist the assault on the right. At

On 1 July a British "flame projector" was used on the front of the 18th Division. With a range of only 40 to 50 yards, this device had to be carried forward, with its fuel, in unwieldy loads, to be assembled before use. Like all large "positional" flamethrowers it used massive quantities of fuel, out of proportion to any practical effect, and was largely a psychological weapon. The Wex flamethrower, unveiled by the German assault pioneers at Verdun in February 1916 with dreadful effect, was a genuinely man-portable weapon, with automatic ignition, a range of about 20 yards, and a capacity of just under three gallons giving about eight bursts' capacity. (IWM Q14938)

Zero Hour the attacking battalions crossed no-man's-land against some opposition, running up against the main German resistance at their support trench and the Castle. Fighting all the way, the infantry of the 18th Division pushed the Germans back trench by trench in a series of battles involving grenades, machine guns and bayonets. By 8.30a.m. most of the division's first objectives had been taken, but the enemy was stubbornly resisting in the centre. Nevertheless, an attack on the Pommiers Redoubt was launched, and this was taken after fierce hand-to-hand fighting.

On the Corps right the reserve brigade of the 30th Division had taken many casualties while moving up to assault Montauban, but despite these and the confusion caused by the loss of officers and the mingling of units, elements of the brigade entered Montauban just after 10a.m. to find it deserted by the enemy. Shortly afterwards Montauban Alley was entered and the second and last objective seized. Many German troops were made prisoner, but many more could be seen retreating northwards, harassed on their way by the British artillery. (It was in this area that infantry of the 30th Division seized the first three German artillery pieces taken in the Somme battle.) Consolidation immediately took place, and the positions seized were put in a state of defence. It had been a good day for the 30th Division, which had cleared the enemy on a frontage of 1,500 yards and to a depth of 2,000 yards, capturing twelve officers and 489 other ranks as well as large quantities of weapons, to establish a commanding position on the Montauban ridge.

On their right the French were well up with them; and on their left the troops of the 18th Division were coming up into line. The parties of German troops holding up the centre of the 18th Division's assault were by now becoming aware of the situation on their flanks, which had been well turned. Some began to fall back, some to surrender, but some remained to fight. Trench by trench the British advanced, until by late afternoon contact had been established with the 30th Division and the whole of the 18th Division's second objective had been captured. In places parties were pushed out to the third objective, and the day's gains consolidated. The day's fighting had cost XIII Corps just over 6,000 casualties, but mercifully it was possible to evacuate the wounded speedily. With virtually no German retaliation it now became possible to repair roads and push forward artillery without interference, and for the full apparatus of supply to swing into action to bring forward the rations, water, forage and ammunition needed.

German reports recorded the British artillery fire of 1 July as "devastating", and that panic measures (the rounding up of clerks, cooks, etc.) had to be taken to man reserve positions. Formations resting in Cambrai were alerted and ordered forward, but in the confusion of the loss of Montauban no effective counter-attack could be mounted.

The French Sector
On the right of XIII Corps, the French XX Corps – the "Iron Corps", a veteran formation once commanded by General Foch, which had distinguished itself at Verdun in February – overcame the whole of the German first position. The French infantry had crossed no-man's-land under

continued on page 74

COLOUR PLATES A–D

Plate A1: General Sir Henry Rawlinson, commanding Fourth Army
Sir Henry Seymour Rawlinson, Bt., KCB, KCVO, was born in 1864 and educated at Eton and Sandhurst before being commissioned into the King's Royal Rifle Corps in 1884. His long and distinguished career included appointment as ADC to Lord Roberts, study at the Staff College, service on the staff of Lord Kitchener, and the post of Commandant of the Staff College. He saw active service in Burma, the Sudan and South Africa. He exchanged into the Coldstream Guards in 1892. He was promoted Lieutenant-Colonel in 1897, Brigadier-General in 1903, Major-General in 1909, Lieutenant-General and Temporary General in 1916. A protégé of Kitchener (who wrote of him that he "possessed the qualities of a Staff officer combined with those of a column commander in the field. Such characteristics always ensure him a front place whatever he sets his mind to"), Sir Henry was bound for high command. Rising rapidly through division and Corps, he took command of the Fourth Army on its formation and remained its leader throughout the Somme battles. As an infantryman his perspective differed from that of cavalrymen such as Haig and Gough, and his appreciation as to how the "wearing" battle should be fought emphasised the conservation of manpower and established the "bite and hold" theory.

Sir Henry is depicted in the Service Dress of a General and wearing an Army Staff brassard. Note the unusual corduroy breeches, stockings and trench boots he was accustomed to wear in 1916. By now the Sam Browne leather officer's equipment had virtually ceased to have practical value, but the belt and single brace had become a form of badge of officer status. The ribbons of his orders and decorations include the KCB, KCVO, CMG, King Edward VII Coronation, King George V Coronation, India GS, Sudan, Queen's South Africa, King's South Africa, Legion of Honour, Khedive's Sudan and a Russian order.

General officers had the distinctions of a red cap band, crossed sword-and-baton cap badge, oakleaf peak lace and "gorget" patches; badges of rank were worn on the shoulder straps – crossed sword-and-baton with a crown and star for General. Staff brassards identified officers at the headquarters of a formation; they were blue for brigade, red for division, red-white-red for Corps, red-black-red for Army, and red-blue for General Headquarters of the BEF. Devices worn on the brassards included a gun for Royal Artillery officers, letters to indicate various appointments, and divisional and Corps signs.

Plate A2: Staff-Sergeant, Military Mounted Police
At this time the red cap covers, so familiar in later years, had only recently been introduced. They were not generally worn, being used when high visibility was necessary, but as they were the same colour as the crown of the pre-war forage cap worn by military policemen they kept the nickname "Redcap" alive. There was also a branch of the Military Foot Police in 1916, but most of the personnel in Provost units were men attached from other regiments as temporary MPs. The Staff-Sergeant is depicted in "modified" Service Dress and is armed with a .455in. revolver and 1908 pattern sword. Note his whistle and chain, gas helmet haversack, "MMP" shoulder titles and "MP" brassard. His mount is tacked-up with the standard British Army harness of the time, including the 1902 pattern bridle and 1912 pattern saddle and wallets.

The "Redcaps" formed part of the fearsome disciplinary machinery of the BEF, into whose hands it was unwise for a Tommy to fall. In an attack a stop-line of "battle police" might arrest an unwounded soldier appearing to be running away from his duty, thus feeding him into a system of summary trial and punishment which might end with field punishment, a term in a military prison, or a firing squad. Much has been written about the degrading wagon-wheel "crucifixion" aspect of field punishment; less about the dreadful conditions prevailing in the "glasshouses" – the military prisons in France and elsewhere – presided over by the Military Provost Staff Corps, an organisation detested by all who had the misfortune to come in contact with them in any capacity. Over 300 British soldiers were executed by firing squad during the course of the war, but these unfortunate men represented only a fraction of the capital sentences handed out by courts martial, most of which were commuted.

Plate B1: Major-General C.E.D.Budworth, Major-General RA, Fourth Army
General Budworth had been General Rawlinson's chief gunner in IV Corps and joined him again in Fourth Army, taking over as MGRA shortly before the Somme battles. He was amongst a number of gunner personalities credited with devising advanced artillery tactics, including those of the "creeping barrage", but, as with a great deal of the innovation in this field, much was copied from the French. A former Chief Instructor at the School of Gunnery, Budworth had no

chance to put his contribution on record as he died shortly after the war, but he was probably one of the best British gunner generals of the Great War. He is depicted in the Service Dress of a general officer, with the breeches, field boots and spurs of a mounted officer. Note the Army Staff brassard and gun device, General's collar patches, and the ribbons of the CB, King George V Coronation, Queen's South Africa, King's South Africa and the French Croix de Guerre.

Plate B2: Driver, Royal Field Artillery, Divisional Ammunition Column, 4th Division

In addition to its four field artillery brigades (with 48 x 18-pounders and 16 x 4.5in. howitzers), each division had a divisional ammunition column. In 1916 these were busily engaged in moving the almost unbelievable quantities of ammunition needed for the destruction of the German defences, and for the barrages in support of the British infantry. Drivers were the private soldiers of the artillery who rode the horse teams which pulled the guns and ammunition limbers; gunners were the men who manned the guns.

The driver is depicted in the short-sleeve working dress typical of the time. His helmet cover bears the stencilled device of his unit, and he wears a "grey-back" shirt with breeches, puttees and spurs. Note the "leg-iron" worn to prevent the leg being crushed between pairs of horses, the driving whip, braces, anti-gas helmet haversack and identity discs. He holds a round of high explosive shell for an 18-pounder field gun; note the colours of the shell and filling bands. Screwed into the nose of the shell is a "Fuse, graze, No. 100", the notoriously dangerous device responsible for so many of the "bore prematures" which destroyed guns and killed and injured their crews. Such ammunition was carried to the guns in limbers when wheeled vehicles could be got up to the battery positions, or on pack animals when this was not possible; as a last resort it was carried forward by man-pack.

The driver represents an arm of service central to the Army's eventual victory; in the attacks of the later battles of the Great War there were often more gunners supporting operations than there were infantrymen going forward. In the line for longer periods than the infantry, closer to the enemy than any other category of artillery, the prime targets for counter-battery high explosive and gas, the Royal Field Artillery manning the 18-pdrs. and 4.5in. howitzers were the hardest used of all the gunners on the Somme.

Plate C1: Lieutenant–Colonel A.W.Rickman, commanding 11th (Service) Battalion, East Lancashire Regiment (Accrington Pals), 94th Infantry Brigade, 31st Division (New Army)

A regular from the Northumberland Fusiliers, Colonel Rickman had commanded the Accrington Pals from the formation of the battalion, and had been instrumental in turning them from a mob of high-spirited volunteers into a keen and disciplined unit. He had the misfortune of watching it destroyed in a matter of minutes on the morning of 1 July, and was himself wounded. He is depicted in steel helmet and Service Dress on which are sewn cuff rank badges, as well as the devices of his battalion on the shoulder and his brigade below the collar. In addition to these marks his men wore tinplate triangles on their packs, and coloured tapes on their shoulders (for the benefit of aerial observers, and for sub-unit identification). Note Colonel Rickman's Sam Browne equipment, anti-gas helmet haversacks, map case and pistol case.

Not all the officers of the British infantry battalions on the Somme wore this style of uniform; by 1916 German snipers and machine gunners knew too well its distinctive cut and open collar. Amongst junior officers it had become common practice to wear a "Tommy jacket" – the other ranks' issue – with rank badges on the shoulder straps, issue personal equipment and a rifle and bayonet, in order to be less conspicuous in the attack.

Plate C2: Scout Sergeant, 11th (Service) Battalion, Royal Fusiliers, 54th Infantry Brigade, 18th (Eastern) Division (New Army)

Typical dress and equipment for British infantry on 1 July 1916 is depicted by this figure. He wears the Mark I "Brodie" steel helmet, introduced earlier in the year and by then available in sufficient numbers for general issue. On his Service Dress he wears his badges of rank, above which is the badge of a 1st Class Scout, the fleur-de-lys. The brass "RF" titles of his regiment are worn on the shoulder straps, its grenade badges on the collar, and the patches on his sleeves and helmet are part of a divisional scheme of unit "battle insignia". The equipment worn is the 1914 leather pattern, which was sometimes manufactured in the khaki/green shade shown. His .303in. Short, Magazine, Lee-Enfield Mark III rifle has a wire-cutting device attached to the muzzle. In addition to two gas helmets in haversacks he carries extra ammunition in bandoliers (200 rounds in all), and empty sandbags tucked into his belt for use in consolidating captured positions. In the haversack on his back are an "iron" (emergency) ration, a cardigan pullover, a woollen cap "comforter", spare socks and a groundsheet; attached to it is his

messtin with his rations for the day, and the waterbottle strapped to his equipment holds two pints. His "first field dressing" for wounds is in a jacket pocket, as are his paybook, personal possessions, and two grenades. An entrenching tool and his bayonet bring the weight of his load up to about 65lbs.(29.5kg).

A scout section of a Scout-Sergeant and about 25 Scouts was part of battalion establishment at this date. They were the pick of the battalion; after selection they were trained in map-reading, the use of compass and telescope, observation and report-writing, judging distances, setting up OPs, concealment, use of aerial photographs, night movement and patrolling. They appear to have been the intelligence section and reconnaissance platoon of their day, their duties merging with those of the battalion snipers as this skill began to be fostered by the BEF.

Behind the Sergeant can be seen an identification device typical of those carried by attacking units, in this case the orange-painted tin semicircle of the 11th Royal Irish Rifles of the 36th (Ulster) Division; and on the ground is one of the tin triangle reflectors worn on pack-flaps.

Plate D1: Daffadar, 20th Deccan Horse, 9th (Secunderabad) Cavalry Brigade, 2nd Indian Cavalry Division

Of the five British cavalry divisions present on the Somme only units from two saw sufficient action to be awarded battle honours; in the case of the 2nd Indian Cavalry Division, troopers saw action on two occasions, at Bazentin and Flers-Courcelette. Large numbers of Indian Army troops had been sent to France in 1914, but by 1916 the 1st and 2nd Indian Cavalry Divisions were the only fighting formations remaining, forming the BEF's Cavalry Corps with the 1st, 2nd and 3rd British Cavalry Divisions. Within the Indian divisions British and Indian units were mixed, one British and two Indian regiments forming a brigade, and all artillery being manned by British gunners. In the 9th Brigade the 20th Deccan Horse were brigaded with the 7th Dragoon Guards when squadrons from both made their charge between Delville Wood and High Wood on 14 July.

This Daffadar (Sergeant) wears the mounted marching order of 1916. He is a "Dekhani Musalman" and wears his pagri headdress tied in the manner of his race; he also wears the kurta, the shirt-like tunic common to Indian troops, with the three-bar chevron of his rank on the right sleeve, and "XDHX" shoulder titles. The rest of his clothing, equipment and saddlery is regulation British issue except for his haversack, waterbottle, and the browband fringe on his mount's bridle – these are distinctive Indian Army items. His rifle is carried on the nearside of his saddle so as not to interfere with free use of his lance; his animal's nosebag is tied to the rifle boot. His sword is carried on the offside; his greatcoat, toilet items and spare kit are rolled in a groundsheet and strapped to the front arch of the saddle. Rifle ammunition is carried in pouches and bandoliers, and a second bandolier is strapped round his mount's neck – in all he carries 230 rounds.

He also carries bayonet, entrenching tool, grenades, messtin and rations – in fact, everything necessary for him to fight as an infantryman once his horse has been led to the rear.

Plate D2: Private John Leak, VC, 9th (Queensland) Infantry Battalion, 1st Australian Division

Born in England in 1892, John Leak was working in Queensland as a carrier in 1914; he enlisted with the Australian Imperial Force, and served at Gallipoli before his arrival on the Western Front. During the fighting for Pozières on 23 July 1916 he won the Victoria Cross when he ran forward under heavy fire to throw grenades into an enemy strongpoint, leaping in after them with rifle and bayonet; when his comrades came forward they found him wiping his bayonet clean with his felt hat. Although wounded and gassed later in the war, John Leak survived to die in 1972 at the age of 80.

He is depicted wearing the Australian Service Dress of 1914, which differed from the British pattern. The jacket was made of a light flannel material which faded with wear to a pale shade; it was cut in the style of a bush jacket, and worn with breeches. The rising sun badge of the AIF was worn on the brim of the hat and as collar badges; shoulder titles were lettered "AUSTRALIA"; and unit and formation patches were worn on the sleeves. In the 1st Australian Division these were rectangular; the lower colour indicated the brigade, and the upper the battalion (on these patches Gallipoli survivors wore a metal "A"). He wears full marching order 1908 pattern infantry web equipment, with entrenching tool, bayonet for the SMLE Mark III rifle, his helmet strapped to his pack, and haversacks for the two anti-gas helmets.

A1: General Sir Henry Rawlinson

A2: Staff–Sergeant, Mounted Military Police

B1: Major-General C.E.D.Budworth

B2: Driver, Royal Field Artillery

PLATE C

C1: Lieutenant-Colonel A.W.Rickman, 11th East Lancs.Regt.

C2: Scout Sergeant, 11th Royal Fusiliers

D2: Private John Leak VC, 9th (Queensland) Bn., AIF

D1: Daffadar, 20th Deccan Horse

E2: Lewis gunner, 1/9th Royal Scots

E1: Lance-Corporal, 143rd Machine Gun Company

F2: Piper James Richardson VC, 16th (BC) Bn., CEF

F1: Gunner, Heavy Section, Machine Gun Corps

G1: Lieutenant–Colonel Bernard Freyberg VC, Hood Bn.

G2: Captain, No.1 Coy., New Zealand MGC

H1: Lieutenant, Royal Flying Corps

H2: Despatch rider, Royal Engineers

Plate E1: Lance-Corporal, 143rd MG Company, Machine Gun Corps, 48th (South Midland) Division, Territorial Force

Along with artillery and mortars, machine guns dominated the Western Front by 1916. The British Army had begun the war with only two sustained-fire weapons per battalion; but by the time of the Somme battles it had created a Machine Gun Corps with 4,000 officers and 80,000 men which provided each division with three MG companies, each with 16 Vickers guns. By this date they were beginning to be recognized as distinctive weapons with tactics of their own – neither those of the infantry from which they had sprung, nor those of the artillery, and even more effective than the lattter against troops in the open out to their effective range of 3,000 yards. On the Somme MG companies fired millions of rounds in barrages to support attacks or to neutralise enemy positions and rear areas; these were invariably "indirect fire" shoots, in which machine guns were layed in the manner of artillery pieces for direction and elevation, and fired according to a plan which ensured maximum coverage of the target area. In defence, sections of guns were sited to cover the wire obstacles before British forward positions so that a cross-fire could be layed along them on call.

The subject is in Service Dress, over which he wears the padded machine gunner's waistcoat intended to protect him when carrying hot, heavy guns. The badge of the MGC is pined to his helmet cover; the insignia on his jacket include the patch of the 143rd MG Coy., the "MG" skill-at-arms badge, and the single chevron of his appointment. His equipment is the 1908 pattern webbing modified for those armed with the .455in. pistol, and he carries the usual anti-gas helmets. By his side is a Vickers Mark I machine gun mounted for action on its Mark IV tripod; note box for 250-round ammunition belt, condenser tube and canvas condenser bag, the auxiliary mounting below the barrel, and the leather carrying straps.

Plate E2: Lewis gunner, 1/9th (Highlanders) Battalion, Royal Scots, 51st (Highland) Division, Territorial Force

The Lewis was not a sustained-fire weapon, its 47-round magazines being unable to match the volume of fire of belt-fed weapons. Its value lay in the ability to keep up with advancing infantry and to produce fully automatic direct fire in their support.

The "Dandy Ninth" were a Territorial battalion from Edinburgh who wore the uniform of Highlanders, unlike the other units of their regiment. This soldier is muffled in a goatskin jerkin, scarf and mittens against the bitter weather in which his division fought the last battle of the Somme campaign. Note the title of his battalion on his jacket sleeve, above the blue stripe which was this battalion's indicator in the 51st Division's scheme of battle insignia; these stripes were frequently painted on helmets. At this date no skill-at-arms proficiency badge had yet been authorised for Lewis gunners. A khaki drill apron protects and subdues his kilt of Hunting Stewart tartan, and his garters are "belled". His equipment is the 1914 pattern leather "fighting order", here with the pouch and pistol case for the gunner's .455in. Colt revolver. The pan-shaped Lewis magazine has been removed so that the weapon will sit comfortably on his shoulder.

Plate F1: Gunner, Heavy Section, Machine Gun Corps

Over their uniforms tank crews were required to wear the light brown "canvas" fatigue jackets and trousers then on issue to the British Army; but within the confines of their fighting vehicles the order of dress illustrated was more commonly worn. The flannel shirt was supposed to be made up from grey material, but wartime shortages resulted in shirts of whatever colour was to hand, including the brown shown here. A leather or fibre helmet gave some minimal protection from accidental injury against the many sharp projections inside a pitching, rolling tank moving over rough ground. Eyes and face were sometimes protected against bullet "splash" within the tank by slotted steel goggles set in a leather-covered mask with a hanging chainmail face curtain. This gunner has the usual anti-gas equipment, and a .455in. Webley revolver, case and pouch on a 1903 pattern belt. On his shoulders he carries two rounds of high explosive shell for his Mark I "Male" tank's 6-pdr. guns.

Plate F2: Piper James Richardson, VC, 16th (British Columbia) Infantry Battalion ("Canadian Scottish"), 1st Canadian Division

Piper James Cleland Richardson is depicted in the uniform of his battalion at the time he won his Victoria Cross. Note the "tam-o-shanter" bonnet with the badge of the Canadian Scottish, the "C" over "16" collar badges, and the "CANADIAN" over "SCOTTISH" shoulder titles. His jacket (British issue had by now replaced the Canadian Service Dress in which the CEF came to France) has

the skirts cut away; kilt and pipe bag are of Lennox tartan – a distinction of pipers of this battalion – and his garters are "double-belled". On his sleeves are the recently adopted battle patches: large red rectangles identify 1st Canadian Division, and blue squares indicate the fourth battalion of the third brigade within the division. He wears 1908 pattern webbing fighting order with pouch and case for the .455in. Webley; in action his bonnet would be replaced by a steel helmet.

Piper Richardson had been born in Scotland in 1895, moving to Canada a few years before the war; he enlisted in 1914, coming to the Canadian Scottish via a Militia unit, the 72nd Seaforths of Canada. In the attack on Regina Trench on 8 October 1916 he was piper to No.4 Company when they advanced behind the barrage. He had orders not to play his pipes. The German wire was found to be uncut, and the leading waves suffered heavy casualties to intense rifle and machine gun fire. Richardson then began to play, walking up and down the enemy wire and inspiring the men of his battalion to get through the obstacle and into the enemy positions. By some miracle he remained unscathed, later taking part in a bombing attack, and helping evacuate the wounded. After this supreme example of courage and coolness in the face of what must have seemed certain death, it is all the more poignant to record that he met his death later the same day while trying to retrieve his mislaid pipes. For some reason his posthumous award of the Victoria Cross was not gazetted for a further two years.

Plate G1: Lieutenant-Colonel Bernard Freyberg, VC, DSO, Hood Battalion, 63rd (Royal Naval) Division

By 1916 the sailors and marines of the Royal Naval Division had adopted the khaki Service Dress of the Army; and the GOC had ordered officers of Royal Navy battalions to wear both naval rank rings on their cuffs and Army badges of rank on their shoulder straps. (Ratings were ordered to wear their naval badges of rank on their left sleeves and the Army equivalent on their right.) Colonel Freyberg is depicted in Service Dress, with the cap and cuff rings of a Royal Navy Commander; note the collar badges of his battalion, and the ribbon of the DSO he had won at Gallipoli. A Sam Browne belt and the leggings and spurs of a mounted officer complete the "number one rig" he was reported to have worn on the morning when he won his Victoria Cross (although drawings of the incident show him wearing a helmet and raincoat and carrying a revolver).

On the dark, foggy morning of 13 November 1916 the division moved off to attack enemy positions north of the Ancre. Freyberg was leading the Hood Battalion, but in the prevailing confusion assumed command of several units. In front of Beaucourt he gave orders to dig in and consolidate. The following morning he led the brigade he was by now commanding in the assault on that village, being knocked down for the first time when a bullet struck his helmet. After the capture of Beaucourt he was hit a second time, and then, far more seriously, a third time. His wounds were dressed, and he refused to go to the rear until he had issued orders and satisfied himself that command had been properly passed on. By then his courage and exemplary leadership had ensured that his men had taken and held the most advanced lodgement of the Corps attack.

Plate G2: Captain, No.1 Company New Zealand Machine Gun Corps, New Zealand Division

The New Zealand Division was formed in March 1916. The uniform worn by New Zealand troops was identical to that of the British Army apart from the felt hat, which by 1916 was worn with the brim down and the crown creased into the "lemon squeezer" (or "Montana peak") shape that became the mark of the "Kiwis". Around the hat were worn khaki bands with different colours inset according to branch of service: red for infantry, blue for gunners, crimson for medical personnel, etc. At first patches called "battalion distinctions" or "blazes" were worn on the hat, but by 1916 these had moved to the backs of Service Dress jackets; later still they were worn on the sleeves.

This officer is shown in the uniform he would have worn out of the line: felt hat with infantry band and badge of the NZMGC; SD jacket with his company "blaze", "NZMGC" titles, and cuff rank badges; Sam Browne belt; and the breeches, spurs and riding crop of an officer required to ride when on the line of march. At this time it was the fashion among junior officers to buy from their tailors and outfitters the very palest shirts, ties, breeches and puttees obtainable.

Plate H1: Lieutenant, Royal Flying Corps

Many officers seconded from other regiments and Corps to the RFC for flying duties continued to wear their former Service Dress and badges, distinguished only by the flying badges of pilots and observers. Officers commissioned directly into the RFC wore the uniform illustrated. This differed from other forms of Service Dress in the jacket, a lancer-fronted garment with concealed buttons, soon nicknamed the "maternity jacket". The subject is depicted with his badges of rank worn on his shoulder straps, the collar badges of the RFC, the flying badge of an observer – introduced in 1915 – and the ribbon of the Military Cross. He wears a fur-lined flying helmet and goggles and thigh-length sheepskin-lined flying boots, and carries the leather coat and gauntlets worn when in the air.

Military flying was exceptionally hazardous in the Great War. Aircraft were flimsy and unstable, and aero-engines unreliable. Pilots were committed to combat after the briefest of training and conversion to the aircraft types they were to fly against the enemy. Accidents were common, and the slightest hits from enemy fire could cause engine failure, airframe damage, or – worst of all – fire. With no parachutes (these were issued only to balloon observers) aircrew stood little chance of survival if shot down.

Much sterling artillery observation work was also carried out by the captive balloon companies of the RFC, which had the advantage of telephone communication between the observer's basket and the ground – sometimes, directly to the battery in action. This was not possible for the crews of aircraft engaged on the "artillery spotting" which was their most important contribution to the ground fighting; they had to employ visual signalling, usually with lamps, or to drop written messages to batteries.

Plate H2: Despatch Rider, Royal Engineers

Signalling above unit (battalion) level was the responsibility of Royal Engineer signal companies. They operated the primitive wireless sets, the sophisticated field telephone systems, and the signal centres through which military communications were channelled. A vital part of their duties was the carriage of messages, a task performed by foot orderlies, riders, and motorcycle despatch riders. This typical "Don-R" is dressed in waterproof coat, leggings and cap cover; note his goggles, gauntlets, signal satchel, and the armbands of a signaller. He is armed with one of the many types of .455in. revolver issued to British troops during the Great War (Webley, Smith and Wesson, Colt, Tracola, etc.).

His machine is a Triumph Model H, of which some 20,000 were supplied to the British Army from 1915 to 1918. They were mainly used for despatch riding duties, and with their 550cc engines, three-speed gearboxes, and belt drive to the rear wheel they could achieve a top speed of 45mph. Note the sign of XIII Corps painted on the side of the machine. Adopted in 1915, its horseshoes represented the "CC" of "Congreve's Corps".

continued from page 62

the cover of a thick morning mist to find the German trenches devastated by the bombardment and barrage of the French artillery. In contrast to the British tactics the *poilus* employed the fluid techniques of infiltration by small parties which they had learned, to their advantage, from the Germans at Verdun. What defenders remained put up a patchy resistance, the exception being at Curlu, and by midday most of the Corps objectives had been taken. An invitation to press on with the attack was turned down by the British, aware as they were of the insecurity of their left flank. By 6.30p.m., following a bombardment lasting over an hour, the village of Curlu was taken.

South of the Somme the story was much the same. Two French Army Corps, I Colonial and XXXV, attacked two hours later than the assault in the north and took the enemy completely by surprise, seizing their objectives and making an attempt at the German second position; 4,000 prisoners were taken.

Summary: The first day

Whatever confusion might have been in the minds of the Allied commanders as to their success or failure on 1 July 1916, the beginning of the offensive had made a clear impression upon General von Falkenhayn, the Chief-of-Staff of the German Field Army. On that day he began moving formations from Verdun to the Somme front; in doing so he was conceding an eventual victory at Verdun to the French, and recognising that although the German front on the Somme had held the strategic indications were bad. The German Army was in for a long and bitter campaign and needed to assemble its forces to fight it. A report written at the time described how the British attack had been contained in the north, but went on to say that "on both sides of the Somme, however, the English and French had driven a deep ridge into our defensive front. On this sector our losses were so considerable that there was no available strength with which to carry out the intended counter-attack".

Losses suffered on the first day of the offensive by the French were considered to be light. The British losses, carefully researched and collated after the war, were: killed or died of wounds, 993 officers, 18,247 other ranks; wounded, 1,337 officers, 34,156 other ranks; missing, 96 officers, 2,056 other ranks; prisoners-of-war 12 officers, 573 other ranks – in total, 57,470 casualties. German losses cannot be so precisely known but are estimated at 40,000 for the period 1–10 July.

There had been no breakdown in morale in any army. French morale was high. The British, although shaken by the events of the day, had yet to absorb the full extent of their reverses and casualties – indeed, so unaware of the realities were Fourth Army headquarters that at 10p.m. that night they issued orders to all Corps to "continue the attack" on the following day. The morale of the Germans was sufficiently good to enable them to restore parts of their line on 2 July. But the bombardment and barrage which had preceded the Allied assault had had an effect; most of the letters, accounts and histories of the time dwell on the horror of being under prolonged bombardment and "drum-fire", and these were the first indicators of a break in morale.

CHAPTER EIGHT

Maintaining the Pressure: 2–11 July 1916

A picture of the true situation at the end of the first day's fighting was slow to emerge at Fourth Army headquarters. Where there had been success, reports made their way back up the chain of command rapidly and with a fair degree of accuracy. But from those parts of the line where attacks had been bloodily repulsed, and especially where contact with forward troops had been lost, situation reports were confused, incomplete, and in some cases misleading. Little by little the true state of affairs was pieced together: that on two-thirds of the front the attack had been repulsed, but that complete or partial success had been won by the British formations on the right.

In taking stock General Rawlinson noted that on his right XIII Corps had taken all its objectives, and that next to it XV Corps was in possession of Mametz with a defensive flank facing Fricourt. North of that village isolated parts of the German front line had been taken, and these were being held by the survivors of the infantry units of the divisions which had made the lodgements. The extent of the day's losses were unknown at Fourth Army headquarters, where Rawlinson thought them to be 16,000; but even had the full casualty lists been available they would have caused no change to the plans being made. Sir Douglas Haig wished the assault to be carried on as soon as possible, and at 10p.m. Rawlinson issued orders for the attack to be continued "under Corps arrangements as early as possible compatible with adequate previous artillery preparations".

XIII Corps was ordered to prepare to attack Mametz Wood in conjunction with XV Corps, which latter was ordered to first capture Fricourt village and its original objective. III Corps was to secure La Boisselle, Ovillers and Contalmaison, with X and VIII Corps renewing their attack on the German front system between Mouquet Farm and Serre. General Rawlinson thus intended to renew the attack on his left and centre, where it had failed, choosing for the time being not to exploit the success achieved on his right. Lieutenant-General Sir Hubert Gough, Commander of the Reserve Army that was to have exploited any breakthrough, was now sent to take command of X and VIII Corps for their renewed assault astride the Ancre. Gough, a cavalryman and protégé of Sir Douglas Haig, was a notorious "thruster", a commander who got results regardless of the cost. "Press on" was to be the order of the day.

The night following the first day of battle was fairly quiet; both sides seemed grateful for the respite and, as the German inactivity extended throughout Sunday 2 July, the British divisions were able to reorganise and reinforce as well as pushing forward supplies and ammunition. Preoccupied as they were with overcoming the confusion in their own lines and with preparations for future operations, they were unaware of the desperate situation they had created for their enemy. On the night of the 1st the Germans were very close to tactical defeat. The whole of the field artillery opposite the French southern assault had been lost, together with six of the eight heavy batteries, all of the German front trench system between the Somme and the Amiens road, and Hem, Hardecourt, Montauban and Mametz. Fricourt was threatened and the situation above Thiepval was critical; Trônes and Bernafay Woods had been abandoned, and in the course of the day contingency plans had been drawn up for the abandonment of the whole first line south of the Ancre. In the event this had not been necessary, and the counter-attacks around Thiepval had restored the situation there.

Preparations were now made for a night attack with the aim of recapturing Montauban. This struck the front of XIII Corps between 3 and 4 a.m. with four large infantry groups in close formation. Warned by the noise the Germans were making, British artillery put down a shrapnel barrage which broke up the German attack with heavy loss. A party of enemy infantry did succeed in getting into Montauban but were bombed and killed. Fricourt was bombarded by the artillery of XV Corps and entered by infantry of the 17th (Northern) Division, a New Army formation, against little resistance at noon on 2 July. On their right infantry of the 7th Division pushed forward in line with them, and on their left units of the 21st Division also advanced; so that by the end of the day XV Corps had, on its right, taken its objective of the previous day as well as Fricourt village and wood.

In the III Corps area Sausage Redoubt was captured by a bombing attack. At 4p.m. an attack was mounted against La Boisselle by a brigade of the 19th (Western) Division. Before the infantry advanced Ovillers had been bombarded for half an hour and smoke was released to mask the assault. The trick worked, focusing German attention on Ovillers and enabling the infantry of the 19th Division to get into the La Boisselle defences and capture the western half of the village. In front of Ovillers the 8th Division had been relieved by the 12th (Eastern) Division, New Army.

On that part of the front held by X and VIII Corps the task set them by Fourth Army – to carry the whole of the German front and intermediate positions – seemed out of the question. Lieutenant-General Gough informed General Rawlinson that nothing could done until the morning of the 3rd. The lodgement of the 36th (Ulster) Division north of Thiepval was reinforced but was under pressure from the enemy, as was the lodgement at the Leipzig Redoubt. The failure at Gommecourt led to a decision not to renew the attack there.

At 10.30a.m. on 2 July Sir Douglas Haig visited Fourth Army headquarters. In discussion with Rawlinson, he told him that there were sufficient reserves of men to replace the losses sustained, but that ammunition was going to limit the courses of action open to them. He was anxious, he said, to exploit the successes on the right, and wished to concentrate

on the Mametz Wood-Contalmaison sector in order to strike at the German second position on the Longueval-Bazentin le Petit ridge. He felt that an advance from the line Montauban-Fricourt would outflank the enemy defences facing westward. In his view Thiepval should be attacked as a diversion, and the enemy kept under threat of attack north of the Ancre. Without first consulting General Foch he could not consider development of the Fourth Army right.

In reply, General Rawlinson said that he was in favour of improving his centre and securing Thiepval; and at noon he issued orders to X and VIII Corps to attack the objectives already set for them, and for III Corps to take Ovillers. Zero Hour was to be 3.15a.m. on 3 July following an hour's intense bombardment. An independent operation was approved for XV Corps to straighten their line at 9a.m. on the 3rd. Haig urged Rawlinson to take action in the Montauban area, and it was agreed to send patrols forward there. On a subsequent visit to General Gough, Sir Douglas countermanded the orders just issued and gave instructions that activities on the left should be reduced to an assault by two brigades.

The subject of exploitation on the right had not been exhausted, however. Later that night, in a conversation with Haig's chief-of-staff, Rawlinson said that he had arranged to see General Foch at 9a.m. the next day to discuss French co-operation. General Kiggell replied that Sir Douglas would back with reserve divisions and extra ammunition any attempt to secure the German positions on Longueval ridge.

Throughout 2 July the French kept up the pressure in their area, especially south of the river, where the Germans were forced to withdraw from the Flaucourt plateau to their third line of defence before Peronne. The loss of this position was to cost General von Below's chief-of-staff his job. He was sacked the next day; at the same time three divisions and three flights of aircraft were ordered from the German general reserve to the support of Von Below, and four additional divisions – two from Verdun – were placed under orders for the Somme. These reinforcements were in addition to the 16 heavy batteries – 15 of them from Verdun –

which had been ordered to march to the Somme on the 1st, and the further 22 who were preparing to move. The German moment of vulnerability was passing, as was the Allied opportunity to exploit it.

3 July: The attacks at Ovillers and Thiepval

By this time the good weather of the previous few days was beginning to deteriorate, but the cloud did not prevent British air reconnaissance from observing the columns of German infantry, horses and guns moving towards Bapaume and Peronne from the east and south-east.

Twenty minutes before the attack by III and X Corps was due to be launched General Gough telephoned III Corps to say that X Corps could not be ready before 6a.m., but that part of the bombardment would be fired and smoke released. In spite of this the attack against Ovillers by the 12th Division went ahead on time at 3.15a.m. Immediately red rockets shot into the air from the enemy's positions to summon up the artillery fire which fell on the British lines. Despite this and the fire from machine guns the leading five battalions got over no-man's-land, through the German wire and into the enemy front trench, which appeared to be empty. Pressing on to the German support line, the British were attacked from the rear by the German infantry who had by now emerged from the deep dug-outs of the first line. When dawn broke little could be seen through the smoke that obscured the German lines, but the noise of battle went on without a pause. Reinforcement was made impossible by the German fire now sweeping no-man's-land. By mid-morning the 12th Division admitted its failure to take Ovillers and reported the loss of the attacking force of nearly 2,400 officers and men. One small success was the action of a company of the 9th Essex who lost their way, captured 220 Germans, and managed to find their way back to a part of the line held by the 19th Division.

Attacks in the 19th Division area resulted in the complete capture of La Boisselle and the German trenches 400 yards beyond, but a German counter-attack retook the eastern end of the village. A series of running fights developed, with constant exchanges of hand grenades; and it was at this

2 July 1916: British artillery bombarding German positions at Fricourt prior to the attack of the 17th Division. (IWM Q114)

gain represented about 100 yards. Attempts to link up with the 19th Division by the 34th Division, still holding the right sector of III Corps, failed.

Further north the 32nd (New Army) Division attack against the Leipzig salient, launched late and with reduced artillery support, failed with the loss of nearly 1,100 men. During the night of 3/4 July the 32nd was relieved by the 25th (New Army) Division.

The operation launched by XV Corps at 9a.m. met with resistance that was only gradually overcome, and then with many casualties, before their objectives were gained and the line in their area "straightened up". At 2p.m. a German counter-attack was beaten off, many prisoners were taken, and the business of consolidating the new positions set in hand. Patrols then found that Mametz Wood and Quadrangle Trench were empty; but units of the 7th Division, pushed forward after dark to occupy the southern edge of the wood, got lost. The position was occupied in daylight the following day. This not very brisk initiative frequently allowed the Germans time to restore their positions, to the cost of the British in days to come.

XIII Corps spent 3 July in consolidation. Patrols discovered Bernafay Wood to be still undefended; and at 9p.m., supported by a 20-minute barrage, two battalions of the 9th (Scottish) Division, New Army, entered and took possession of the wood. Caterpillar Wood, reported empty by the RFC, was occupied by the 18th Division on the 4th, and the same division recovered five abandoned German field guns while taking possession of a section of enemy trench near the wood. These events gave rise to a feeling among the officers of XIII and XV Corps that the enemy before

time that Lieutenant-Colonel Carton de Wiart found himself leading not only his own battalion – the 8th Glosters – but the 10th Royal Warwicks as well. In these bombing brawls Carton de Wiart, who had lost an eye in a previous war and an arm at Ypres (earning him the nickname of "Nelson"), strode ahead of his men pulling the pins with his teeth before hurling grenades at the enemy. In this episode he set a precedent that has been emulated by film actors (though by few soldiers) to this day; more importantly, his "dauntless courage and inspiring example" won him a Victoria Cross. At the end of the battle the British

Men of the 10th Notts.& Derby Regiment (Sherwood Foresters), 17th Division, after the attack on Fricourt, posing with their trophies – the ever-popular Pickelhaube helmets, caps, Luger pistols, bayonets, but also including the dog at left. The cloth discs on their sleeves were brown, and part of a scheme of insignia worn throughout the 17th Division to indicate unit and brigade. (IWM Q130)

them were beaten and that a determined advance might keep them on the run. Their Army commander, however, was not anxious to create a deeper salient opposite XIII Corps.

General Rawlinson's meeting with General Foch on the morning of the 3rd failed to obtain a promise of co-operation from the French while the British XIII Corps remained inactive. Later that day, when Haig met with General Joffre, he was told that the French wanted the future main British effort to be made further north in the area from Pozières to Thiepval, and not against the Longueval-Contalmaison front; indeed, Joffre went so far as to order Sir Douglas to carry out this operation. Haig recorded: "General Joffre exploded in a fit of rage...he ordered me to attack Thiepval and Pozières. If I attacked Longueval, I would be beaten! I waited calmly till he had finished. His breast heaved and his face flushed. The truth is the poor man cannot argue, nor can he easily read a map." The British Commander-in-Chief declined to comply, saying that his artillery ammunition was insufficient, and that he must concentrate his efforts upon one part of his line whilst attempting to hold the enemy elsewhere. He went on to say that in his opinion

3 July: German prisoners under escort carry a stretcher case back from La Boisselle. The groundsheets worn by some of the Tommies remind us that the weather began to deteriorate on the 3rd. (IWM Q759)

the area Longueval-Contalmaison was the most promising. The German defences were weaker there and the enemy garrison was clearly shaken. He had, therefore, decided to attack in the south. Joffre persisted, forcing Sir Douglas to point out that he was responsible solely to his own government, and would not pursue a plan of which he did not approve. He would follow Joffre's strategy, but would go no further. Joffre accepted this, and the meeting closed amicably. Haig's views had been accepted by the French staff, and arrangements were made to discuss Allied co-operation in the capture of Longueval.

A conference of Corps commanders was held that afternoon at Fourth Army headquarters, following which an Army order was issued at 9.45p.m.; this required preparations to be made for an attack on the German second position Longueval-Bazentin le Petit, before which the British front was to be advanced to assaulting distance and artillery deployed to support the attack. Specifically, XIII Corps was to secure Bernafay and Caterpillar Woods (which it did in the course of the night); XV Corps was to occupy Mametz Wood; and III Corps was to capture Contalmaison and establish itself upon a line from Mametz Wood to La Boisselle. In the north what was now called the Reserve Army – Gough's command – was to carry out raids, bombing attacks and artillery barrages in order to pin the enemy on its front. X Corps was to extend its footings in the German front system.

4–6 July: Preparing to attack in the south

The weather, which had been fine apart from occasional thunderstorms, broke on 4 July; heavy rain filled the trenches and turned tracks into quagmires. The shell-torn ground absorbed the downpour, melting into tracts of

The entrance to a German dug-out in Bernafay Wood, captured by the 9th (Scottish) Division on 3 July 1916, gives an indication of the scale of field engineering undertaken by the Germans on the Somme. Most of their fortifications were less photogenic, being deep beneath the surface of the ground. This massive exercise in fortification guaranteed most of the infantry protection from the Allied bombardment; but would have a distinct disadvantage once Allied artillery tactics became more sophisticated, allowing assaulting infantry to follow close behind a creeping barrage and to get into the German trenches before the defenders could emerge from their bunkers. (IWM Q4307)

marshland. Starting on the 4th, the British and French spent three days improving their positions and preparing for the attacks on Hardecourt, Trônes Wood, Mametz Wood and Contalmaison which were to take place on 7 July. Artillery bombardment of the objectives began, and roads were repaired and improved.

At 8.30a.m. on the 4th an attempt was made to complete the capture of La Boisselle, with units of the 19th Division bombing their way up the trenches supported by machine guns and mortars. Against determined German resistance progress was made, and by 2.30p.m. the village was in British hands. Elsewhere, elements of the 17th Division advanced along trenches towards Contalmaison, and that night troops of the 18th Division occupied Marlboro Wood, 500 yards beyond Caterpillar Wood.

A XV Corps operation planned for midnight of 4/5 July was delayed by a heavy rainstorm, but under its cover battalions of the 7th and 17th Divisions were able to approach to within a hundred yards of the enemy unobserved. The surprise thus gained enabled the British to seize the German positions on the southern edge of Mametz Wood, but any further progress was held up by severe enemy machine gun fire. Between Mametz Wood and La Boisselle the 23rd Division fought a difficult battle in an attempt to extend its position before Contalmaison. Further north in the X Corps area infantry of the 25th Division improved their holding in the Leipzig salient.

There was much activity among the commanders and their staffs. Sir Douglas Haig visited General Rawlinson on 4 July, and stressed to him the importance of the seizure of Contalmaison, Mametz Wood and Trônes Wood. Afterwards he visited the commanders of XIII, XV and III Corps and urged them to be energetic and enterprising in the coming battles. Formal orders issued by GHQ on the 4th restated the objectives of the Fourth Army, and warned the Reserve Army to prepare to attack Ovillers and the Leipzig salient. (By this time General Gough's Reserve Army's area of responsibility had been extended south to the Amiens-Bapaume road.) Also on the 4th, General Foch informed Rawlinson that the French XX Corps would attack the position north of Hardecourt, and requested action by Fourth Army against Trônes Wood and Maltz Horn Farm.

On 5 July Sir Douglas was back at Fourth Army to discuss with Rawlinson the French request and to order the Reserve Army to take Ovillers. Information now released on artillery ammunition availability for the forthcoming operations showed it to be very unsatisfactory. There were only 70,000 rounds of 18-pounder and 5,800 rounds of 6in. howitzer for both Armies. Once again the French came to the aid of their allies, loaning General Rawlinson four batteries of 120mm guns and a battery of 220mm howitzers with an ample supply of ammunition. Further conferences with the French were conducted to overcome problems with their mutual flank.

On 6 July the Fourth Army received an extraordinary intelligence memorandum from Haig's chief-of-staff. General Kiggell informed them that the enemy were confused and demoralised, and went on to say that the line La Boisselle-Hardecourt was being held by only 15 German battalions, eleven of which had suffered severely in the recent fighting. (In fact, 33 German battalions held this position with 40 in reserve.)

7 July: Mametz Wood, Contalmaison and Ovillers

The 7th was yet another day of gusty wind and heavy showers, grounding aircraft and deepening the slime through which the forward troops had to wade. Movement was such a struggle that men collapsed from exhaustion, and at times teams of 14 horses were required to draw a single wagon. On the right XIII Corps were awaiting the French, who could not be ready to advance until the 8th and so took no part in the day's fighting.

In the centre, the divisions of XV Corps were to launch their attacks upon Mametz Wood and Contalmaison after preliminary attacks by the 17th Division at 2a.m. had secured an intermediate position. These were only partly successful, and at 8a.m. the division was ordered to try again. By now the Germans were thoroughly alerted and kept up a heavy bombardment of the British positions. In the prevailing atmosphere of confusion the British barrage lifted from the German front trenches before the infantry of the 17th Division were within assaulting distance. Unsupported, they were driven back by German machine gun fire.

At 8.30a.m. the 38th (Welsh) Division, New Army, set off to attack Mametz Wood but were soon held up by machine guns. Further attempts were made at 10.15a.m. and 3.15p.m., both supported by artillery, but the Welshmen were again held up and could get no closer to the Wood than 250 yards. Both divisions were ordered to renew their attacks at 5p.m. after a further artillery barrage, but in the rain and mud the battalions of the 17th Division could not be organised in time and their advance was postponed until 8p.m., when they struggled through the mud to be caught once again by the enemy machine gun and artillery fire. With no hope of success the attack of the 17th Division was abandoned. In the 38th Division units could not be got ready in time to follow the British barrage; and XV Corps finished the day with nothing to show for its casualties.

On the Fourth Army left, the III Corps attacks were disrupted by the failure of the 17th Division, which had the effect of holding back the attack of the 23rd Division. The 19th Division, however, after waiting for a quarter of an hour, went into the attack at 8.15a.m., following their orders to "approach the objective as near as possible before the bombardment lifts". Unfortunately the infantry of the 19th ventured too close to the barrage, and suffered the consequences. Despite this setback they recovered sufficiently to seize the whole of their objective. The attack of the 23rd Division got under way at 9.15a.m.; against fierce German opposition elements of the 1st Worcesters fought their way into Contalmaison, only to be forced to withdraw through lack of support and ammunition. Further attempts to renew the attack came to nothing, the combination of deep mud and heavy enemy fire having defeated the infantrymen of the 23rd Division. In these appalling conditions they established a line short of their objective.

Further north, in the Reserve Army area, the infantry of X Corps were preparing to attack Ovillers at 8a.m. Prior to this troops of the 49th (West Riding) Division, Territorial Force, holding the positions north of Thiepval, came under fierce attack and were driven back to their old front line, losing the Ulster lodgement won at such cost on the 1st. A similar attack at the Leipzig salient was contained by the British, who managed to improve their position.

Major-General Maxse, commander of the 18th (Eastern) Division, New Army, and later of XVIII Corps. (IWM Q6165)

18th (EASTERN) DIVISION

Acknowledged as the best of all the "Kitchener" divisions, the 18th had the good luck to have as its commander one of the best general officers in the British Army, Major-General Ivor Maxse. A visionary, an exceptional leader, but most of all a "trainer" dedicated to preparing his command for the reality of battle, Maxse developed the 18th Division, and saw his methods and leadership justified in the Somme battles. His division remained an elite formation after he left it for a Corps, retaining its high morale and always fighting well.

Conversely, there were several "hard luck" divisions, not all of them New Army, whose records show consistent failure. The reasons for their low morale and performance are hard to define, but probably lay in poor leadership and training. Certainly most formations started equal in the quality of their men and equipment; but in the campaigns of the Western Front some fought with distinction and some with discredit. Once the cancer of low morale developed in a division it was hard to eradicate. One division noted to have "run away" on the Somme was also noted to have "broken and fled" in the face of the German counterattack at Cambrai over a year later.

According to plan, five battalions of the 12th and 25th (New Army) Divisions attacked Ovillers in the face of severe enemy artillery and machine gun fire, and persisted in their efforts until the first three lines of German trenches were taken. Casualties were heavy and the captured positions deep in mud, but the survivors clung to their gains until reinforced that night.

Hearing the news, Sir Douglas Haig ordered General Gough to complete the capture of Ovillers and link up with III Corps at La Boisselle. That evening he ordered forward reinforcements including three Australian divisions, two additional New Army divisions, and the 51st (Highland) Division, Territorial Force. His blooded battalions, struggling in the mud, were approaching exhaustion, and fresh troops were needed for the fray.

8 July: Trônes Wood

The Allied attacks for this day were to start at 8a.m., with the French advancing on the knoll north of Hardecourt while the British went for Trônes Wood "as far as the railway line". In the early hours the objectives were bombarded and the infantry of the 30th Division formed up in Bernafay Wood for the assault. At the appointed time they advanced, only to be stopped by heavy enemy fire before they had gone far. Subsequent attempts to renew the attack were similarly checked; but eventually parties of British infantry infiltrated the German positions south of Trônes Wood and into the south-eastern edge of the wood itself. After dark reinforcements were sent forward, the positions were consolidated, and the division was ordered to renew the attack upon the wood before dawn the next day.

Elsewhere, the regulars of the 3rd Division began to relieve the 18th Division; and the 17th Division pressed forward in an attempt to improve its position. The 38th Division were ordered to attack Mametz Wood after dark, and chose 2a.m. on 8 July as their time to do so; but a solitary platoon which they sent forward found it impossible to get on owing to the conditions in the mud-filled trenches

Loading 18-pdr. ammunition onto General Service wagons, Acheux, July 1916. Acheux was behind the Beaumont Hamel area of the line, and several of these men wear the divisional sign of the 29th Division. The rough handling which ammunition received on its way up to the gun positions was almost certainly a contributory cause of the lethal rate of premature detonations. (IWM Q727)

and over the shell-pocked open ground. Similar difficulties were experienced by the units of the 23rd Division who were ordered to push forward towards Contalmaison. Movement was almost impossible, with men sinking into the mud to such a depth that they had to be hauled out by their comrades. In these conditions little progress was possible, although the 19th Division managed to extend their front by nearly a thousand yards.

On the front of the Reserve Army further attempts were made to capture Ovillers, elements of the 12th and 25th Divisions trying to bomb their way forward along the waterlogged trenches; to their great credit, some gains were made. But it was the situation at Mametz Wood which occupied the mind of Sir Douglas Haig. General Rawlinson had reported to him his dissatisfaction with some of the commanders involved, and they were subsequently sacked.

9-13 July: Trônes Wood, Mametz Wood and Contalmaison

The weather from the 9th to the 13th was generally fine, favouring offensive operations and allowing the RFC to go ahead with artillery observation and bombing raids against the enemy rear. The 30th Division kept up its attempts to take Trônes Wood in a series of battles during which positions were captured and lost repeatedly as the casualties mounted. Exhausted, the division was relieved by the 18th Division on 13 July; they too attempted to secure the wood, but had failed to do so by the next day.

On 10 July the 38th Division made another attempt to secure Mametz Wood, which by now – like Trônes Wood – was an insane tangle of fallen and shattered trees and branches, laced with barbed wire, through which movement was extremely difficult. Following a creeping barrage battalions of the division set off at 4.15a.m., and fought their way forward against the resistance of the terrain and the enemy in a series of confused battles which ended that night with the Welshmen in possession of most of the wood. On the following day the position was extended and consolidated, and on the 12th the division was relieved by

July 1916: men of a Motor Machine Gun Battery – Corps troops – pose with their souvenirs at Contalmaison. Their machines are the Vickers-Clyno 5-6hp motorcycle combinations, used to move the Vickers machine guns and the enormous amounts of ammunition they consumed from place to place. Once again, the Pickelhaube is the souvenir of choice, but at least one German M1916 helmet can be seen in this group.(IWM Q6231)

elements of the 21st Division, who completed the consolidation of Mametz Wood.

The 23rd Division had been working their way forward towards Contalmaison since the morning of 9 July, defeating a German counter-attack and entering the ruins of the village on the 10th. After a brisk fight the village was captured, along with over 200 German prisoners and nine machine guns. (At this point enemy infantry were streaming away from Contalmaison, but could not be properly engaged because the buffer springs of many of the supporting 18-pounders were unserviceable.) Consolidation proceeded, and a further enemy counter-attack was beaten off. On 11 July the division was relieved by elements of the 1st (Regular) Division.

The fall of Contalmaison and Mametz Wood placed the Germans between them, in Quadrangle Support Trench, in great danger. Attacks on this position by the 17th Division were rewarded when it fell on 10 July. In the Reserve Army area fighting went on for Ovillers. In the French area their forces remained on the defensive except for an operation south of the river.

On 11 July a German attack at Verdun had failed despite a supreme effort by their exhausted infantry, and the use of their deadly new phosgene gas. A handful of survivors of their 140th Regiment had actually reached the cupolas of Fort Souville, the final French ridge bastion above the Meuse, only to be driven off by a sortie. German forces before Verdun were now ordered on to the "strict defensive", and numerous artillery units were withdrawn from the sector and sent north to the Somme. This date, therefore, marked the achievement of the primary aim of the Allied offensive.

CHAPTER NINE

The Attack on the Second Position: "The Battle of Bazentin Ridge"

After the Great War a committee apportioning "battle honours" gave names to all the actions that made up the Allied campaign on the Somme. "The Battle of Albert" was conferred upon the events of the first two weeks – the initial attacks and the series of battles fought immediately afterwards to secure vital ground and to keep up the pressure on the Germans. As has been described, many of these later battles were fought under atrocious conditions of weather and terrain, in circumstances that were sometimes confused or even chaotic, and sometimes with inadequate support. Nearly all were fought by troops who were at best tired, sometimes exhausted, and among whom there had been no opportunities for analysis of tactics or scope for tactical innovation.

The British Army, however, in common with all other armies, believes in "concurrent activity", which includes the planning and preparation of future operations whilst fighting the current ones. If the weary infantry and gunners of the Fourth Army had no time to digest and act upon the lessons of the recent fighting, their leaders had. On 8 July, while the Fourth Army had yet to secure Trônes Wood, Mametz Wood and Contalmaison, General Rawlinson had issued a warning order for an attack on the German second position, setting in train the preparations behind the battlefront required for such an undertaking, and a ground and aerial reconnaissance of the German second and third positions.

A meeting was held with Corps commanders and their Brigadiers RA at which, with the setbacks of recent days clearly in mind, it was decided that the main attack should be made at dawn, before the enemy machine gunners could see and shoot to effect. XIII Corps was chosen to attack the line Longueval-Bazentin le Grand village with two divisions, which were to form up silently in no-man's-land under cover of darkness. XV Corps was to attack Bazentin le Grand Wood and Bazentin le Petit village from the cover of Mametz Wood. On the left, a division of III Corps would carry out an attack to protect the flank.

Secrecy was vital. If the Germans had a suspicion of British intentions disaster might ensue, but General Rawlinson judged the risk to be acceptable. Sir Douglas Haig, on the other hand, was not enthusiastic about the plan, considering the task of assembling in the dark to be beyond the capabilities of his men. He felt that they lacked the necessary training and discipline, that their staff officers were too inexperienced for such a task, and that the proposed approach march and forming up would be a diffi-cult undertaking even on peacetime manoeuvres. He suggested an alternative plan which did not stake all on surprise. After a further conference Rawlinson reported to his chief that he, his Corps and divisional commanders were all strongly in favour of the original plan.

Sir Douglas remained unmoved, and issued orders that

XV Corps should attack first, with XIII Corps standing ready to exploit any success. He was not the only sceptic; the French also felt that an operation of this type could not be kept secure, and did not believe that the British could overcome the problems inseparable from the task of forming up large bodies of troops at night. They refused to have anything to do with "an attack organised for amateurs by amateurs", but consented to provide some fire support.

Bombardment began on the 11th, with counter-battery work, wire-breaking, and the destruction of enemy defences. At night the enemy rear areas were bombarded, particularly Waterlot Farm, Flers, High Wood, Martinpuich, Le Sars and Bapaume. The artillery of the Reserve Army was incorporated into this fire plan, as were some French batteries. Once again, reserves of artillery ammunition gave cause for concern, especially that for the heavy howitzers, which had to be limited in some cases to 25 rounds per gun per day. The state of the ground made transportation of ammunition difficult, but the complete air supremacy won by the RFC allowed ammunition to be brought up by day and night, and for Allied batteries to shoot from open positions unmolested.

On 12 July, following an appeal from General Rawlinson, Haig relented and gave permission for both XII! and XV Corps to attack together, a decision made that much easier now that British troops had substantial lodge-ments in both Trônes and Mametz Woods. Orders were now issued for the infantry assault to take place at 3.25a.m. on the 14th, preceded by a barrage of all available guns. This was to be of only five minutes' duration, after which a creeping barrage was to be fired ahead of the advancing infantry, in which all high explosive shells were to be fitted with time fuses instead of the customary "graze". The reason given for this departure was that graze fuses might cause danger to the advancing infantry by detonating prematurely against trees and buildings. (This type of barrage was to prove so effective that few barrages consisting entirely of shrapnel were ever fired again.) In the final orders the initial objectives were given as the enemy's front and second trenches from the south-west corner of Delville Wood, through the centre of Longueval, the southern ends of Bazentin le Grand village and wood and the southern edge of Bazentin le Petit wood. The second objective included Delville Wood, Longueval, and Bazentin le Petit wood and village. Three cavalry divisions were to be held ready to move at 4a.m.; their objectives were High Wood, Leuze Wood and Martinpuich.

The attacks of 14 July

The divisions chosen for the attack were the 3rd and 9th (Scottish) of XIII Corps, and the 7th and 21st of XV Corps. The 18th Division, still struggling in Trônes Wood, were to provide a defensive flank on the right, and on the left the 1st Division were to do the same. After dark on 13 July the troops of the assaulting brigades, over 22,000 men, began to move forward to the forming-up positions, which were mostly within 500 yards of the enemy. Unit by unit and in absolute silence the deployment was perfectly conducted until, at 3a.m., all were in place. Great pains had been taken to ensure secrecy, including a telephone deception, sure to have been overheard by the enemy, "postponing" the operation. Standing patrols had been pushed forward to guard against enemy interference during the assembly, and lanes and approaches had been marked with white tape to guide companies and platoons to their forming-up places. The night was remarkably quiet, with little enemy shelling and no patrol activity.

At 3.20a.m. the five-minute intensive barrage began, and by this time many of the assault battalions had crept forward to within 50 yards of where the British shells now fell. Behind them the whole sky seemed to ripple in a continuous curtain of flame as the Allied artillery fired at a rapid rate. Before them the ground shook and trembled with bursting shells, and streams of bullets from supporting machine guns crackled above their heads. At 3.25a.m., when the barrage began to move onward, the leading companies of the assault battalions (all except one of them New Army units) advanced behind it through a ground mist. There was just sufficient light to distinguish friend from foe. Surprised by the shortness and the intensity of the bombardment, by the use of high explosive in the creeping barrage, and by the immediate arrival of the infantry in its wake, enemy resistance was feeble. Most of the leading British waves were through the barbed wire and had captured the German first position before the German infantry emerged from the dug-outs and the counter-barrage fell. Leaving the task of "mopping-up" to the following waves, the assault battalions pressed on.

On the right the 9th (Scottish) Division encountered increasing opposition as it took two lines of trenches and got into Longueval. By 10a.m. they had captured all their objectives including a lodgement in Delville Wood. Parties of the enemy were still holding out in Longueval, however, and it proved impossible to secure Waterlot Farm. Consolidation went ahead, and on the right contact was made with the 18th Division who, after an heroic struggle, had captured Trônes Wood.

Next to the Scots the 3rd Division, after some difficulty with the German wire, pressed on to secure their objectives exactly on time. Bazentin le Grand was captured and consolidation proceeded. Further left, the infantry of the 7th Division had no difficulty with the enemy wire and moved straight onto the second line behind the barrage, arriving there at 3.35a.m. From here large numbers of the enemy were seen falling back towards High Wood, and these were brought under rifle and machine gun fire. At 4.25a.m., when the barrage lifted off Bazentin le Grand wood, it was quickly cleared and a line established beyond it. A brigade was pushed forward whilst consolidation proceeded, and this formation secured the village of Bazentin le Petit by 7.30a.m., capturing the headquarters of the 16th Bavarian Regiment and over 200 prisoners. A series of counter-attacks were driven off and the village was consolidated.

The assault companies of the 21st Division also got into the enemy's front trenches as the barrage lifted, and against

Indian troopers of the Deccan Horse photographed in Carnoy Valley on 14 July. The cavalry's failure to exploit the German confusion at High Wood after the successful night attack was one of the three great lost opportunities of the Somme battles. (IWM Q823)

sporadic resistance pushed on to secure the second line by 4a.m. From here they advanced to take Bazentin le Petit wood, from where they got into Bazentin le Petit and helped units of the 7th Division in capturing the village.

Thus, in an operation which took the enemy completely by surprise, troops of the Fourth Army had established themselves on the main Ginchy-Pozières ridge in a matter of hours. Two German regimental commanders, 40 other officers and 1,400 of their men had been captured, while the ground taken was littered with German dead and wounded. (It is worth noting that much greater execution could have been done had the musketry of the British infantry been better. Through lack of training many of them could not hit a target at 300 yards. There had been too much emphasis, it was apparent, on the cult of the "bomb".)

If the Germans had been taken by surprise, so too had the French. Before the attack General Rawlinson's chief-of-staff had promised his French counterparts that if the British were not on the Longueval ridge at 8.00a.m. the next morning he would eat his hat. In having to admit that they had underestimated the British they also had to concede that *"Montgomery ne mange pas son chapeau"*. It had been a splendid demonstration by the British, who with great dash had pulled off one of the most difficult operations of war.

In Longueval and Delville Wood fighting continued all

day as the Germans pressed the vulnerable British right flank, but on the front of the 3rd and 7th Divisions the enemy appeared to have withdrawn. At about 10a.m. reconnaissance towards High Wood discovered no enemy, but requests for permission to probe forward were denied. Overcaution and rigid adherence to plans now conspired to rob the British of the full fruits of victory. High Wood was due to be taken by the cavalry, and the cavalry were on their way to carry out this task. And so time passed as the British waited for the arrival of the exploitation force, and as the Germans reinforced their defences.

At 7.40a.m. the 2nd Indian Cavalry Division had been ordered forward from Morlancourt; they began to move at 8.20a.m., making slow progress over ground that was badly cut up by old trench systems and shell holes. The division's leading elements were approaching Montauban in the early afternoon; but by then the Fourth Army had ordered infantry of the 7th Division to advance on High Wood, only to have them halted by the commander of XV Corps until Longueval had been secured. Little by little the initiative was slipping from the grasp of the British.

As German reaction strengthened, mistaken reports reached XV Corps that Longueval was in British hands. The 7th Division was ordered to advance on High Wood with cavalry screening their right flank. After a great deal of confusion the advance began at 7p.m.; the wood was entered and part of it occupied, but consolidation was interrupted by fierce German counter-attacks which now began

to develop. Squadrons of the 7th Dragoon Guards and the Deccan Horse, moving forward to occupy high ground between Delville Wood and High Wood, came under German fire and charged, killing a number of Germans with sabre and lance and capturing others. As it grew dark the horses were got into shelter and a line was established from near Longueval to the southern corner of High Wood.

So ended the day. The British objectives on the ridge had been taken at the cost of over 9,000 casualties. The Germans had suffered even worse, the 16th Bavarian Regiment alone losing nearly 2,300 officers and men. The sight of British cavalry had alarmed the Germans, one report stating that "the British had broken through northwards between Longueval and Pozières...had reached the line Flers-High Wood-Martinpuich and were still advancing". In the area of the Reserve Army inconclusive fighting had gone on during the day at Ovillers and at the Leipzig salient.

15-22 July

While the fighting of the 14th was still in progress General Rawlinson had issued orders for exploitation on the

19 July: men of the 26th (Highland) Infantry Brigade, 9th (Scottish) Division, make their way back from the fighting at Longueval and Delville Wood. The division lost 314 officers and 7,303 other ranks in their part of the battle. The piper and two others are from the 7th Seaforth, and the other two from the 8th Black Watch and 5th Camerons. (IWM Q4012)

19 July: men of the 8th Black Watch rest after counter-attacking at Longueval. Most wear the coloured arcs of cloth stitched to their shoulders which in this brigade identified the wearer's company. (IWM Q4009)

following day. But the 15th dawned misty and overcast, and a persistent rain set in that was to last for 48 hours. In addition, sufficient German reinforcements to counter British intentions were now arriving. To add to the difficulties of the Fourth Army, artillery ammunition had to be rationed pending the arrival of further supplies.

On the right the 9th (Scottish) Division, which included a brigade of South Africans, were still fighting in the ruins

MAJOR W.La T.CONGREVE, VC, DSO, MC

Major William La Touche Congreve of the Rifle Brigade was among the many soldiers who met their deaths in Delville Wood. Major Congreve, Brigade Major of the 76th Infantry Brigade, 3rd Division, was shot dead on 20 July while in the act of writing a report in the front line. He was posthumously awarded the Victoria Cross, "for most conspicuous bravery during a period of fourteen days preceding his death in action", during which time he performed numerous acts of gallantry in and about Delville Wood, Longueval, Montauban and the Bazentin ridge. The son of Lt.Gen.Sir Walter Congreve, VC, commanding XIII Corps, "Billy" Congreve was only 25 years old at the time of his death, but had previously been mentioned in despatches four times, had been awarded the French Legion of Honour, the Military Cross and the Distinguished Service Order. Had he lived he would undoubtedly have had a brilliant career in both World Wars.

of Longueval and Waterlot Farm and attempting to capture Delville Wood. At first the South Africans made good progress into this tangle of fallen trees and hazel thickets; having seized a substantial lodgement they dug in to resist the German counter-attacks now directed against them.

Fighting went on all day, throughout the night and into the following day, during which the wood was progressively shattered by the high explosive barrages and machine gun concentrations fired by both sides. On the morning of 16 July the 9th (Scottish) Division made an attempt to seize the remainder of the wood and that part of Longueval still in German hands; the attack failed, but was pressed again later in the day, and again that night, only to be beaten back again by intense German fire, which now included gas in addition to high explosive and machine gun fire. By noon on the 17th the Scots and South Africans admitted failure and arrangements were made for the 3rd Division to renew the attack.

The squadrons of cavalry which had held the line between Longueval and High Wood on the night of the 14th/15th were withdrawn the following morning, while the British troops holding part of High Wood attempted to seize the rest of it during the day. A fierce battle developed as the Germans launched a series of counter-attacks, but by nightfall the battalions of the 7th Division in High Wood were still holding on. At 11.25p.m. they were ordered to withdraw from the wood, their Corps commander, Lieutenant-General Horne, mistakenly believing their position to be untenable. His order was carried out with very little fighting. The Germans followed up and occupied the whole wood.

While the 7th Division had been attempting to capture High Wood, on their left the 33rd (New Army) Division were going forward as part of a III Corps operation attacking Pozières. By the afternoon of the 15th the attacking battalions of the 33rd Division had been driven back to their starting positions, but the remainder of the III Corps assault fared better. The 1st (Regular) Division captured parts of the German first and second line, while

the 34th (New Army) were halted about a quarter of a mile from Pozières. On 16 July the 1st Division launched a further attack which resulted in the capture of their original objectives, but Pozières remained in German hands.

Whilst these battles were being fought orders were again being drawn up for future operations, including attacks on Guillemont, Ginchy, the German positions between High Wood and Martinpuich, and Pozières. These were to be supported by the French on the right, the Reserve Army on the left, and the cavalry, who were to be held in readiness for their usual role in the event of a breakthrough. On 16 July High Wood was added to the list of objectives, and the date for the assault was given as the 18th. The usual instructions to the artillery for registration, bombardment, etc. were issued. There were, however, many factors at work to delay the operation, and postponement followed postponement.

The Reserve Army
At 2a.m. on 15 July X Corps of the Reserve Army launched a further attack against Ovillers. Fighting went on until the evening of the 16th, when the remnants of the German garrison surrendered and the village was reported clear of the enemy. On the morning of the 17th the British line was pushed further forward beyond the ruins of Ovillers.

As a consequence of Haig's decision to shorten the Fourth Army front, the capture of Pozières now became a task of the Reserve Army. I ANZAC Corps, which had recently joined the Reserve Army, were ordered to relieve the Fourth Army formations before Pozières.

German prisoners help to push a water cart out of the mud near Contalmaison, July 1916. Painted on the tank is the Geneva Cross, "21 FA" indicating the 21st Field Ambulance, and the white disc which was the sign of the 7th Division. (IWM Q810)

THE BANTAM DIVISIONS

In 1914 the desire of small men to serve their country led to the enlistment of recruits below the minimum standards of height and physique. They were formed into "Bantam" battalions, which went to form the 35th and 40th (New Army) Divisions. At first great care was taken to enlist men who, though small, were physically tough; there were many miners, for example, in the ranks of the Bantams. In December 1916, however, the commander of the 35th Division reported that the replacements for the casualties sustained by his units on the Somme were of "low physical and moral standard", not real Bantams but city-dwellers who were unfit and physically underdeveloped. Subsequent medical inspections rejected 2,784 men for service, replacing them with men of normal physique, mostly dismounted cavalrymen; the rejects were posted to labour battalions and base depots. The sign of the 35th Division, a bantam cockerel, was replaced (by a shape representing seven fives), and the "Bantam" subsidiary titles were dropped.

The 40th Division was never entirely a Bantam formation. It arrived late on the Somme, and one of its brigades took part in the final battle of the campaign.

The Fourth Army

On the afternoon of 18 July General Rawlinson held a conference with his Corps commanders and their Brigadiers Royal Artillery. They discussed the consequences of the shortening of the Fourth Army front and reliefs which were to take place. The general attack was further postponed. After consultation with the French, it was arranged to assault the line Guillemont-Pozières on 22 July. On the 19th Sir Douglas Haig, worried about the possibilities of a German counter-attack, issued orders for the widening of the Fourth Army salient in order to secure the battery positions now crowded behind the British front. Subsequently General Rawlinson arranged for his XIII Corps, in conjunction with the French XX Corps, to attack the German second position from Waterlot Farm south to the Somme on 23 July; and – as a result of Sir Douglas's orders – for XV Corps to attack High Wood on 20 July, at the same time as XIII Corps made another attempt to secure Longueval and Delville Wood.

It was at this last location that the 3rd Division had gone into action on 18 July. Linking up with the Scots and South Africans of the 9th (Scottish) Division, the regulars of the 3rd made some gains in Longueval and in the shattered wood; but German artillery fire became so intense that they had to withdraw in conditions made even more miserable by the heavy rain now falling. A series of German counter-attack were contained with small arms fire and support from British batteries, after which a British counter-attack, launched at 6p.m., regained the ground lost. On the morning of 19 July battalions of the 18th Division, reinforcing the Scots, cleared the southern part of Delville Wood. Fighting went on all day, and that night the relief began of the 9th (Scottish) Division.

Other reliefs were carried out as the components of the Fourth Army prepared for the forthcoming attack. Further efforts were made to capture Longueval and Delville Wood, but with little success, and on the night of the 20th the South African Brigade was at last relieved. They had gone into battle at Delville Wood on the 15th with a strength of 121 officers and 3,032 other ranks; 29 officers and 751 other ranks answered their names at roll call on 21 July. In spite of these losses the South Africans had steadfastly endured the German bombardment and had fought off repeated counter-attacks to hold Delville Wood, which will forever be associated with them and is today their national memorial. But the fighting proved that the lesson had yet to be learned by the British that objectives such as Delville Wood were better by-passed and enveloped rather than taken head on. The concentrations of fire poured into the wood by both sides over the course of a week had turned it into a killing ground in which the infantry of both sides were devoured.

In the early hours of 20 July the 5th and 7th Divisions, both regular formations of XV Corps, set out to secure the approaches to High Wood while the 33rd Division attempted to take the wood itself. The regulars fought their way to their second objective, but were driven back to their first by German machine gun fire. The 33rd Division managed to get into High Wood and clear the southern part of it. Fighting went on all day, during which elements of the division reached the northern end of the wood before being forced to withdraw by a German bombardment of gas and high explosive. German infantry then re-occupied the

north of the wood, and both sides settled down to consolidate their positions.

On the right of the British line an unsuccessful attempt to capture enemy positions near Maltz Horn Farm was made by battalions of the 35th (New Army) Division – a "Bantam" formation, in which the infantry were mostly men below the minimum standards of height and physique.

On the 21st the artillery of the Fourth Army began their preparatory bombardment for the forthcoming attack. Haze and cloud made aerial observation and therefore registration difficult. A consequence of this was an order in at least one Corps that a higher proportion of high explosive shell was to be used in protective barrages so that greater accuracy could be obtained. The ammunition situation momentarily worsened on this day when a German air raid started a fire in a British ammunition dump, resulting in the loss of 500,000 rounds of 18-pounder and 10,000 rounds of heavy howitzer ammunition.

A Fourth Army conference issued details of Corps objectives for the attack. XIII Corps were to clear Delville Wood, XV Corps were to secure Longueval and High Wood, and III Corps were to capture the German line westward to Martinpuich in conjunction with the Reserve Army's operations against Pozières. Later XIII Corps would assault the German second position from Falfemont Farm to Waterlot Farm in co-operation with the French XX Corps. Zero Hour was to be 9.50p.m. on 22 July for the main attack, and 12.30a.m. on the 23rd for the attack of XV and

THE ANZAC VCs

The fighting spirit of the Australian and New Zealand troops resulted in six Victoria Crosses being awarded to them during the Somme battles. The first two were won at Pozières on 23 July, by Private John Leak of the 9th (Queensland) Battalion and Lieutenant Arthur Blackburn of the 10th (South Australia) Battalion; both were in the thick of bombing fights. Also at Pozières, over the course of the following two days, Private Thomas Cooke of the 8th (Victoria) Battalion operated his Lewis gun in a dangerous part of the line until killed, setting "a splendid example of determination and devotion to duty" which earned him a posthumous VC. The fourth Pozières VC, also posthumous, was won by Sergeant Claude Castleton of the 5th Australian Machine Gun Company on 29 July; Castleton had rescued two wounded men and was bringing in a third when he was himself shot and killed.

Private Martin O'Meara won his VC in August, in the fighting north-west of Pozières. A member of the 16th (South & West Australia) Battalion, O'Meara repeatedly went through artillery barrages to bring up supplies and evacuate the wounded; over the course of four days he was credited with the rescue of over 25 men.

Sergeant Donald Brown of the Otago Regiment, New Zealand Division, won his VC for a succession of attacks on enemy machine-gun posts during the Battle of Flers-Courcelette. He was killed performing a similar act on 1 October 1916.

29 July: men of the 89th Infantry Brigade attend a religious service in the Carnoy valley before going into the line. Three New Army battalions of the King's (Liverpool) Regiment were in this brigade of the 30th Division, along with the 2nd Bedfords. (IWM Q4069)

July 1916: soldiers of the 1st Australian Division rest and clean up after the capture of Pozières. The Digger in the foreground is using the mirror of a heliograph, hlaf hidden under the pile of other signalling equipment. (IWM Q4041)

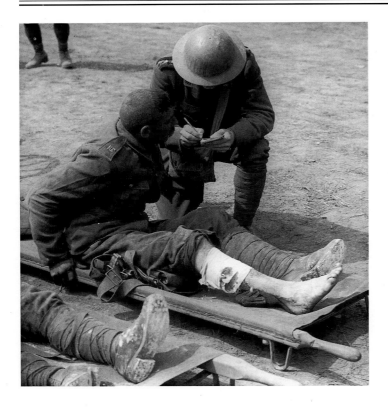

30 July: the Battle of Pozières Ridge. A chaplain taking details from a wounded sapper at a dressing station on the Fricourt-Carnoy-Montauban road. The fate of a wounded man could be something of a lottery. He might have to make his own way to the aid posts and dressing stations; and if he was unable to move he might lie out in the open for hours or even days waiting to be found, evacuated and treated. (IWM Q4056)

III Corps in order to synchronise with the operations of the Reserve Army.

On 22 July the French declared that they could not be ready before the 24th; the objectives on the right were consequently limited to the capture of Guillemont, and adjustments in timings were made. On the front of the Reserve Army the 1st Australian Division took over the line before Pozières, and the Germans were kept on the alert with bombardments and raids. General Gough had received orders to "carry out methodical operations against Pozières with a view to capturing that important position with as little delay as possible". He in turn had ordered the 1st Australian Division to carry out this task in the early hours of 23 July.

Fromelles
North of the Somme a subsidiary attack was mounted on 19 and 20 July to draw German attention away from the operations about to be undertaken. This diversionary action took place in the region of the Aubers ridge, north of Loos, and centred on the village of Fromelles. The operation was on a front of only 4,000 yards but the bombardment was on such a scale as to give the enemy the impression that a major offensive was in the offing. But the attack, which was made by one Australian division and one British division, met with fierce German resistance, resulting in very high casualties for the attackers; the 5th Australian Division alone lost 5,500 men. No enemy forces were diverted to counter the attack at Fromelles, for the enemy realised the true scope of the operation when British orders were captured.

23 July to early September: Clearing Bazentin Ridge

The battles now about to be fought were to occupy the British until the early part of September, during which time the French Sixth Army were to make gains along the north bank of the Somme, up to Clery. Their attempt to take Combles was to fail, following which the Allies agreed that an attempt should be made to envelop the town and cut it off. But deteriorating weather was to turn the battlefield once more into a quagmire, delaying all movement and hampering offensive operations. It was to take until 12 September before encircling attacks began, and these were only partially successful. Nevertheless, by early September the French had accomplished a turning movement on the Allied right upon which the British hoped to capitalise.

The night attacks by the Fourth Army began on time on the night of 22/23 July, and suffered a universal fate — all the participating formations were driven back to their starting trenches, and no ground whatsoever was gained. Several reasons were subsequently advanced for this failure, including the difficult positions from which the British attacked, the lack of precision in the artillery bombardment due to hindered observation, the varied Zero Hours, and the lack of opportunity for reconnaissance by the attacking units. What was particularly disappointing was that the attack had been made by some of the "best" formations, including a number of regular divisions.

The Australians at Pozières

The story at Pozières was quite different. Here the Australians had crept forward so that they might spring upon the German positions as soon as the barrage lifted. Amongst other innovations, a field gun was dragged to within 200 yards of a German strongpoint, which was then devastated with over a hundred rounds at short range. The "Diggers" were soon into the German front trench, and by 1a.m. on the 23rd they were among the ruins of the village. Here, in small parties, they fought their way from cellar to cellar in a grim sport which they called "ratting" — rolling phosphorous grenades into the enemy dug-outs — in order to clear the village and to attempt a link-up with the infantry on their left, the Territorials of the 48th (South Midland) Division.

For several days the fighting went on as the artillery of both sides bombarded the ruins of Pozières. The 2nd Australian Division relieved the 1st, and the Germans were driven slowly from the village and back up the slope behind it. As July drew to a close plans were made to maintain the offensive around Pozières, while the cost was counted. The fighting of the previous eight days had been particularly bloody, with the 2nd Australian Division alone losing nearly 3,500 officers and men.

On the front of the Fourth Army the fighting flared as further attempts were made to secure Delville Wood, Longueval, High Wood and Guillemont, where the Germans still hung on tenaciously to deny the British full possession of the Bazentin ridge. From 27 to 29 July the 2nd and 5th Divisions (both of regulars) fought their way northward through Longueval and Delville Wood to improve the British lodgements there; and on the 29th the 51st (Highland) Division made an attempt to take High Wood. Attempts elsewhere to improve the Fourth Army position met with little success.

At 4.45a.m. on 30 July Guillemont was attacked by the

30th Division, who were heavily shelled with gas and high explosive as they formed up. Nevertheless the attack was pressed into Guillemont itself; but in the face of the German fire and counter-attacks the gains could not be held and the infantry were driven back to their start line, retaining only parts of the German trench on the division's right. An attack by battalions of the 2nd Division on the north of Guillemont met with a similar fate. The subsidiary attacks mounted elsewhere by the Fourth Army on the 30th met with only limited success, but the British line was extended on either side of High Wood and beyond Longueval.

If the fighting had been costly for the British it had been equally so for the enemy. The German battalions defending Guillemont lost nearly 5,500 men between 14 and 31 July, while the units holding the Delville Wood area lost nearly 9,500 men in the same period. One division recorded that it had lost 5,000 men up to 3 August – "rather more than had been sustained before Verdun in May".

August 1916: Hard fighting for little gain

Throughout the month of August attacks were made on the German strongpoints which continued to defy the British. Guillemont was again attacked on the 8th, but the assault met with no more success than previous attempts. On the 18th it was again attacked as part of a XIV Corps offensive in conjunction with the French XX Corps. This seized most of the German front trench and brought the British line closer to Ginchy and into the outskirts of what was left of Guillemont before it ran out of impetus. On the left of XIV Corps infantry of XV Corps also attacked on the 18th to seize parts of the German front line. Further left still, III Corps also took part of the German front on that day.

From 19 to 31 August pressure was kept up along the whole Fourth Army front by a series of hard-fought actions which extended the British position in some places. On 24

August XV Corps made yet another attempt to clear the enemy from Delville Wood and establish a line beyond it; this was partially achieved, but on the 31st a German counter-attack recovered some of these gains, forcing part of the British line back into the rotting ruins of the wood.

In the Reserve Army area operations went on to secure Posières ridge and to push the British line towards Thiepval. In a series of attacks over the course of the month I ANZAC Corps and II Corps steadily pushed forward the British line along the Bapaume road, towards Mouquet Farm and beyond the Leipzig salient. The battles were costly for the divisions concerned, but they represented an achievement to counterbalance the disappointments of the Fourth Army. As the month drew to a close the commander of the Reserve Army drew up his plans for an attack upon Thiepval, which was to be launched in conjunction with attacks by the Fourth Army and the French in a resumption of the general offensive.

September 1916: Planning and preparations

Sir Douglas Haig's plan for his September offensive was to be carried out in three phases. First, the infantry of the Fourth and Reserve Armies were to capture the remaining parts of their first line still held by the Germans on the Bazentin ridge. In this endeavour they were to be helped by the new British secret weapon, the "tank", whose development the Commander-in-Chief had observed with interest. In phase two, while the Reserve Army held the ground captured in phase one, the Fourth Army would attempt to breach the German line between the Albert-Bapaume road and Flers, to open the way for phase three, which involved

August 1916: an Australian 9.2in. howitzer battery in action at Fricourt. This weapon could hurl a 290lb. shell containing 34 pounds of high explosive to a maximum range of 10,000 yards. (IWM Q4408)

August 1916: striking photograph of an advanced dressing station at Fricourt. Note (right foreground) the Geneva flag and the Union Jack that these stations were required to display. The markings painted on the nearest motor ambulance are the divisional sign of the 23rd (New Army) Division and the oakleaf of its 69th Field Ambulance. (IWM Q4086)

September 1916: eight heavy draught horses move a 60-pdr. near Beaucourt Wood – this was the largest gun to be towed by horses. Note the way in which the piece was retracted for movement. (IWM Q917)

passing five cavalry divisions through the breach to fall upon the enemy rear. Haig's plan was, broadly, that of 1 July, but on a front cut down to 12,000 yards. There would be 14 fresh divisions for the forthcoming battles, along with (it was hoped) about 70 tanks.

The Reserve Army's push towards Thiepval had as one of its aims the seizure of ground that would provide security for the position from which General Gough would launch his Army's part of the September attack. The Canadian Corps were sent to the Reserve Army to take their place in these operations, relieving the Australians of the ANZAC Corps.

Relief formations arrived for the Fourth Army too, and by the time the preliminary bombardment began on 12 September the German strongpoints which had held out for so long on the Bazentin ridge – Guillemont, Falfemont Farm and Leuze Wood – had at last been taken by divisions of XIV Corps between 3 and 6 September. Operations against Ginchy and the enemy line between High Wood and Delville Wood by XV Corps from 3 to 9 September extended the British position and led to the capture of Ginchy. Fighting went on in places until the 13th as British positions were developed and consolidated.

On the front of the Reserve Army an attack astride the Ancre was launched on 3 September but was beaten back with the usual heavy losses. At the same time attacks against German positions on the Pozières ridge further to the south resulted in some small gains. To offset these dismal results, four companies of the 11th Division, advancing behind what has been described as an "excellent" barrage at 6.30p.m. on 14 September, broke into the German front line to seize the "Wonder Work", together with 250 yards of the Hohenzollern trench adjoining it. All this was accomplished at little cost, although many casualties were sustained in the enemy shelling that followed.

Conscious of the surprise that the appearance of tanks would achieve, GHQ had stressed in orders that "exploitation of success to the full during the first few hours is essential to a decision and it must be impressed on all Corps and divisional commanders that the situation calls for great boldness and determination on their part.... the necessity for great vigour...in this attack...must be impressed on all ranks". And so, no doubt with these words ringing in their ears, the Allied artillery went about the business of the pre-attack bombardment, as the infantry and tanks prepared for Z Day, 15 September.

A German review of tactics

It was at this time that the German High Command came to the conclusion that their tactics for defence were unsound. Resolutely clinging to positions at all costs had led to unacceptable losses and a consequent lowering of morale. Few German divisions relieved from the Somme fighting had taken less than 4,500 casualties, and many had suffered even more grievously. The deep dug-outs in which infantry had sheltered from bombardment had frequently become man-traps. Too much reliance was being placed on the use of grenades and too little on the use of the rifle. Orders were consequently issued to the effect that in future front lines were to be held more lightly. Deep dug-outs were to be destroyed, and positions were to be given up if holding

NOEL CHAVASSE, VC

The heroism of medical officers is legendary, and none more so than Captain Noel Chavasse, VC and Bar, MC, Royal Army Medical Corps. Chavasse was regimental medical officer to the Liverpool Scottish, 55th Division, when he won his first Victoria Cross at Guillemont in August 1916. He tended wounded in the open all day, under heavy fire, and at night he went up to the enemy positions and searched for four hours for more wounded. He carried on his work next day, despite a wound in his side, and again went up to the enemy positions at night to find the wounded, bury the dead, and collect identity discs. Chavasse already held the Military Cross; and at Ypres in 1917 he was posthumously awarded a bar to his Victoria Cross for his unsurpassed devotion to the wounded, though he himself was mortally wounded. Noel Chavasse was one of only three men ever to have won the supreme award twice.

September 1916: artillery horses being taken to water, east of Mametz and south of Bazentin le Grand. The picture gives a small insight into the monumental task of managing the hundreds of thousands of horses the Army needed. Huge amounts of forage were shipped to France to feed the animals and each division required its own veterinary unit. (IWM Q4348)

The Battle of Ginchy, 9 September: a view from Trônes Wood of the British bombardment of Ginchy. The trenches in the foreground and the wood on the left have suffered a bombardment of their own. (IWM Q4226)

The Battle of Ginchy, 9 September: supporting infantry follow up the attacking waves. Away in the middle distance can be seen the earlier waves following the "creeping" barrage, its shell-bursts visible on the horizon. (IWM Q1306)

THE CANADIAN VCs

The first Canadian Victoria Cross to be won in the Somme fighting went to Corporal Leo Clarke of the 2nd Battalion, Canadian Infantry, 1st Canadian Division. On 9 September Clarke was engaged in building a "block" in a section of newly-captured trench near Martinpuich when he was attacked by 20 Germans. He immediately advanced on them, armed only with a revolver, and put them to flight, shooting five and capturing a sixth. He died of wounds received in this fight a month later; his VC was gazetted the following week.

Private John Kerr of the 49th Battalion, Canadian Infantry, 3rd Canadian Division, was a bayonet man to a party of bombers when he won his VC on 16 September. Fighting in a German trench near Courcelette, he ran along the parapet shooting at the enemy below; 62 Germans surrendered to Kerr, who was wounded in the hand and side.

On 8 October Piper James Richardson of the 16th Battalion, Canadian Infantry, 1st Canadian Division, won the supreme decoration when he marched up and down the line of the wire in front of Regina Trench, playing his pipes and inspiring the men of the Canadian Scottish battalions of his brigade to greater effort. Later in the battle he went in search of his mislaid pipes, and was killed.

them were likely to cause heavy losses. Instructions were given for the preparation of a rear defensive line, later to be known as the Hindenburg Line; eleven supplementary divisions were formed to reinforce the Western Front; and a programme was put into effect for the production of larger quantities of ammunition, artillery and machine guns. These measures were to have the effect of restoring to the Germans a considerable measure of tactical initiative in the battles to come.

While they waited for the expected attack their pilots and balloon observers noted the activity in the rear of the British lines, including what were reported as "large armoured cars" moving behind the British front. This report appears not have attracted the attention it deserved, in view of the effect the appearance of the tanks was to have upon the German infantry. The commencement of the Allied bombardment, especially the extent of the wire-breaking, confirmed German suspicions as to where the attack would fall, and approximately when.

CHAPTER TEN

Enter the Tank:
"The Battle of Flers-Courcelette"

The idea of a mobile fortress, a landship able to cross the battlefield impervious to enemy fire while pouring out fire from its own weapons, was not a new one. Taking the broadest view, its lineage may be traced from the war chariots which revolutionized Middle Eastern warfare 1,500 years before Christ, via the war elephants of Hannibal, to the drawings of Leonardo da Vinci, right up to the various designs going the rounds of the world's military ministries in the early 1900s.

Wheeled military armoured cars (limited to movement over roads or other good surfaces), and the less warlike but more versatile commercial track-laying vehicles, had been developed before 1914, the latter being purchased by the British Army to tow heavy guns. In the search for ways to overcome the barriers of barbed wire, the trenches and the fire that swept no-man's-land from the end of 1914, these track-laying vehicles came under the scrutiny of personalities such as Major Swinton, RE, who began attempts in 1914 and 1915 to get his project for a "machine gun destroyer" taken up. In early 1915 a demonstration of a Holt track-laying vehicle in this role was deemed unsatisfactory, and Swinton's idea might have been rejected at that point. But Mr Winston Churchill, at this time First Lord of the Admiralty, came to hear of the discussions engendered

by Swinton's proposals; and these added weight to a project of his own for a similar vehicle. Churchill's energy led to further trials, and the development, via the Admiralty and the Armoured Car division of the Royal Naval Air Service, of a "landship".

In June 1915 the War Office became involved with this project, and in February 1916 the first "tank" was demonstrated before a group of notables which included Lord Kitchener, the Chief of the Imperial General Staff, and Mr Lloyd George, then Minister of Munitions. The demonstration resulted in an order being placed for 100 of the model known as "Big Willie" or "Mother", the prototype for the Mark I tank.

Personnel for the units that were to operate the new fighting vehicles were recruited into the Machine Gun Corps and called variously the "Heavy Section" or "Heavy Branch". Commanded by Swinton, the men came from the motorcyclists of the Motor Machine Gun batteries then in

September 1916: a Mark I "Female" tank moves up to the front. Note the "dazzle"-painted camouflage, the frame and netting to protect the top hatches from enemy grenades, and the overalls and medieval-looking leather crash helmet of the Corporal taking a breather through a roof hatch – on a summer day the temperature inside could easily reach 120F (45C). (IWM Q2488)

15 September: a Mark I "Male" tank of C Coy. (C19, "Clan Leslie") advances with attendant infantry. Note the tail wheels, a steering aid. (IWM Q5575)

the process of disbandment, and mechanical transport drivers of the Army Service Corps; officers were selected from volunteers. The first establishment provided for six companies each of 25 tanks, 28 officers and 255 other ranks, and their training was carried out in great secrecy at various camps in England. On 13 August 1916, C and D Companies of the new corps began their move to France.

From the beginning choosing a name for the new vehicle proved to be a problem, and there are several different stories claiming to explain how the creatures came to be called "tanks", the name adopted in December 1915; the most likely is that they looked like large water cisterns and were given the name "tank" as a security measure to hide their real purpose.

Two types of Mark I tank were used in the Somme battles: a "Male" armed with two 6-pounder guns and four machine guns, and a "Female" armed only with machine guns. The basic technical details of the Male tank were:

Length (with tail): 32ft.6in.
Length (without tail): 26ft.5in.
Width: 13ft.9in.
Height: 7ft.4½in.
Weight (fully equipped): 28 tons
Engine: 6-cylinder 105hp Daimler
Maximum speed: 3.7mph
Petrol capacity: 46 gallons
Range: 23 miles
Max. trench crossing: 10ft.
Ammunition: 324 rounds 6-pdr., 6,272 rounds MG
Crew: 1 officer, 7 other ranks

The "tail" was an attachment with two heavy wheels at the rear of the tank which aided its steering and helped reduce the shock of travel over broken ground. Female tanks were designed to deal with infantry at close quarters with their four Vickers and one Hotchkiss machine guns; Male tanks, to take on "harder" targets such as fortifications. Pigeons were carried for communications with the rear, while flags and semaphore devices were used to signal to infantry and other tanks.

Viewed from the outside tanks appeared to be huge, but their interiors were very cramped indeed. The commander and driver sat side by side in an elevated position at the front. Two gearsmen crouched either side of the vehicle's

transmission at the rear, their job being to assist the driver in steering by stopping the appropriate track. The four gunners squeezed themselves into the sponsons bolted to the sides of the hull. As the tank moved its unsilenced and largely unshielded engine roared and thrashed and smoked in the centre of the box that was the tank's hull — and which it almost filled, leaving only the narrowest of spaces for the crew to move around it. The tracks screeched and clattered along the skidways surrounding each side of the hull. The noise was deafening, almost maddening; speech was quite

The Battle of Flers-Courcelette, 15 September 1916: follow-up infantry units crossing captured German trenches during the advance to Flers. (IWM Q188)

impossible, instructions being passed by hand signal. The heat generated by the engine was oppressive, and its fumes dizzying. Vision was extremely limited, and once the ports were closed for action the crew became – to all intents and purposes – deaf, dumb, almost blind and condemned to slow asphyxiation. In action the noise and sickening cordite fumes of the tank's weapons added to the discomfort of the crew, who were jerked and tumbled around as the tank lurched unnervingly over even the least obstacle. The hammering of enemy small arms fire on the hull flaked off particles of metal inside called "splash", which flew around the tank's interior, wounding men and damaging machinery when they struck home.

Mark I tanks were mechanically unreliable, and on the Somme were operated by novice crews – comparatively new to their machines and certainly to war. Nevertheless, they took these contraptions into battle, and from time to time, in actions such as the capture of Flers, proved the enormous potential of their new "weapons system". In time more reliable tanks were designed, tactical experience was gained, and the MGC Heavy Branch evolved into the Tank Corps with, at war's end, 27 battalions of which 18 served in France. Their contribution to the final victory – by which time they had almost 2,000 machines in the field – was immeasurable, and possibly the best example of the ability of the British Army to devise and develop new weapons and tactics while fighting a war.

15-22 September: "The Battle of Flers-Courcelette"

Sir Douglas Haig had taken a keen interest in the progress being made to get tank units to France. He was aware of their potential as a means of destroying barbed wire, bridging trenches and bringing close quarter fire to bear on their occupants. There is no doubt that had tanks been available on 1 July Sir Douglas would have used them. Early indications were that 150 tanks would be available in September, but an important factor in their readiness was the time needed to train their crews. There were also differing opinions as to the wisdom of using these new weapons piecemeal, one lobby insisting that they should be held back until early 1917 when 500 might be ready. In the end the demands of the Somme fighting prevailed, and the decision was made to get tanks into action before the campaign was closed down by the weather. Following their arrival in August the first tanks were used for a series of demonstrations; these may have been beneficial in introducing the new machines to the rest of the BEF, but had the unfortunate effect of wearing those machines out, contributing to the number of mechanical failures suffered in their first battle.

Over the course of 14 September the units earmarked for the attack made the usual preparations and moved forward to their assembly trenches. It was a cold day, but the cold was not felt within the confines of the tanks as they moved forward; to escape the heat, smoke, noise and stink the

15 September: New Zealand infantry digging in near Martinpuich. The devices on their backs show them to be from the 2nd NZ Infantry Brigade, and their collar badges identify them as men of the 4th Otago Rifles. (IWM Q193)

Mark I "Male" ditched and later destroyed by artillery on 15 September. The mechanically immature tanks were prone to break-downs, and once immobilised tended to draw shellfire. The crew had the choice of staying within the protection of what was now a stationary bullet-proof pillbox, or risking the cover of a shellhole before the artillery got the range. The Mark I carried its high octane aviation spirit in gravity tanks in the front horns, and the armour was not proof against shellfire. (The Tank Museum)

gunners, not involved with the steering of the tanks or in the operation of their gears, walked alongside their machines as they were guided forward. Such was the mechanical unreliability of these first armoured fighting vehicles that not all reached their starting points.

Only 49 tanks were available out of the hoped-for 150, and of these 42 were allotted to the Fourth Army. Six got into position behind the Canadians, two fell in behind the 15th (Scottish) Division, two with the 50th (Northumbrian) Division, three before High Wood, four made it to the 2nd New Zealand Division, and seven took up station with the

41st (New Army) Division. Only one reached the vicinity of Delville Wood, and only nine of the 16 allotted to XIV Corps arrived.

One of the tanks which did reach its correct station was "D1" commanded by Lieutenant Mortimore. At 5.20a.m. it advanced up the road leading from Delville Wood to Ginchy, firing its guns and followed by two companies of infantry. The Germans in the area were astounded by its appearance and began to surrender, but within a short time of its arrival in battle "D1" was hit by two shells which immobilised the tank and killed two of its crew. It had, however, the distinction of being the first tank in history to see action, and of helping to secure vital ground before Zero Hour.

At sunrise on 15 September, 5.40a.m., the Allied barrage began. Behind the Fourth Army 720 18-pdrs., 200 4.5in. howitzers, 92 6in. howitzers, 82 60-pdrs., 48 9.2in. howitzers, 48 8in. howitzers, 20 4.7in. guns, 14 6in. guns, eight 12in. howitzers, three 9.2in. guns, two 15in. howitzers, one 12in. gun and the divisional mortar batteries poured the usual hurricane of shells and mortar bombs onto the German positions. At Zero Hour, 6.20a.m., the infantry left their trenches and advanced behind the shelter of the

September 1916: the ruins of the main street of Flers, up which, it was reported in the press, a tank was "walking…with the British Army cheering behind". (IWM Q4271)

barrage, which began to creep towards the enemy at the rate of 50 yards a minute. The tanks with the Canadian Corps went forward on either side of the Bapaume road towards Courcelette, but were outstripped by the infantry of the 2nd and 3rd Canadian Divisions who kept pace with their barrage, and pushed on steadily throughout the day to capture the village despite strong German resistance. Of their supporting tanks, one broke down behind the line, while three others became "ditched" – immobilised among the German trenches. But the two remaining stayed the course, and gave the German infantry they encountered such a fright that they surrendered in large numbers.

On the right of the Canadians the 15th (Scottish) Division also pressed forward close behind its barrage, followed by one tank (the other having been disabled by shellfire at the start of the attack), which proved of great help to the Scots in the clearance of trenches. By 3p.m. the division had taken Martinpuich, along with a large number of prisoners and several pieces of German artillery.

THE GUARDS DIVISION

Said by many to be the best division in the BEF, the Guards Division had been formed in France in 1915 from regular and wartime-raised battalions of the Grenadier Guards, the Coldstream Guards, the Scots Guards, the Irish Guards and the newly-raised Welsh Guards. On 15 September it was part of the XIV Corps attack on Lesboeufs and Morval. Setting off from Ginchy at 6.20a.m., the 1st Guards Brigade immediately came under intense machine gun fire which halted the attack before 100 yards had been covered. At this moment Lieutenant-Colonel John Vaughan Campbell of the Coldstream Guards blew a note on his hunting horn, rallied the brigade, and then led the 2nd and 3rd Coldstream in a headlong charge that took them as far as the German first line. Ordered to press on towards Lesboeufs, Campbell led his men on, sounding his hunting horn, until the enemy third line was reached and taken. He was awarded the Victoria Cross.

While Campbell was winning his VC, a young Lance-Sergeant of the 1st Scots Guards, Fred McNess, was busy "bombing" his way along a German communication trench. Running out of grenades, he found a stock of enemy grenades and started throwing those. McNess fought on until a German grenade burst in front of his face, after which he carried forward supplies of bombs until he passed out from loss of blood. He too was awarded the Victoria Cross.

Observing from a captured German trench during the Battle of Flers-Courcelette, 15 September. Getting the results of such observation to the rear was a chancy business. Telephone field cable was often cut by shelling or the passage of troops and vehicles, and runners ran the risks both of enemy fire and of arrest by "battle police". Visual signalling by flag or lamp was the most effective method, but was dependent on better visibility than was often available under battle conditions. Note, in front of the officer's hole, a discarded German M1916 steel helmet and cap. (IWM Q190)

To the right of the Scots were the 50th and 47th (London Territorial) Divisions. The Londoners had the task of capturing High Wood, and their Corps commander, General Pulteney, insisted that they take their supporting tanks into the wood. Of these one became ditched at the start, one was destroyed by shellfire after raking the first German trench with its machine guns, and the other two were unable to find a way through the nightmarish maze of broken treetrunks, stumps, shellholes and undergrowth. They turned back, and in their confusion fired on infantry of the division they were supporting. Once again, a British attempt to take High Wood had become bogged down, and the German machine guns there were able to pour enfilade fire on the infantry of the 50th Division advancing on the left of the 47th. Caught in such a deadly fire the 50th Division was driven back. Grimly the Londoners battled on, and at about 11a.m., following a trench mortar barrage, they advanced into the wood – to discover to their amazement that the German garrison had at last had enough. Exhausted, the Bavarians surrendered in their hundreds, and High Wood finally passed into British hands, two months and one day after it had been discovered unoccupied and there for the taking.

On the right wing of the Fourth Army was XIV Corps with its three divisions in line: the Guards, the 6th (Regular) and the 56th (London Territorial) Divisions. In front of them the wire before the German positions lay mostly uncut but, helped by the tanks supporting them, the infantry managed to take the German first trench line; they were unable to get across the Ginchy-Combles road, however. The objective of the Guards Division was the village of Lesboeufs, but their supporting tanks had either broken down, succumbed to enemy fire, or lost direction and wandered off. At 11a.m., led with great gallantry by Lieutenant-Colonel Campbell of the Coldstream, the Guards attack was relaunched and pressed on to just over half way to Lesboeufs.

Between the Guards and the Londoners in High Wood were the three divisions of XV Corps: the New Zealanders, the 41st and the 14th (Light) Divisions, the latter two New Army formations. By 7a.m. they had taken their first objectives, but when the advance was resumed the New Zealanders were held up by uncut wire and machine guns. Despite heavy losses and confusion as leaders became casualties, the assaulting infantry of the 41st Division pressed on towards Flers village with the aid of tank "D17" commanded by Lieutenant Hastie. Three other tanks which had got forward ("D6", "D9", and "D16") added their fire to Hastie's, and the British infantry dashed forward to secure the village. From the air an observer of the RFC saw this part of the battle and reported it to XV Corps headquarters at 11a.m. It was a critical moment, for with the capture of Flers the enemy line had almost been broken. The breach in the German lines that had been sought for so long and at such cost was tantalisingly near.

Unfortunately, the headquarters of the German First Army knew of the imminent rupture of their line almost as soon as General Rawlinson. Every German reserve unit forward of Bapaume was ordered to seal the breach, and every available gun was trained on the area of Flers and its approaches. Their fire caused heavy casualties amongst

British infantry moving into the village, knocking out four of the six commanding officers on the scene; despite this the village was reinforced and put into a state of defence as darkness fell. But with their troops also digging in, the Germans had beaten the British to the punch.

Above the battlefield the Royal Flying Corps had flown more hours and taken part in more fighting than on any previous day of the war. No less than 150 enemy batteries were observed on the Fourth Army front, and 70 of these were engaged. Aerial combats resulted in 19 enemy aircraft being either destroyed or "driven down", and two enemy observation balloons destroyed. The British pilots were reported to have flown with "reckless daring", strafing enemy trenches and batteries with machine gun fire, and flying low over British troops in order to ascertain their progress. A bombing raid was made upon trains in the Bapaume area.

The following day was spent by the British in moving forward batteries and improving their newly-won front; and the cavalry, which had moved forward to ride through the breach, turned about and rode instead to their bivouacs. German artillery maintained a heavy fire all along the British line. As the rain began to fall on friend and foe, it soaked the five German divisions marching forward to reinforce their line.

Despite the lost opportunities, British gains had been considerable. Along the whole front the German position had been driven in to a depth of 2,500 yards, and at Flers, 3,500 yards. But the rain continued to fall; and the date for the renewal of the British assault was postponed, postponed again, and eventually cancelled. A German counter-attack, when it came, fell upon the French, who contained it, but in so doing used up the last of their reserves. The main Battle of Flers-Courcelette had lasted only one day, but fighting continued on a smaller scale, resulting in gains for the British on 16 and 17 September, and petering out in patrol activity by the 22nd.

September 1916: Highlanders of the 8th Seaforth carrying forward defence stores at Martinpuich. The weather, fine for several days, broke on the 17th, when it rained heavily. Once a position had been taken tons of wire, sandbags, timber, revetting material, ammunition and tools had to be carried forward on the backs of infantrymen to refortify it against the inevitable counter-attacks. (IWM Q4358)

Led by their pipes and drums the 8th Black Watch, 15th (Scottish) Division, march back to the rear from Martinpuich in September 1916. The countryside about them is unscarred by war, and the road beneath their feet has not yet disintegrated. (IWM Q4424)

Several weeks later reports on the use of tanks in action were collated at General Headquarters. Amongst these was that of General Rawlinson, who considered that tanks were not sufficiently reliable to justify departure from the tactical methods then in use. Other reports recommended the provision of greater engine power, stronger armour and more effective weapons than those carried by the Mark I tanks. Better technical and tactical training was needed by the men of the tank companies; better workshop provision was essential; but the general opinion was that tanks had a future in war if their mechanical weaknesses could be overcome. It was felt that at present their employment should not interfere with the combined action of infantry and artillery, especially if their use meant depriving the infantry of protective barrages. Tanks were, in short, a "valuable accessory". There is no doubt, however, that their use in the Battle of Flers-Courcelette had pointed up many valuable lessons, and these were to be put to good use in the remaining Somme battles and in those of 1917 and 1918.

September 1916: the ruins of the former German trench system viewed from the Albert-Bapaume road looking towards Ovillers. Digging threw up chalk spoil, making concealment of defensive positions impossible. Bombardment then churned the earth more and stripped trees of foliage and branches. Even today the chalk scars of the trench lines are still visible. (IWM Q4123)

CHAPTER ELEVEN

British Infantry Tactics

As the Somme battles were being fought British gunners found ways to progressively overcome the technical problems which beset them, while at the same time developing better artillery tactics. Gunnery, after all, had always been a technical art. Within the ranks of the British infantry the problems faced had their roots in the ingrained attitudes of their commanders and were, therefore, harder to expose and to address. They stemmed from the regime of the pre-war regular army, of which – naturally – the senior officers of 1916 were all products. Applied to the training of the New Armies, this ethos ruthlessly suppressed the initiative of the volunteers, failed to recognise their human potential, and squandered their best men.

British officers were unaccustomed to dealing with recruits of high quality. Put in the most simplistic terms, the old regular army had attracted into the ranks of its infantry the lowest elements of British society, who were then turned into useful soldiers by the application of stern discipline and rote learning, much of which was administered by long-service NCOs. Like the worst kind of horse-breakers, these disciplinarians first broke any spirit shown by recruits, and then accustomed them to instant and unquestioning obedience of commands. Infantry officers came from the middle and upper classes, seeking a career which would provide a comfortable lifestyle with plenty of sport and games. Few were ambitious, most being content to spend their service careers within the family of their regiment.

Service life in peacetime was built around a leisurely annual cycle of "training" which culminated in large-scale manoeuvres in the autumn and then, after suitable furloughs, went back again to individual training to begin the cycle all over again. There was time aplenty in such a system to teach next year what had not been grasped this season. Initiative was discouraged in a system where men learned to do only as they were told, and in which repression was the order of the day. An ideal regular infantry battalion "turned out" well, marched and drilled with precision, kept their barracks spotless, and never disgraced the name of the regiment by getting drunk and fighting with other soldiery in public. Clean, quiet and obedient; and if they were not, there was a disciplinary process ending with a military prison, to make them so.

The effect of the Kitchener volunteers on senior officers accustomed to such a system may be imagined. They saw only a vast, undisciplined mob, patriotic and cheerful maybe, but questioning of authority and used to expressing their grievances in a forthright manner. They immediately set this rabble to drill: to march and countermarch, to wheel and halt, to form fours, to salute, to slow march, quick march, double march, to form two deep, to mark time, to form close column of platoons, to form mass, to advance in column of companies from the right....For weeks and months, without uniforms or rifles, the New Army men drilled until their boots wore out – and on again, until they could perform without thought the complicated gyrations that were the regular army benchmark of soldierly proficiency. At the same time discipline was forced into the unruly by the traditional methods of the British Army, later supplemented in the field by gun-wheel "crucifixion" and capital court-martial sentences. In time, clothed in khaki and armed and accoutred, the New Army battalions presented the outward appearance of soldiers, especially to the British press and public.

In reality, they had acquired the habits of the British regular soldier with none of his skills. Subdued by their exposure to the regimentation of the regulars, few New Army formations were to show the dash and fighting spirit of the volunteers from Australia, Canada or New Zealand who had not undergone such "training". Few Kitchener men had learned much about practical soldiering, or had fired more than the recruit instructional practices on gallery ranges. The experiences of trench warfare filtering back from France had served to promote the newest infantry wonder weapon, the "bomb" (hand grenade), while musketry and the minor tactics of the 1902-1914 period became downgraded. (This was probably inevitable, for there were very few instructors of tactics for the New Armies.)

The bomb was, from the end of 1914, seen as the ideal weapon for use in trenches, where all fighting was at close quarters and victory invariably went to the side which could hurl most high explosive with greatest effect. As far as the British infantry establishment were concerned what was needed were more bombs, more effective bombs, and a plentiful supply of volunteers to throw them. Early British grenades had been primitive devices, almost as lethal to their users as to the enemy. Considerable training in their use had been necessary, and those so trained wore a special badge to mark their proficiency and their hazardous role in action. By 1916 the "Mills bomb" (the Grenade, Hand, No.5) had replaced most other types, and was safe and effective. It was, however, still the prerogative of the "bomber".

Such tactics as there were for the attack were simple and crude. Gangs of bombers and their accomplices, the bayonet men, were to get across no-man's-land and into the enemy trenches; bomb and skewer the occupants; and then bomb their way down the communication trenches towards the enemy rear. The remainder of the infantry were there to carry forward extra grenades and to occupy the trenches won. It was thought that as long as a plentiful supply of bombs could be got forward the impetus of an attack could be maintained. Most of all, the simple blood-and-thunder aspect of bombing appealed to those senior officers of the former "cold steel" school of tactics. They had always seen the bayonet, sword and lance as war-winning weapons, and to this unlovely company they freely admitted the bomb.

1 July 1916: 11th Royal Irish Rifles, 108th Inf.Bde., 36th (Ulster) Division advance to the attack, in a realistic painting by James Prinsep Beadle − the artist was advised by Lt.Francis Thornley, the young officer seen here with raised arm, while he was recovering from wounds received. The riflemen are preceded by "bombers", carrying grenades in canvas buckets. (Courtesy Belfast City Hall)

A lethal problem for infantry in the attack was the crossing of no-man's-land, when they were vulnerable to enemy fire of all kinds. British senior officers had pre-war experience of infantry firepower in a small arms firefight, and of the fire-and-movement "dribbling" tactics by which infantry could get forward to close with the enemy. But they had long made up their minds that their New Army infantry were not capable of fighting in this way, and had never attempted to train them to do so. On 1 July strict orders were issued against taking cover, resulting in many men marching on to death and wounds sooner than disobey. On the British right flank French infantry − who had learned about crossing open ground the hard way in 1914-15, and now copied German tactics observed most recently at Verdun − fought their way forward in small groups, taking advantage of cover and local covering fire. But British generals relied entirely on artillery to get their infantry safely across no-man's-land. Where this worked the infantry got into the German trenches and got down to bombing, bayoneting and snap-shooting their way around the traverses. Where it did not, they were shot down helplessly out of bombing range of the enemy trenches.

A big disadvantage of the "bomber" cult was that it squandered the bravest men to the smallest effect. Human resources in the average infantry unit break down into the minority with that special quality that is called guts, dash or aggression; those others who will follow them if given a lead; and the remainder, who are mainly bent on survival but will fight if forced to do so. It was the courageous who chose the hazards of bombing, and the high casualty rate among them deprived the infantry of junior leaders who might have been better employed. In time the Mills grenade was seen to be sufficiently safe for all to use, and was also adapted to enable it to be projected from a rifle to much greater distances than it could be thrown. This had the effect of making redundant the specialist bomber and causing a revision of infantry tactics.

The Somme fighting pointed up the many shortcomings of the British infantry of 1916 − over-reliance on the bomb and abysmal rifle marksmanship were but two. Perhaps the greatest lesson was the need for the platoon to be the group around which minor tactics should be practised. Led by a junior officer or a sergeant, it was to have its own light automatic, the Lewis gun; its own "pocket artillery" provided by rifle grenades; its own scouts, and its own snipers. Able to produce its own smoke, the platoon could manoeuvre on the battlefield under the covering fire of its light automatic and rifle grenades. In the fighting of 1917, when the enemy had given up linear defence, these tactics were to prove invaluable in dealing with isolated German strongpoints.

Vickers machine guns − the belt-fed, sustained fire weapons operated from heavy mounts − had been taken from infantry battalions before the Somme fighting, and by July 1916 were being used by the Machine Gun Corps to support the infantry rather in the manner of artillery, whose fire-control methods they had copied. The Lewis guns which replaced the Vickers within the infantry battalion were thought at first to be poor substitutes for the heavier weapons; but in the Somme battles their portability and flexibility as a source of automatic fire came to be appreciated. The infantry demanded more Lewis guns, and in time it got them − two for every platoon.

After-action reports continued to show that New Army infantry in the attack frequently lost direction in the confusion of battle and failed to react effectively to the unexpected. Early attempts to correct these faults included the "gingering up" of Kitchener divisions with an infusion of regulars. This involved swapping brigades between divisions, and battalions between brigades. Schools of all types were set up to teach a variety of subjects ranging from the command of a battalion to the better handling of a Lewis gun. Gradually change began to be affected, as natural leaders came to the fore, common sense solutions began to be circulated, and the lessons that had been so dearly bought in lives were put into practice. But even as late as September 1916, some infantry commanders were still emphasising the importance of the "dressing" of the assault waves in the attack, regardless of the target that straight ranks of soldiers present to enfilade machine-gun fire from a flank.

Perhaps the greatest tactical lesson of the early Somme fighting was that assault infantry could only get across no-man's-land behind a creeping barrage, which could not protect following infantry. If infantry "lost" their barrage, they lost the battle. As creeping barrages were fired by field artillery, the limit of an infantry advance was the limit of their supporting gun range. Field artillery took the infantry into the enemy positions to effect a "bite", which the infantry were required to "hold" until the guns were towed forward, dug in, registered, and generally made ready to take another "bite". If the enemy could prepare trench lines faster than attacking artillery could be got forward, a rupture of his line was unlikely. The race became gun versus shovel.

★   ★   ★

Of course, not all British generals were so set in their ways that they could not adapt to the better human and material resources now available to them. While the Somme battles were only four weeks old one Corps commander issued the following notes, which are worth quoting at length (with original punctuation rationalised):

BOMBS

The "Grenade, Hand, No.5" – the "Mills bomb" – made its appearance in 1915; by 1918 more than 67,000,000 Mills bombs had been made in their No.5, No.23 or No.36 variants. The Mills weighed 1lb.7oz. and could be thrown about 25 yards. It had a danger area much greater than this, so the thrower needed to be behind cover. Once the safety pin was pulled the grenade remained safe until the safety lever was released on throwing; this allowed the striker to fire the fuse, which burned for five seconds before detonating the grenade.

The "Grenade, No.26" or "P-bomb" was a tin cylinder, 5ins. long, filled with red phosphorous and with a nine-second Brock fuse connected to a detonator inside the tin. "P-bombs" were thrown into dug-outs to smoke out the occupants.

The photograph shows "bombers" priming No.5 grenades; the boxes at right each contain twelve grenades, and a tin of cap, fuse and detonator sets. The paper label visible on the inside of the lid is reproduced below the photograph.

The widely circulated 1915 pamphlet *Grenade Warfare: Notes on the Training and Organisation of Grenadiers* by Lt.G.Dyson, Brigade Bombing Officer of 99th Inf.Bde., goes into considerable detail as to the composition and tactics of the bombing party under various circumstances. Bombers were trained to throw when standing or lying in the open; from trench to trench; and from bay to bay of a trench, over one or two traverses. Two "bayonet men" led each eight-man party along the enemy trench, rounding the traverse ready to stab or shoot as soon as the grenades detonated. Two "barricaders" carried tools and empty sandbags, and were trained to work quickly to block off the trench from either side.

TO USE THE MILLS HAND GRENADE.
GRENADE, HAND No. 5, MARK 1.

1. Before use, remove the Aluminium plug in base (Key will be found under box lid), Insert Cap chamber, Fuse and Detonator in same position as packed in tin box, then replace plug, and screw hard home.

2. Grasp the Grenade as illustrated.

3. With the other hand pinch the ends of the split pin "A" together. Pull the same out by means of ring "B." Keep the lever "C" against the side of the Grenade, then throw at your convenience. If found inconvenient to throw replace split pin.

4. The act of letting go when throwing allows the lever "C" to fly out and fires a five second fuse.

(J 4614.) Wt. 22936—325. 750m. 6/16. D & S.

THE LEWIS GUN

Developed from an American design, the Lewis was adapted to fire the standard .303in. service ammunition, and began to be issued to British infantry battalions in 1915. By 1916 each platoon had a Lewis gun, handled by a section of about eight men commanded by a junior NCO; between them they carried the gun, the tools and spares, 44 magazines and over 2,000 rounds of ammunition. The gun itself weighed 27lbs.(12.25kg), and could thus be carried and brought into action by one man. Fully autumatic, it fired at a cyclic rate of 550 rounds per minute, and had a maximum effective range of 800–1,000 yards. The "pan" magazines held 47 rounds and were carried, in 1916, in panniers resembling canvas buckets.

The photographs show men of the 1/6th Glosters, 48th Division (TF) in a trench at Ovillers, July 1916 (IWM Q3987); and a magazine and pannier (author's collection).

Tactical Memoranda, circulated by
GOC XIV Corps

Without wishing in any way to curb the initiative of Divisional Commanders, I should like to impress the following short memoranda on the minds of all, which are based on the experience of this battle, backed by the teaching of our text books:

1. All attacks must be in depth of units so as to *keep order and control as long as possible*. Subordinate Commanders are responsible for maintenance of order in their formations; Brigadiers, for the direction and engagement of their echelons behind the assaulting line; Divisional Commanders, for ensuring at any instant the co-operation of his [sic] Artillery and Infantry.

2. We are still fighting against prepared positions. These selected parts of them are first destroyed and broken by our Heavy Artillery, which also has the effect of driving the enemy and his machine guns into deep dugouts, but this is not enough to enable infantry to advance without heavy losses – and the only way to do this is methodical progression from point to point, *right underneath the protection of our*

18-pounders firing shrapnel.

3. It has been the experience of many Brigadiers that the *first* waves of Infantry must seize, clear and hold the *first* trench – otherwise the enemy get up and shoot the first waves in the back; then, knowing this cannot happen, the *second* echelons can *cross* the first trench and advance still under cover of our own shrapnel to the support trench. Sentries are wanted for every dugout and care must be taken that prisoners do not overwhelm their escort and outnumber the attackers, as has happened recently. If prisoners will not come out of the dugouts the P-bomb is the weapon to throw down.

4. The most difficult point of all is how to cross NO MAN'S LAND once the enemy has got the alarm and put his barrage on. In my opinion this can only be done:

(i) By tunnelled trenches and by very rapid digging by parties specially detailed, who should begin work at the same second as the assault carries the first trench.

(ii) By getting as many men across as possible while the element of surprise lasts. On the tunnellers and diggers depend not only the supply of the attacks with food, water,

---

BATTLE INSIGNIA

Amid the noise and confusion of battle the need arose for the rapid identification of formations, units, even companies. Expedients such as coloured tapes and tinplate reflectors were used, even on 1 July 1916; but these were gradually replaced by coloured cloth patches sewn to sleeves, collars, shoulder straps or helmet covers, or painted on helmets. Such insignia identified men in battle without the need to risk crossing fire-swept ground to question them; and allowed other insignia (titles, badges, etc.) to be removed, making identification difficult for the enemy. Patches worn on the back made the progress of a unit visible from the rear. Schemes of battle insignia were usually devised by divisional headquarters, and most divisions present on the Somme had such schemes.

(Top) The 24th Division, a New Army formation stiffened with a regular brigade, wore patches in red (17th Infantry Brigade), green (72nd Inf.Bde.) and yellow (73rd Inf.Bde.) respectively. The senior battalion in each brigade wore the colour as a rectangular patch on each sleeve, the second senior as a saltire, the third as a triangle and the fourth as a square. Above these devices were worn diamond-shaped patches indicating the wearer's company: blue for A, green for B, red for C and yellow for D. Thus a yellow diamond above a red rectangle identified D Coy., 8th Buffs (see Appendix Two for seniority order of units within formations).

(Centre) The 4th (Regular) Division stencilled devices on the sides of the helmet; again, colour indicated the brigade (respectively green, yellow and red); and shape the battalion (horizontal bar, vertical bar, square, diamond). Some battalions wore patches of tartan, cloth titles or silhouettes of regimental devices on the sleeves, but for 1 July they were ordered to stitch on pieces of white cloth cut to prescribed shapes; e.g. the 2nd Seaforths wore a large C-shape, and the 2nd Royal Dublin Fusiliers – helmet and sleeve patch illustrated – a grenade shape. When the 38th (Welsh) Division fought at Mametz Wood the infantry wore sleeve patches indicating the brigade by shape (respectively triangle, circle and square) and the unit by colour (red, blue, yellow and green).

(Bottom) In the 46th (North Midland) Division, a Territorial formation, the 137th Inf.Bde. consisted of two battalions each from the South Staffordshires and North Staffordshires; they wore the Stafford Knot in various colours as a sleeve badge.

In time these devices would become a source of pride, marking their wearers as veteran Western Front infantrymen; but in summer 1916 they were a recent and strictly utilitarian addition to uniform.

GAS WARFARE

The threat of gas attack was ever-present from 1915 onwards; acute respiratory irritants such as chlorine and phosgene were widely used by summer 1916, and anti-gas equipment had to be carried at all times in the forward areas. That issued to British troops consisted of goggles to ward off the worst effects of lachrymatory (tear) gas; and two types of "smoke helmets" – flannel and cotton hoods impregnated with chemicals, carried in small haversacks. The earlier "hypo" helmet was a crude affair, basically a bag with a single celluloid window; but the later "PH" (phenate-hexamine) helmet had proper glass eyepieces and a mouth exhalation valve.

Once the gas alarm was given troops donned their helmets, tucking the lower end into their collars, and drew breath through the layers of chemically impregnated material. In the PH helmet the valve was clenched between the teeth like a pipe stem, as the wearer snorted air into his lungs through his nose and blew it out through the valve. To add to the obvious discomfort, eyepieces would steam up unless coated inside with wax; this melted as the temperature within the hood rose, forming (ideally) a smooth, transparent film upon which moisture would not settle. The wearing of anti-gas equipment severely limited a soldier's ability to see, speak, hear and shoot – and especially to serve artillery, hampering the tasks of sight-setting and fuzing shells.

After the Somme battles effective respirators were devised and issued – but so were more deadly gases, including the dreaded blister agents or "mustard gas".

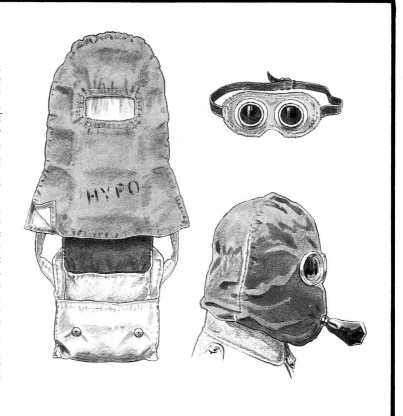

bombs and ammunition, but the flow of reinforcements and the whole continued progress of the fight.

Once masters of the German first trench we have their communications [trenches] for further progress, but until ours are made across NO MAN'S LAND the bravest and most successful assault cannot be definitely considered successful.

I therefore appeal to all Divisional Commanders to make this point paramount in their preparations all along the line.
5. Every advance except the first assault should be preceded by Battle patrols to avoid "fire surprise".
6. Communications by runners, pigeons, visual and signal to the air. Runners should have special armbands, to save any mistake of shirking of duty if stopped when running to the rear. In several instances pigeons have proved the only means of communication.
7. If a captured trench is being shelled it is useless to reinforce that trench unless:
(i) A further immediate advance is contemplated.
(ii) An enemy counter-attack is expected.
8. The first assaulting line cannot be equipped too lightly [i.e. should not be equipped too heavily]: 50 rounds SAA [small arms ammunition], 4 to 6 bombs, haversack with rations, waterbottle full [and] rifle and bayonet have been found to meet all requirements.

CAVAN
Lieutenant-General
Commanding XIV Corps

3rd August 1916

CHAPTER TWELVE

The Last Battles: from Morval to the Ancre

Allied agreement to pursue offensive operations led to plans being made to capture ground on the front of the Fourth Army from Gueudecourt to Morval, and for the Reserve Army to capture the Thiepval ridge. The Fourth Army's objectives were to be mainly those which it had failed to take during the battle of Flers-Courcelette. In a three-phase operation they planned to capture Gueudecourt, then the Combles-Gueudecourt road, and finally the ground east of Morval and Lesboeufs. Continuing bad weather delayed the start of these operations until 25 September; attacks by the French Army were to begin on the 26th.

The British attacks followed the pattern which had by now become well established, in that success attended the early stages of the assaults, which then became bogged down. In the XIV Corps area the attack on Morval and Lesboeufs went smoothly, and by 6p.m. the infantry of the Guards, 5th, 6th and 56th Divisions were established in both villages. XV Corps failed at Gueudecourt, however, as did III Corps at Martinpuich. On 26 September the Germans evacuated Combles, which was immediately occupied by the British and the French. Later the enemy also evacuated Gueudecourt, which was then occupied by infantry of XV Corps. On the 27th and 28th part of the XIV Corps sector was handed over to the French, following which the battle of Morval terminated on the 28th. It had been for the Allies a moderately successful operation.

In the Reserve Army area on 26 September the Canadian Corps attacked to seize the German positions before them to a depth of 1,000 yards, while on their left the 11th and 18th Divisions of II Corps advanced in line with them, battalions from the 18th Division capturing the ruins of Thiepval. Over the course of the next few days the Canadian Corps made further gains north-east of Courcelette, and infantry of II Corps pushed on beyond Thiepval; but on neither Corps front was the crest of the Thiepval ridge, the main objective, taken. Once again, the Germans fought stubbornly to deny the British this vital feature.

Sir Douglas Haig now decided to broaden the frontage of his offensive by bringing the Third Army into the battle. His staff began to prepare for another great attack on 12 October in which the objectives were to be, for the Fourth Army: Le Transloy, Beaulencourt, the ridge beyond Thilloy-Warlencourt, and Loupart Wood. The Reserve Army's objectives were from Loupart Wood westward to Miraumont, and Puisieux; the Third Army's, Gommecourt.

The steadily deteriorating weather, under which the battlefield and rear areas alike were by now becoming a sea of mud, was to seriously hamper the October operations. The roads and tracks, which had never been built to withstand the heavy traffic of the past months, broke up and disappeared into the mud, making the movement of ammunition and rations extremely difficult. Aerial observation was almost impossible, resulting in poor counter-battery work and inaccurate barrages. Simply existing in the open in such conditions was a severe physical trial, but fighting battles in them stretched men to the limits of endurance.

In the Fourth Army area the battle for the Transloy ridges started on 1 October, with an attack in the area of Le Sars and Eaucourt-l'Abbaye. By 5 October all objectives had been taken, and divisions of the Fourth Army were poised for the main attack which began on the 7th with assaults by III, XV and XIV Corps. In better weather the attacks might have had a chance of success, but in the terrible conditions prevailing the British gained very little. By the evening of 12 October General Rawlinson was "conscious that most of what he planned to accomplish ... still remained to do". He issued orders for the attack to be renewed on 18 October, when the infantry struggled forward in the darkness through a landscape of water-logged shellholes and flooded hollows, slipping and falling to clog their weapons with mud. The troops were quickly exhausted. In all their struggles there loomed before them the Butte de Warlencourt, a chalk

The Battle of Morval, 25 September 1916: the 12th Glosters ("Bristol's Own"), 5th Division, move forward in support of the attack on Morval. British artillery is firing to suppress the enfilade fire from Combles, away to the right. On the opposite flank the Guards and 6th Divisions were having trouble getting on to Lesboeufs. (IWM Q4287)

25 September: Private T.A.Jones of the 1st Cheshires, 5th Division, bringing in some of the 102 German prisoners he had just captured single-handedly at Morval, for which act he was awarded the Victoria Cross. Despite a bullet through his helmet and another through his coat, Jones went forward to shoot a sniper, and then accounted for two more of the enemy before collecting his extraordinary "bag". (IWM Q1322)

The Battle of the Transloy Ridges, October 1916: manhandling a 60-pdr. into position through the mud of Bazentin le Petit. (IWM Q4365)

mound blasted clear of all foliage and topsoil. Situated at the side of the Bapaume road, this ugly grey fortress defied all attempts at its capture, and marked forever the limit of the British advance here in 1916.

In the Reserve Army area the Canadians attacked northwards and were involved in very heavy fighting between 7 and 10 October in an attempt to take part of the German line north of Courcelette known as Stuff Trench, but rechristened Regina Trench by the Canadians. On their left the divisions of II Corps also battled northwards towards the Schwaben Redoubt, from which the Germans were finally ejected on 14 October by infantry of the 39th Division.

At this time Sir Douglas Haig estimated that 70 German divisions had been employed in the Somme battles, 40 of them against his own army, and that 370,000 casualties had been inflicted on them. Despite the deteriorating weather he intended to maintain his offensive where possible. He was unable to assess how close to breaking point the enemy might be, but felt that there was still a chance for a breakthrough and that it must be pursued. On 17 October he stood down the Third Army, and warned the Reserve Army to prepare to attack astride the river Ancre, probably on the 23rd, with the Fourth Army putting in an attack at Le Transloy on the 26th in conjunction with the French. On 18 October, in view of the disappointing results of the Fourth Army operations, he set out a series of revisions of future operations "weather permitting". In the event none of these operations took place, and it was not until 3 November that the weather began to improve.

In the area of the Reserve Army (re-named Fifth Army at the end of October) the Battle of the Ancre Heights was resumed between 21 October and 11 November, resulting in an extension of the British position towards Grandcourt by the 4th Canadian, 18th, 25th and 29th Divisions. On the front of the Fourth Army XIV Corps attacked towards Le Transloy in co-operation with the French Army on the 23rd, to make one of the few gains of the several operations mounted in this area in late October and early November.

13-18 November: "The Battle of the Ancre"

In their preparations for an attack astride the Ancre the Fifth Army enjoyed certain advantages not shared by their comrades further south. There the roads were in an appalling condition, making the crossing of five or six miles of former battlefield a slow and exhausting undertaking. But in front of Beaumont Hamel the British were in the trenches they had occupied in July, with behind them communications that were in fairly good condition. The enemy in this area had every reason to feel confident. They had repelled every British attack launched against them, and the weather, which had put paid to the Fourth Army's offensive, might well be putting an end to the whole British effort. Unfortunately for the Germans, the rain ceased on 8 November and, although the weather remained cold, the ground began to dry out. After discussions with his Corps commanders General Gough decided to launch his attack on the 13th.

Supporting the Fifth Army were 282 heavy guns in addition to their field artillery. A mine containing 30,000lbs. of high explosive lay ready under the crater of the mine exploded at the Hawthorn Redoubt on 1 July; and gas was available to be used against the German positions if required. The infantry earmarked for the attack included the 2nd, 3rd, 37th (New Army), 51st (Highland) and 63 (Royal Naval) Divisions in V Corps, and the 18th, 19th, 32nd, 39th (New Army) and 4th Canadian Divisions in II Corps.

The formations of V Corps were to bear the brunt of the attack in an operation that was divided into three phases. The first involved an assault on the German positions between Beaucourt and Serre, the second and third phases involving the deepening of this lodgement. South of the Ancre the divisions of II Corps were to make an attempt on the German positions between St.Pierre Divion and the Schwaben Redoubt. For several days preceding the attack the German positions had been shelled for an hour early each morning, and at 5.45a.m. on 13 November this routine barrage was followed by the firing of the mine at the Hawthorn crater and the advance of the creeping barrage, behind which the British infantry attacked.

On the II Corps front all went to plan. By shortly after 8.15a.m. both the 19th and 39th Divisions had achieved their objectives with relatively few casualties. The right hand division of V Corps was the 63rd, a composite division

of Royal Navy reservist, Royal Marine and Army battalions. Despite fierce enemy resistance they fought their way up to Beaucourt, but could get no further. On the left of the Royal Naval Division, the 51st (Highland) Division also faced a determined enemy, but they fought their way through the "Y" Ravine salient and into Beaumont Hamel, eventually establishing a line on the village's eastern edge. On the left of the Highlanders the 2nd Division made a limited advance, but on the left of the V Corps front the 3rd Division was defeated by the German defences in front of Serre, just as the unfortunate 31st Division had been on 1 July. By an extraordinary quirk of fate this same formation, part of XIII Corps, attacked on the left of the 3rd Division, going forward against the German line north of Serre. After a successful start, the battalions of the 31st Division found themselves halted by a counter-attack and then forced to retire.

However, by the close of the day's fighting General

November 1916: the Lesboeufs road, outside Flers. The two Royal Field Artillery horses up to their knees in mud demonstrate the conditions of the Fourth Army's lines of communications at this stage of the battles. (IWM Q2982)

51st (HIGHLAND) DIVISION

The 51st (Highland) Division, Territorial Force, ended the war with a reputation as an elite fighting formation. As one Corps commander expressed it, "the Division fights with gallantry, and can be depended on to carry out any reasonable task which may be allotted to it in battle. For this reason I venture to place it among the three best fighting divisions I have met in France." The first real success of the Highland Division was the Battle of the Ancre. Its battalions had received a mauling at High Wood in July and as a result the stock of the division was not very high. But the manner in which, in November, its infantry seized "Y Ravine" and the ruins of Beaumont Hamel (over ground "horrible with the dead and the litter of the struggle in the previous July"), along with a huge bag of prisoners, established the Highland Division as one of the best in the BEF. It is altogether fitting that a divisional memorial consisting of the figure of a Highland infantryman stands today in the Beaumont Hamel memorial park.

Gough had reason to feel pleased with the performance of his troops. II Corps had achieved its objectives, and the divisions on the right of V Corps had got up to Beaucourt and taken Beaumont Hamel. He issued orders for the 2nd, 51st and 63rd Divisions to push on the following day.

The Germans had been surprised and shaken by the British attacks. They had imagined that the deteriorating weather had brought an end to offensive operations for the year, and the strong British thrusts astride the Ancre had caught them off guard. Worse was to come. A British barrage began at 6a.m. on 14 November, and at 6.20a.m. it began to creep forward as the British infantry came on yet again. During the early part of the morning Beaucourt was captured by the Royal Naval Division, and it was in this battle that Lieutenant-Colonel Freyberg of the Hood Battalion won the Victoria Cross. The advance by battalions of the 51st (Highland) Division started well, but much of

November 1916: British troops in what is described as the mine crater at Beaumont Hamel. If the description is accurate, this is where the mines of both 1 July and 13 November were detonated. The men in the foreground are from the 22nd West Yorks, a labour battalion and Fifth Army troops at that time. (IWM Q2005)

Prisoners taken by the 51st (Highland) Division in the attack on Beaumont Hamel being counted into the divisional "cage". (IWM Q4500)

the ground gained had to be given up when, at 11a.m., two battalions were shelled by a British heavy battery. Troops of the 2nd Division also had to relinquish ground gained when they found their flanks unsupported. General Gough, characteristically, had issued orders by early afternoon for a resumption of the attack on the following day; these were later countermanded by Haig. The operations that did take place on the 15th were small actions aimed up tidying up the boundary between the 2nd and 51st Divisions. Even so, they resulted in heavy casualties and gained nothing.

It was on 15 November that General Kiggell, Haig's chief-of-staff, visited the headquarters of the Fifth Army to explain to General Gough that the campaign was at an end and that the Commander-in-Chief wished there to be no further offensive operations. But Gough refused to accept this ruling, and sought permission for one final attack. That evening Haig gave his consent.

On 16 and 17 November the weather remained cold, but clear. Aerial reconnaissance proceeded and on the 17th observers reported that the enemy were abandoning trenches near Grandcourt. Orders were issued for them to be occupied that night. Preparations went ahead for an attack on the 18th by II and V Corps, but the instructions for this final operation were not precise, describing its aim

63rd (ROYAL NAVAL) DIVISION

The decision to use the surplus reservists of the Royal Navy and Royal Marines on land was that of Mr Winston Churchill when First Lord of the Admiralty. A brigade of marines and two of sailors were sent to Antwerp and fought in the defence of that port before being evacuated to England. In 1915 the division fought at Gallipoli, and in May 1916 was sent to the Western Front. By the time of the Battle of the Ancre the division had been transferred from the Admiralty to the War Office and had two battalions of marines, six of sailors and five of soldiers as its infantry component. The artillery, sappers, medical units, etc., were all Army.

The Royal Naval Division fought with great distinction in the final battle of the Somme campaign, and amongst its officers and men none fought more gallantly than Lieutenant-Colonel Bernard Freyberg, DSO. Commanding the Hood Battalion in the fighting for Beaucourt, he led the 190th RN Brigade into the village despite being wounded three times, to win the Victoria Cross – the last of 51 awarded during the Somme battles. Freyberg survived his wounds and went on to further distinction in a career which saw him rise to general officer's rank and the command of New Zealand troops in the Mediterranean in the Second World War, and subsequently appointment as Governor-General of New Zealand.

INTO THE BARRAGE

One of the most vivid descriptions of an infantry assault is in *Her Privates We* by "Private 19022", a work of fiction by Frederic Manning, who served with the 7th King's Shropshire Light Infantry in the 3rd Division; this passage describes their attack on the Ancre in November:

"He didn't know whether they had heard any orders or not: he only knew they moved. It was treacherous walking over that greasy mud. They crossed Monk Trench, and a couple of other trenches, crowding together, and becoming confused....Suddenly the Hun barrage fell: the air was split and seared with shells....As they hurried, head downward, over their own front line, they met men, some broken and bleeding, but others whole and sound, breaking back in disorder....They pressed forward, struggling through the mud like flies through treacle....turning their faces wide-eyed, in all directions to search the baffling fog. It shook, and twitched, and whirled about them: there seemed to be a dancing flicker before their eyes as shell after shell exploded, clanging, and the flying fragments hissed and shrieked through the air....

"He avoided some shattered bodies of men too obviously dead for help. A man stumbled past him with an agonized and bleeding face....For a moment they might have broken and run themselves...but they struggled on as Sergeant Tozer yelled at them....He knew, they all did, that the barrage had moved too quickly for them, but they knew nothing of what was happening about them. In any attack, even under favourable conditions, the attackers are soon blinded; but here they had lost touch almost from the start. They paused for a brief moment....Their casualties, as far as he could judge, had not been heavy. They got going again, and, almost before they saw it, were on the wire. The stakes had been uprooted, and it was smashed and tangled, but had not been well cut.

"Jakes ran along it a little way, there was some firing, and bombs were hurled at them from the almost obliterated trench, and they answered by lobbing a few bombs over, and then plunging desperately among the steel briars, which tore at their puttees and trousers. The last strand of it was cut or beaten down, some more bombs came at them, and in the last infuriated rush Bourne was knocked off his feet and went practically head-long into the trench; getting up, another man jumped on his shoulders, and they both fell together, yelling with rage at each other. They heard a few squeals of agony, and he saw a dead German, still kicking his heels on the broken boards of the trench at his feet....The trench was almost obliterated: it was nothing but a wreckage of boards and posts...."

The ruins of Beaumont Hamel after its capture, November 1916. An objective for 1 July, it fell in the final battle, having been pulverised in the meantime to the condition seen here. (IWM Q1558)

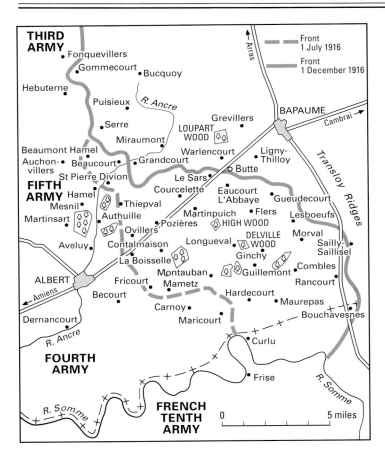

as an attempt to tidy up the British position using Grandcourt as a pivot. The orders were followed by a series of amendments and changes which continued to be published right up to the start of the operation. Such confusion had, in the past, not boded well for operations.

In the event the attack of 18 November and the subsequent fighting, which went on in places until the 19th, were more successful than the cynics amongst the troops of the Fifth Army expected. South of the Ancre the 4th Canadian Division took all its set objectives, and the 19th Division almost got to Grandcourt. North of the Ancre the 63rd and 51st Divisions had been relieved by the 37th Division, who pushed forward to extend the British front 1,000 yards beyond Beaucourt and Beaumont Hamel. Snow had begun to fall during the night before the attacks; these were delivered into a driving sleet which gradually turned to rain, producing conditions that were truly abominable.

And so, as the fighting of 19 November 1916 petered out and the wind and rain swept across the tortured downland of Picardy, so too ended the four-and-a-half month campaign that came to be known as the Battle of the Somme.

Beaumont Hamel, December 1916: the fighting on the Somme had by now died down, and the front lines were in the immobilising grip of winter. Muffled against the cold, a British sentry mans a gas alarm. (IWM Q1717)

CHAPTER THIRTEEN

Epilogue

When the Somme fighting died down the Germans found themselves occupying improvised trench lines which were much weaker than those they had occupied before the battles, and much less capable of withstanding further determined attacks. Twenty miles to their rear a system of fortifications was nearing completion, as thousands of prisoners and civilians laboured to complete what the Germans called their *"Siegfried Stellung"* – known to the Allies as the Hindenburg Line. It was the German intention to withdraw to this line as soon as possible, abandoning what had become an irregular salient of poorly constructed trenches for a shorter, stronger line that would require fewer troops to garrison.

On 24 February 1917 British patrols found the German trenches empty in the areas of Miraumont and Serre. An enemy withdrawal on a vast scale was under way. Over the course of the next few days British troops entered, without opposition, places such as Warlencourt, Miraumont, Serre, Loupart Wood and Le Transloy – charnel houses where so much British blood had been spilled, and which had always resisted capture throughout months of savage fighting. During the next few weeks the British cautiously followed enemy units as they withdrew through Bapaume and Peronne and behind the vast belts of barbed wire shielding their new fortifications. As they went they laid a spiteful waste to the countryside, demolishing bridges and buildings, wrecking roads, and even felling orchards. By April 1917 the Allies had closed up to the Hindenburg Line and had begun the task of constructing trench lines before it. From Arras in the north to Soissons in the south, the Germans had chosen to give up a great tract of French territory on either side of the Somme sooner than face any further confrontation there.

The Somme had cost the Germans dear, as it had the Allies. Even today there is argument over the grisly statistics of attrition, but German casualties have been put in the region of 660,000 to 680,000. History is more certain of the Allied losses, which are reckoned at something under 630,000. (By comparison, the French and German armies are estimated to have suffered between 340,000 and 380,000 casualties each during the ten months of the Verdun fighting.) At the height of the Somme fighting General von Falkenhayn wrote: "Beneath the enormous pressure which now rests on us we have no superfluity of strength. Every removal in one direction leads eventually to dangerous weaknesses in another place, which may lead to our destruction if even the least adjustment in the enemy's disposition is made." At the end of 1916, when Hindenburg had replaced Falkenhayn as chief of the German General Staff, his Quartermaster-General, Ludendorff, wrote that "The German Army had been fought to a standstill and was utterly worn out." Later Hindenburg declared, "We must

save the men from a second Somme battle". Attrition, the *"Material-Schlact"* or battle of materiel, had eroded the strength and confidence of the German Army. In the words of two of its officers: "No art of the commander could give them back the trained artillery which had been destroyed"; and "The immense material superiority of the enemy did not fail to have its psychological effect on the German combatants".

If the Somme campaign of 1916 saw the beginning of the decline of the German Army, it saw the transformation of a British Army which had begun the battles as a vast, enthusiastic collection of amateurs, but emerged from them as a seasoned, professional, battle-winning force. At all levels, from the divisional commanders who had mostly commanded nothing larger than a battalion in peacetime, down through their novice staffs to the raw officers and men in the battalions and batteries, all had learned their business in the hard school of the Somme battles. They had absorbed shocking new experiences and sustained dreadful casualties, returning to the fight again and again, each time with a growing and hard-won expertise. Nearly five months of slogging forward against a determined foe had been a hideously costly way to acquire the skills that should have

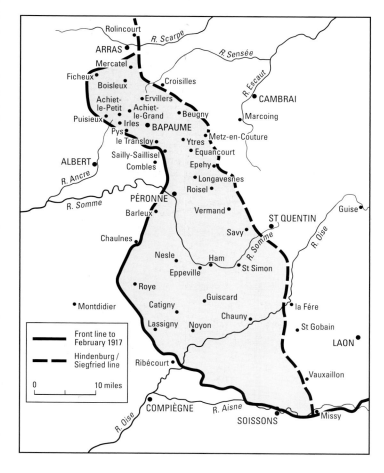

been taught in the training areas and practice camps of England, and at times it must have seemed to some that the task set them was impossible.

And yet on three occasions this army of amateurs had come close to achieving the breakthrough sought by their commanders, and the defeat of the most professional army on earth: at Montauban on 1 July, when its defenders ran away; in the aftermath of the brilliant night attack of 14 July, when the cavalry were too late to exploit the enemy confusion at High Wood; and at Flers on 15 September, when a handful of tanks in their first battle came so close to driving through the German defences. On each occasion the aggressive spirit and stamina of the British infantry – the men with rifle, bayonet and grenade – created an opportunity which their senior commanders found themselves, for one reason or another, unable to exploit. Their failure is all the more striking when one remembers that cavalry is the arm of exploitation and pursuit, and that the majority of British commanders in 1916 were cavalrymen.

If the business of learning the soldier's trade had begun during the battles of 1916, it developed in deadly earnest once those battles had died away. There was much serious debate as the lessons of the recent offensive were absorbed. Schools of all kinds flourished, and training notes and pamphlets were circulated in France and Britain. New infantry and artillery tactics were devised, notably the perfection of the "creeping barrage"; safer fuses, gas and smoke shells were issued to the gunners. The lessons of Flers were studied by the tank arm, who devised more practical tactics as they awaited the delivery of more mechanically reliable machines.

The years 1917 and 1918 would see the British Army committed to battles the equal of those it had fought on the Somme. General Nivelle's disastrous offensive in spring 1917 finally demanded too much of the long-suffering *poilu*, throwing much of the weight and cost of the rest of that year's fighting onto the British Expeditionary Force. The German Army remained dangerous to the last, and during Ludendorff's stunning offensive of spring 1918 the struggle would rage back and forth once again over the battlefields of 1916 until the Germans accepted defeat, sought an armistice, and marched back to their homeland. Following close behind were the armies of the Allies, now including the United States, to set up a "watch on the Rhine". For the British Army it had been a long, hard road to Cologne, a journey that began on the fields of Picardy with the "Big Push". In seeking an epitaph for that army the last words are perhaps best left to a junior oficer who fought on the Somme, and went on to survive the war:

"The British Army learned its lesson the hard way, and during the middle part of the Somme battle and for the rest of the war, was the best army in the field."

Captain Charles Carrington
1/5th Royal Warwickshires
48th Division

APPENDICES

APPENDIX ONE

Commanders and Principal Staff Officers

British Expeditionary Forces

July – November 1916

GENERAL HEADQUARTERS

Commander-in-Chief: General Sir Douglas Haig

Chief of the General Staff: Lt.Gen.Sir L.E.Kiggell

Major-General Royal Artillery: Maj.Gen.J.F.N.Birch

THIRD ARMY

General Officer Commanding: General Sir E.H.H.Allenby

FOURTH ARMY

General Officer Commanding: General Sir H.S.Rawlinson,Bt.

Major-General General Staff: Maj.Gen.A.A.Montgomery

Deputy-Adjutant & Quartermaster-General:
Maj.Gen.H.C.Holman

Major-General Royal Artillery: Maj.Gen.C.E.D.Budworth

Chief Engineer: Maj.Gen.R.U.H.Buckland

Deputy-Director Signals: Col.R.G.Earle

RESERVE ARMY
(Numbered as FIFTH ARMY from 30 October 1916)

General Officer Commanding: General Sir H.D.Gough

Major-General General Staff: Maj.Gen.N.Malcolm

Deputy-Adjutant & Quartermaster-General:
Maj.Gen.H.N.Sargent

Major-General Royal Artillery: Maj.Gen.H.C.C.Uniacke

Chief Engineer: Maj.Gen.R.P.Lee

Deputy-Director Signals: Col.E.G.Godfrey-Faussett

CAVALRY CORPS

General Officer Commanding: Lt.Gen.C.T.McM.Kavanagh

Brigadier-General General Staff: Brig.Gen.A.F.Home

Brigadier-General Royal Artillery: Brig.Gen.H.H.Tudor

II CORPS

General Officer Commanding: Lt.Gen.C.W.Jacob

Brigadier-General General Staff: Brig.Gen.P.Howell
(killed 7/10/16),
Brig.Gen.S.H.Wilson

Brigadier-General Royal Artillery: Brig.Gen.C.E.Lawrie

III CORPS

General Officer Commanding: Lt.Gen.W.P.Pulteney

Brigadier-General General Staff: Brig.Gen.C.F.Romer

Brigadier-General Royal Artillery: Brig.Gen.H.C.C.Uniacke
(to 25/7/16)
Brig.Gen.T.A.Tancred

V CORPS

General Officer Commanding: Lt.Gen.E.A.Fanshawe

Brigadier-General General Staff: Brig.Gen.G.F.Boyd

Brigadier-General Royal Artillery: Brig.Gen.A.Stokes

VII CORPS

General Officer Commanding: Lt.Gen.Sir T.D.Snow

Brigadier-General General Staff: Brig.Gen.F.Lyon

Brigadier-General Royal Artillery:
Brig.Gen.C.M.Ross-Johnson

VIII CORPS

General Officer Commanding:
Lt.Gen.Sir A.G.Hunter-Weston

Brigadier-General General Staff:
Brig.Gen.Hon.W.P.Hore-Ruthven

Brigadier-General Royal Artillery: Brig.Gen.T.A.Tancred
(to 12/7/16)
Brig.Gen.W.Strong

X CORPS

General Officer Commanding: Lt.Gen.Sir T.L.N.Morland

Brigadier-General General Staff: Brig.Gen.A.R.Cameron

Brigadier-General Royal Artillery:
Brig.Gen.C.C.Van Straubenzee

XIII CORPS

General Officer Commanding: Lt.Gen.W.N.Congreve,VC

Brigadier-General General Staff: Brig.Gen.W.H.Greenly

Brigadier-General Royal Artillery: Brig.Gen.R.StC.Lecky

XIV CORPS

General Officer Commanding: Lt.Gen.Earl of Cavan

Brigadier-General General Staff:
Brig.Gen.Hon.J.F.Gathorne-Hardy

Brigadier-General Royal Artillery: Brig.Gen.A.E.Wardrop

XV CORPS

General Officer Commanding: Lt.Gen.H.S.Horne

Brigadier-General General Staff: Brig.Gen.L.R.Vaughan

Brigadier-General Royal Artillery:
Brig.Gen.E.W.Alexander,VC

MACHINE GUN CORPS (HEAVY SECTION)

Commander: Col.E.D.Swinton

Commander in France: Lt.Col.R.W.Bradley
(from 1/9/16 to 28/9/16)
Col.H.J.Elles

Brigade-Major: Capt.G.LeQ.Martel

APPENDIX TWO

British and Dominion Infantry present on the Somme, 1916

The divisional signs which illustrate this Appendix are those in use in 1916. In 1914 unit designations were lettered on vehicles, signboards and flags; but by 1916 these had been replaced by a device which was the sign of the division in which the unit served. These were chosen at random: sometimes for their simplicity, sometimes as a visual pun on the divisional number, and sometimes reproducing the "proprietorial" mark of the commander. In time these signs became familiar, even famous. A few divisional signs were worn on uniform, and this practice became popular later in the war; but in the main the devices worn on uniform were "battle insignia" designed to conceal the unit identity from the enemy. (Where colours are known, other than black and white, they are noted.)

Guards Division
(Blue shield, red edge)

GUARDS DIVISION – Regulars
GOC: Maj.Gen.G.P.T.Fielding
1st Guards Brigade: 2nd Grenadier Guards; 2nd Coldstream Guards; 3rd Coldstream Guards; 1st Irish Guards
2nd Guards Brigade: 2nd Grenadier Guards; 1st Coldstream Guards; 1st Scots Guards; 2nd Irish Guards
3rd Guards Brigade: 1st Grenadier Guards; 4th Grenadier Guards; 2nd Scots Guards; 1st Welsh Guards
Pioneers: 4th Coldstream Guards

1st DIVISION – Regulars
GOC: Maj.Gen.E.P.Strickland
1st Brigade: 10th Glosters; 1st Black Watch; 8th Royal Berks; 1st Camerons
2nd Brigade: 2nd Royal Sussex; 1st Loyal North Lancs; 1st Northampton; 2nd King's Royal Rifle Corps
3rd Brigade: 1st South Wales Borderers; 16th Glosters; 2nd Welsh; 2nd Royal Munster Fusiliers
Pioneers: 1st/6th Welsh

2nd DIVISION – Regulars and New Army
GOC: Maj.Gen.W.G.Walker,VC
5th Brigade: 17th Royal Fusiliers; 24th Royal Fusiliers; 2nd Oxford & Buckingham Light Infantry; 2nd Highland Light Infantry
6th Brigade: 1st King's; 2nd South Staffs; 13th Essex; 17th Middlesex
99th Brigade: 22nd Royal Fusiliers; 23rd Royal Fusiliers; 1st Royal Berks; 1st King's Royal Rifle Corps
Pioneers: 10th Duke of Cornwall's Light Infantry

3rd DIVISION – Regulars and New Army
GOC: Maj.Gen.J.A.L.Haldane (to 6/8/16), Maj.Gen.C.J.Deverell
8th Brigade: 2nd Royal Scots; 8th East Yorks; 1st Royal Scots Fusiliers; 7th King's Shropshire Light Infantry
9th Brigade: 1st Northumberland Fusiliers; 4th Royal Fusiliers; 13th King's; 12th West Yorks
76th Brigade: 8th King's Own; 2nd Suffolk; 10th Royal Welsh Fusiliers; 1st Gordons
Pioneers: 20th King's Royal Rifle Corps

4th DIVISION – Regulars
GOC: Maj.Gen.Hon.W.Lambton
10th Brigade: 1st Royal Warwick; 2nd Seaforth; 1st Royal Irish Fusiliers; 2nd Royal Dublin Fusiliers
11th Brigade: 1st Somerset Light Infantry; 1st East Lancs; 1st Hampshire; 1st Rifle Brigade
12th Brigade: 1st King's Own; 2nd Lancs Fusiliers; 2nd Essex; 2nd Duke of Wellington's

5th DIVISION – Regulars and New Army
GOC: Maj.Gen.J.Ponsonby
13th Brigade: 14th Royal Warwick; 15th Royal Warwick; 2nd King's Own Scottish Borderers; 1st Royal West Kent
15th Brigade: 16th Royal Warwick; 1st Norfolk; 1st Bedford; 1st Cheshire
95th Brigade: 1st Devons; 12th Glosters; 1st East Surrey; 1st Duke of Cornwall's Light Infantry
Pioneers: 1st/6th Argyll & Sutherland Highlanders

6th DIVISION – Regulars and New Army
GOC: Maj.Gen.C.Ross
16th Brigade: 1st Buffs; 8th Bedford; 1st King's Shropshire Light Infantry; 2nd York & Lanc
18th Brigade: 1st West Yorks; 11th Essex; 2nd Durham Light Infantry; 14th Durham Light Infantry
71st Brigade: 9th Norfolk; 9th Suffolk; 1st Leicester; 2nd Sherwood Foresters
Pioneers: 11th Leicester

7th DIVISION – Regulars and New Army
GOC: Maj.Gen.H.E.Watts
20th Brigade: 8th Devon; 9th Devon; 2nd Border Regiment; 2nd Gordons
22nd Brigade: 2nd Royal Warwick; 2nd Royal Irish; 1st Royal Welsh Fusiliers; 20th Manchester
91st Brigade: 2nd Queen's; 1st South Staffs; 21st Manchester; 22nd Manchester
Pioneers: 24th Manchester

8th DIVISION – Regulars
GOC: Maj.Gen.H.Hudson
23rd Brigade: 2nd Devon; 2nd West Yorks; 2nd Middlesex; 2nd Scottish Rifles
24th Brigade: 1st Worcester; 1st Sherwood Foresters; 2nd Northampton; 2nd East Lancs
25th Brigade: 2nd Lincoln; 2nd Royal Berks; 1st Royal Irish Rifles; 2nd Rifle Brigade
Pioneers: 22nd Durham Light Infantry

9th (SCOTTISH) DIVISION – New Army and South Africans
GOC: Maj.Gen.W.T.Furse
26th Brigade: 8th Black Watch; 7th Seaforth; 5th Camerons; 10th Argyll & Sutherland Highlanders
27th Brigade: 11th Royal Scots; 12th Royal Scots; 6th King's Own Scottish Borderers; 9th Scottish Rifles
SA Brigade: 1st Regt (Cape Province); 2nd Regt (Natal & Orange Free State); 3rd Regt (Transvaal & Rhodesia); 4th Regt (Scottish)
Pioneers: 9th Seaforth

11th (NORTHERN) DIVISION – New Army
GOC: Lt.Gen.Sir C.L.Woollcombe
32nd Brigade: 9th West Yorks; 6th Green Howards; 8th Duke of Wellington's; 6th York & Lanc
33rd Brigade: 6th Lincoln; 6th Border Regiment; 7th South Staffs; 9th Sherwood Foresters
34th Brigade: 8th Northumberland Fusiliers; 9th Lancashire Fusiliers; 5th Dorset; 11th Manchester
Pioneers: 6th East Yorks

6th Division	7th Division	8th Division (Red & white)	9th Division (Blue thistle)	11th Division (Red motif, white edge)

| 1st Division | 2nd Division (Two white stars, one red) | 3rd Division (Yellow on black) | 4th Division | 5th Division (Yellow on blue) |

12th (EASTERN) DIVISION – New Army
GOC: Maj.Gen.A.B.Scott
35th Brigade: 7th Norfolk; 7th Suffolk; 9th Essex; 5th Royal Berks
36th Brigade: 8th Royal Fusiliers; 9th Royal Fusiliers; 7th Royal Sussex; 11th Middlesex
37th Brigade: 6th Queen's; 6th Buffs; 7th East Surrey; 6th Royal West Kent
Pioneers: 5th Northampton

14th (LIGHT) DIVISION – New Army
GOC: Maj.Gen.V.A.Couper
41st Brigade: 7th King's Royal Rifle Corps; 8th Royal Rifle Corps; 7th Rifle Brigade; 8th Rifle Brigade
42nd Brigade: 5th Oxford & Bucks Light Infantry; 5th King's Shropshire Light Infantry; 9th King's Royal Rifle Corps; 9th Rifle Brigade
43rd Brigade: 6th Somerset Light Infantry; 6th Duke of Cornwall's Light Infantry; 6th King's Own Yorkshire Light Infantry; 10th Durham Light Infantry
Pioneers: 11th King's

15th (SCOTTISH) DIVISION – New Army
GOC: Maj.Gen.F.W.N.McCracken
44th Brigade: 9th Black Watch; 8th Seaforth; 8th/10th Gordons; 7th Camerons
45th Brigade: 13th Royal Scots; 6th/7th Royal Scots Fusiliers; 6th Camerons; 11th Argyll & Sutherland Highlanders
46th Brigade: 10th Scottish Rifles; 7th/8th King's Own Scottish Borderers; 10th/11th Highland Light Infantry; 12th Highland Light Infantry
Pioneers: 9th Gordons

16th (IRISH) DIVISION – New Army
GOC: Maj.Gen.W.B.Hickie
47th Brigade: 6th Royal Irish; 6th Connaught Rangers; 7th Leinster; 8th Royal Munster Fusiliers
48th Brigade: 7th Royal Irish Rifles; 1st Royal Munster Fusiliers; 8th Royal Dublin Fusiliers; 9th Royal Dublin Fusiliers
49th Brigade: 7th Royal Inniskilling Fusiliers; 8th Royal Inniskilling Fusiliers; 7th Royal Irish Fusiliers; 8th Royal Irish Fusiliers
Pioneers: 11th Hampshires

17th (NORTHERN) DIVISION – New Army
GOC: Maj.Gen.T.D.Pitcher (to 12/7/16); Maj.Gen.P.R.Robertson
50th Brigade: 10th West Yorks; 7th East Yorks; 7th Green Howards; 6th Dorset
51st Brigade: 7th Lincoln; 7th Border Regiment; 8th South Staffs; 10th Sherwood Foresters
52nd Brigade: 9th Northumberland Fusiliers; 10th Lancashire Fusiliers; 9th Duke of Wellington's; 12th Manchester
Pioneers: 7th York & Lancs

18th (EASTERN) DIVISION – New Army
GOC: Maj.Gen.F.I.Maxse
53rd Brigade: 8th Norfolk; 8th Suffolk; 10th Essex; 6th Royal Berks
54th Brigade: 11th Royal Fusiliers; 7th Bedford; 6th Northampton; 12th Middlesex
55th Brigade: 7th Queen's; 7th Buffs; 8th East Surrey; 7th Royal West Kent
Pioneers: 8th Royal Sussex

19th (WESTERN) DIVISION – New Army
GOC: Maj.Gen.G.T.M.Bridges
56th Brigade: 7th King's Own; 7th East Lancs; 7th South Lancs; 7th Loyal North Lancs
57th Brigade: 10th Royal Warwick; 8th Gloster; 10th Worcester; 8th North Staffs
58th Brigade: 9th Cheshire; 9th Royal Welsh Fusiliers; 9th Welsh; 6th Wiltshire
Pioneers: 5th South Wales Borderers

20th (LIGHT) DIVISION – New Army
GOC: Maj.Gen.W.Douglas Smith
59th Brigade: 10th King's Royal Rifle Corps; 11th King's Royal Rifle Corps; 10th Rifle Brigade; 11th Rifle Brigade
60th Brigade: 6th Oxford & Bucks Light Infantry; 6th King's Shrophire Light Infantry; 12th King's Royal Rifle Corps; 12th Rifle Brigade
61st Brigade: 7th Somerset Light Infantry; 7th Duke of Cornwall's Light Infantry; 7th King's Own Yorkshire Light Infantry; 12th King's
Pioneers: 11th Durham Light Infantry

21st DIVISION – New Army and Regulars
GOC: Maj.Gen.D.G.M.Campbell
62nd Brigade: 12th Northumberland Fusiliers; 13th Northumberland Fusiliers; 1st Lincoln; 10th Green Howards
63rd Brigade: 8th Lincoln; 8th Somerset Light Infantry; 4th Middlesex; 10th York & Lancs
64th Brigade: 1st East Yorks; 9th King's Own Yorkshire Light Infantry; 10th King's Own Yorkshire Light Infantry; 15th Durham Light Infantry
Pioneers: 14th Northumberland Fusiliers

23rd DIVISION – New Army
GOC: Maj.Gen.J.M.Babington
68th Brigade: 10th Northumberland Fusiliers; 11th Northumberland Fusiliers; 12th Durham Light Infantry; 13th Durham Light Infantry
69th Brigade: 11th West Yorks; 8th Green Howards; 9th Green Howards; 10th Duke of Wellington's
70th Brigade: 11th Sherwood Foresters; 8th King's Own Yorkshire Light Infantry; 8th York & Lancs; 9th York & Lancs
Pioneers: 9th South Staffs

| 12th Division | 14th Division (White on green) | 15th Division (Red on white) | 16th Division (Green motif) | 17th Division (Red on white) |

  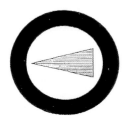  

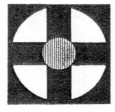

| 18th Division | 19th Division (Blue) | 20th Division (Red bullseye) | 21st Division (Red motif) | 23rd Division (Red Maltese cross) |

24th DIVISION – New Army and Regulars
GOC: Maj.Gen.J.E.Capper
17th Brigade: 8th Buffs; 1st Royal Fusiliers; 12th Royal Fusiliers; 3rd Rifle Brigade
72nd Brigade: 8th Queen's; 9th East Surrey; 8th Royal West Kent; 1st North Staffs
73rd Brigade: 9th Royal Sussex; 7th Northampton; 13th Middlesex; 2nd Leinster
Pioneers: 12th Sherwood Foresters

25th DIVISION – New Army and Regulars
GOC: Maj.Gen.E.G.T.Balnbridge
7th Brigade: 10th Cheshire; 3rd Worcester; 8th Loyal North Lancs; 1st Wiltshire
74th Brigade: 11th Lancashire Fusiliers; 13th Cheshire; 9th Loyal North Lancs; 2nd Irish Rifles
75th Brigade: 11th Cheshire; 8th Border Regiment; 2nd South Lancs; 8th South Lancs
Pioneers: 6th South Wales Borderers

29th DIVISION – Regulars
GOC: Maj.Gen.H.DeB.De Lisle
86th Brigade: 2nd Royal Fusiliers; 1st Lancashire Fusiliers; 16th Middlesex; 1st Royal Dublin Fusiliers
87th Brigade: 2nd South Wales Borderers; 1st King's Own Scottish Borderers; 1st Royal Inniskilling Fusiliers; 1st Border Regiment
88th Brigade: 4th Worcester; 1st Essex; 2nd Hampshire; Royal Newfoundland Regiment
Pioneers: 2nd Monmouth

30th DIVISION – New Army and Regulars
GOC: Maj.Gen.J.S.M.Shea
21st Brigade: 18th King's; 2nd Green Howards; 2nd Wiltshire; 19th Manchester
89th Brigade: 17th King's; 19th King's; 20th King's; 2nd Bedford
90th Brigade: 2nd Royal Scots Fusiliers; 16th Manchester; 17th Manchester; 18th Manchester
Pioneers: 11th South Lancs

31st DIVISION – New Army
GOC: Maj.Gen.R.Wanless O'Gowan
92nd Brigade: 10th East Yorks; 11th East Yorks; 12th East Yorks; 13th East Yorks
93rd Brigade: 15th West Yorks; 16th West Yorks; 18th West Yorks; 18th Durham Light Infantry
94th Brigade: 11th East Lancs; 12th York & Lancs; 13th York & Lancs; 14th York & Lancs
Pioneers: 12th King's Own Yorkshire Light Infantry

32nd DIVISION – New Army and Regulars
GOC: Maj.Gen.W.H.Rycroft
14th Brigade: 19th Lancashire Fusiliers; 1st Dorset; 2nd Manchester; 15th Highland Light Infantry
96th Brigade: 16th Northumberland Fusiliers; 15th Lancashire Fusiliers; 16th Lancashire Fusiliers; 2nd Royal Inniskilling Fusiliers
97th Brigade: 11th Border Regiment; 2nd King's Own Yorkshire Light Infantry; 16th Highland Light Infantry; 17th Highland Light Infantry
Pioneers: 17th Northumberland Fusiliers

33rd DIVISION – New Army and Regulars
GOC: Maj.Gen.H.J.S.Landon
19th Brigade: 20th Royal Fusiliers; 2nd Royal Welsh Fusiliers; 1st Cameronians; 5th Scottish Rifles
98th Brigade: 4th King's; 1st/4th Suffolk; 1st Middlesex; 2nd Argyll & Sutherland Highlanders
100th Brigade: 1st Queen's; 2nd Worcester; 16th King's Royal Rifle Corps; 1st/9th Highland Light Infantry
Pioneers: 18th Middlesex

34th DIVISION – New Army
GOC: Maj.Gen.E.C.Ingouville-Williams (killed 22/7/16); Maj.Gen. C.L.Nicholson
101st Brigade: 15th Royal Scots; 16th Royal Scots; 10th Lincoln; 11th Suffolk
102nd (Tyneside Scottish) Brigade: 20th Northumberland Fusiliers; 21st Northumberland Fusiliers; 22nd Northumberland Fusiliers; 23rd Northumberland Fusiliers
103rd (Tyneside Irish) Brigade: 24th Northumberland Fusiliers; 25th Northumberland Fusiliers; 26th Northumberland Fusiliers; 27th Northumberland Fusiliers
Pioneers: 18th Northumberland Fusiliers

35th (BANTAM) DIVISION – New Army
GOC: Maj.Gen.R.J.Pinney
104th Brigade: 17th Lancashire Fusiliers; 18th Lancashire Fusiliers; 20th Lancashire Fusiliers; 23rd Manchester
105th Brigade: 15th Cheshire; 16th Cheshire; 14th Glosters; 15th Sherwood Foresters
106th Brigade: 17th Royal Scots; 17th West Yorks; 19th Durham Light Infantry; 18th Highland Light Infantry
Pioneers: 19th Northumberland Fusiliers

36th (ULSTER) DIVISION – New Army
GOC: Maj.Gen.O.S.W.Nugent
107th Brigade: 8th Royal Irish Rifles; 9th Royal Irish Rifles; 10th Royal Irish Rifles; 15th Royal Irish Rifles
108th Brigade: 11th Royal Irish Rifles; 12th Royal Irish Rifles; 13th Royal Irish Rifles; 9th Royal Irish Rifles
109th Brigade: 9th Royal Inniskilling Fusiliers; 10th Royal Inniskilling Fusiliers; 11th Royal Inniskilling Fusiliers; 14th Royal Irish Fusiliers
Pioneers: 16th Royal Irish Rifles

| 33rd Division | 34th Division | 35th Division (White on red) | 36th Division (Red on white) | 37th Division (Yellow motif) |

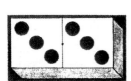

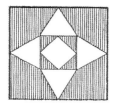

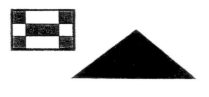

24th Division (Red & white)	25th Division (Red & white)	29th Division (Red)	30th Division	31st Division (Red & white)	32nd Division (Red motif)

37th DIVISION – New Army

GOC: Maj.Gen.Count Gleichen

110th Brigade: 6th Leicester; 7th Leicester; 8th Leicester; 9th Leicester

111th Brigade: 10th Royal Fusiliers; 13th Royal Fusiliers; 13th King's Royal Rifle Corps; 13th Rifle Brigade

112th Brigade: 11th Royal Warwick; 6th Bedford; 8th East Lancs; 10th Loyal North Lancs

Pioneers: 9th North Staffs

38th (WELSH) DIVISION – New Army

GOC: Maj.Gen.C.G.Blackader

113th Brigade: 13th Royal Welsh Fusiliers; 14th Royal Welsh Fusiliers; 15th Royal Welsh Fusiliers; 16th Royal Welsh Fusiliers

114th Brigade: 10th Welsh; 13th Welsh; 14th Welsh; 15th Welsh

115th Brigade: 10th South Wales Borderers; 11th South Wales Borderers; 17th Royal Welsh Fusiliers; 16th Welsh

Pioneers: 19th Welsh

39th DIVISION – New Army and Territorials

GOC: Maj.Gen.G.J.Cuthbert

116th Brigade: 11th Royal Sussex; 12th Royal Sussex; 13th Royal Sussex; 14th Hampshire

117th Brigade: 16th Sherwood Foresters; 17th Sherwood Foresters; 17th King's Royal Rifle Corps; 16th Rifle Brigade

118th Brigade: 1st/6th Cheshire; 1st/1st Cambridge; 1st/1st Herts; 4th/5th Black Watch

Pioneers: 13th Glosters

41st DIVISION – New Army

GOC: Maj.Gen.S.T.B.Lawford

122nd Brigade: 12th East Surrey; 15th Hampshire; 11th Royal West Kent; 19th King's Royal Rifle Corps

123rd Brigade: 11th Queen's; 10th Royal West Kent; 23rd Middlesex; 20th Durham Light Infantry

124th Brigade: 10th Queen's; 26th Royal Fusiliers; 32nd Royal Fusiliers; 21st King's Royal Rifle Corps

Pioneers: 19th Middlesex

46th (NORTH MIDLAND) DIVISION – Territorial Force

GOC: Maj.Gen.W.Thwaites

137th Brigade: 1st/5th South Staffs; 1st/6th South Staffs; 1st/5th North Staffs; 1/6th North Staffs

138th Brigade: 1st/4th Lincoln; 1st/5th Lincoln; 1st/4th Leicester; 1st/5th Leicester

139th Brigade: 1st/5th Sherwood Foresters; 1st/6th Sherwood Foresters; 1st/7th Sherwood Foresters: 1st/8th Sherwood Foresters

Pioneers: 1st Monmouth

47th (2nd LONDON) DIVISION – Territorial Force

GOC: Maj.Gen.C.StL.Barter

140th Brigade: 1st/6th London (City of London); 1st/7th London (City of London); 1st/8th London (Post Office Rifles); 1st/15th London (Civil Service Rifles)

141st Brigade: 1st/17th London (Poplar and Stepney Rifles); 1st/18th London (London Irish Rifles); 1st/19th London (St Pancras); 1st/20th London (Blackheath and Woolwich)

142nd Brigade: 1st/21st London (First Surrey Rifles); 1st/22nd London (The Queen's); 1st/23rd London; 1st/24th London (The Queen's)

Pioneers: 1/4th Royal Welsh Fusiliers

48th (SOUTH MIDLAND) DIVISION – Territorial Force

GOC: Maj.Gen.R.Fanshawe

143rd Brigade: 1st/5th Royal Warwick; 1st/6th Royal Warwick; 1st/7th Royal Warwick; 1st/8th Royal Warwick

144th Brigade: 1st/4th Glosters; 1st/6th Glosters; 1st/7th Worcester; 1st/8th Worcester

145th Brigade: 1st/5th Glosters; 1st/4th Oxford & Buckingham Light Infantry; 1st/1st Bucks; 1st/4th Royal Berks

Pioneers: 1st/5th Royal Sussex

49th (WEST RIDING) DIVISION – Territorial Force

GOC: Maj.Gen.E.M.Perceval

146th Brigade: 1st/5th West Yorks; 1st/6th West Yorks; 1st/7th West Yorks; 1st/8th West Yorks

147th Brigade: 1st/4th Duke of Wellington's; 1st/5th Duke of Wellington's; 1st/6th Duke of Wellington's; 1st/7th Duke of Wellington's

148th Brigade: 1st/4th King's Own Yorkshire Light Infantry; 1st/5th King's Own Yorkshire Light Infantry; 1st/4th York & Lancs; 1st/5th York & Lancs

Pioneers: 3rd Monmouth

50th (NORTHUMBERLAND) DIVISION – Territorial Force

GOC: Maj.Gen.P.S.Wilkinson

149th Brigade: 1st/4th Northumberland Fusiliers; 1st/5th Northumberland Fusiliers; 1st/6th Northumberland Fusiliers; 1st/7th Northumberland Fusiliers

150th Brigade: 1st/4th East Yorks; 1st/4th Green Howards; 1st/5th Green Howards; 1st/5th Durham Light Infantry

151st Brigade: 1st/5th Border Regiment; 1st/6th Durham Light Infantry; 1st/8th Durham Light Infantry; 1st/9th Durham Light Infantry

Pioneers: 1st/7th Durham Light Infantry

51st (HIGHLAND) DIVISION – Territorial Force

GOC: Maj.Gen.G.M.Harper

152nd Brigade: 1st/5th Seaforth; 1st/6th Seaforth; 1st/6th Gordons; 1st/8th Argyll & Sutherland Highlanders

153rd Brigade: 1st/6th Black Watch; 1st/7th Black Watch; 1st/5th Gordons; 1st/7th Gordons

154th Brigade: 1st/9th Royal Scots; 1st/4th Seaforths; 1st/4th Gordons; 1st/7th Argyll & Sutherland Highlanders

Pioneers: 1st/8th Royal Scots

38th Division (Red motif)	39th Division (Blue & white)	41st Division (White bar, various colours)	46th Division (Red over green)	47th Division

| 48th Division | 49th Division | 50th Division (Red motif) | 51st Division | 55th Division (Red rose) |

55th (WEST LANCASHIRE) DIVISION – Territorial Force

GOC: Maj.Gen.H.S.Jeudwine
164th Brigade: 1st/4th King's Own; 1st/8th King's; 2nd/5th Lancashire Fusiliers; 1st/4th Loyal North Lancs
165th Brigade: 1st/5th King's; 1st/6th King's; 1st/7th King's; 1st/9th King's
166th Brigade: 1st/5th King's Own; 1st/10th King's; 1st/5th South Lancs; 1st/5th Loyal North Lancs
Pioneers: 1st/4th South Lancs

56th (1st LONDON) DIVISION – Territorial Force

GOC: Maj.Gen.C.P.A.Hull
167th Brigade: 1st/1st London (RF); 1st/3rd London (RF); 1st/7th Middlesex; 1st/8th Middlesex
168th Brigade: 1st/4th London (RF); 1st/12th London (Rangers); 1st/13th London (Kensington); 1st/14th London (London Scottish)
169th Brigade: 1st/2nd London (RF); 1st/5th London (LRB); 1st/9th London (QVR); 1st/16th London (QWR)
Pioneers: 1st/5th Cheshire

63rd (ROYAL NAVAL) DIVISION

GOC: Maj.Gen.A.Paris
188th Brigade: Anson Bn; Howe Bn; 1st Royal Marine Bn; 2nd Royal Marine Bn.
189th Brigade: Hood Bn; Nelson Bn; Hawke Bn; Drake Bn
190th Brigade: 1st HAC; 7th Royal Fusiliers; 4th Bedford; 10th Royal Dublin Fusiliers
Pioneers: 14th Worcester

1st AUSTRALIAN DIVISION

1st (NSW) Brigade: 1st Bn; 2nd Bn; 3rd Bn; 4th Bn
2nd (Victoria) Brigade: 5th Bn; 6th Bn; 7th Bn; 8th Bn
3rd Brigade: 9th (Queensland) Bn; 10th (S.Austr.) Bn; 11th (W.Austr.) Bn; 12th (S.& W.Austr.,Tasmania) Bn
Pioneers: 1st Australian Pioneer Bn

2nd AUSTRALIAN DIVISION

5th (NSW) Brigade: 17th Bn; 18th Bn; 19th Bn; 20th Bn
5th (Victoria) Brigade: 21st Bn; 22nd Bn; 23rd Bn; 24th Bn
7th Brigade: 25th (Queensland) Bn; 26th (Queensland, Tasmania) Bn; 27th (S.Austr.) Bn; 28th (W.Austr.) Bn
Pioneers: 2nd Australian Pioneer Bn

4th AUSTRALIAN DIVISION

4th Brigade: 13th (NSW) Bn; 14th (Victoria) Bn; 15th (Queensland, Tasmania) Bn; 16th (S.& W.Austr.) Bn
12th Brigade: 45th (NSW) Bn; 46th (Victoria) Bn; 47th (Queensland, Tasmania) Bn; 48th (S.& W.Austr.) Bn
13th Brigade: 49th (Queensland) Bn; 50th (S.Austr.) Bn; 51st (W.Austr.) Bn; 52nd (S.& W.Austr., Tasmania) Bn
Pioneers: 4th Australian Pioneer Bn

5th AUSTRALIAN DIVISION

5th Brigade: 29th (Victoria) Bn; 30th (NSW) Bn; 31st (Queensland, Victoria) Bn; 32nd (S.& W.Austr.) Bn
14th (NSW) Brigade: 53rd Bn; 54th Bn; 55th Bn; 56th Bn
15th (Victoria) Brigade: 57th Bn; 58th Bn; 59th Bn; 60th Bn
Pioneers: 5th Australian Pioneer Bn

1st CANADIAN DIVISION

1st Brigade: 1st (Ontario) Bn; 2nd (E.Ontario) Bn; 3rd Bn (Toronto Regt); 4th Bn
2nd Brigade: 5th (Western Cav.) Bn; 7th Bn (1st BC); 8th Bn (90th Rifles); 10th Bn
3rd Brigade: 13th Bn (R.Highlanders); 14th Bn (R.Montreal Regt); 15th Bn (48th Highlanders); 16th Bn (Canadian Scottish)
Pioneers: 1st Canadian Pioneer Bn

2nd CANADIAN DIVISION

4th Brigade: 18th (W.Ontario) Bn; 19th (Cent.Ontario) Bn; 20th (Cent.Ontario) Bn; 21st (E.Ontario) Bn
5th Brigade: 22nd (Canadien Francais) Bn; 24th Bn (Victoria Rifles); 25th Bn (Nova Scotia Rifles); 26th (New Brunswick) Bn
6th Brigade: 27th (City of Winnipeg) Bn; 28th (North-West) Bn; 29th (Vancouver) Bn; 31st (Alberta) Bn
Pioneers: 2nd Canadian Pioneer Bn

3rd CANADIAN DIVISION

7th Brigade: PPCLI; R.Cdn.Regt; 42nd Bn (R.Highlanders); 49th (Edmonton) Bn
8th Brigade: 1st Cdn.MR; 2nd Cdn.MR; 4th Cdn.MR; 5th Cdn.MR
9th Brigade: 43rd Bn (Cameron Highlanders); 52nd (New Ontario) Bn; 58th Bn; 60th Bn (Victoria Rifles)
Pioneers: 3rd Canadian Pioneer Bn

4th CANADIAN DIVISION

10th Brigade: 44th Bn; 46th (S.Saskatchewan) Bn; 47th (BC) Bn; 50th (Calgary) Bn
11th Brigade: 54th (Kootenay) Bn; 75th (Missisauga) Bn; 87th Bn (Canadian Grenadier Guards); 102nd Bn
12th Brigade: 38th (Ottawa) Bn; 72nd Bn (Seaforth Highlanders); 73rd Bn (R. Highlanders); 78th Bn (Winnipeg Grenadiers)
Pioneers: 67th Canadian Pioneer Bn

NEW ZEALAND DIVISION

1st NZ Brigade: 1st Auckland; 1st Canterbury; 1st Otago; 1st Wellington
2nd NZ Brigade: 2nd Auckland; 2nd Canterbury; 2nd Otago; 2nd Wellington
3rd NZ Brigade: 1st NZRB; 2nd NZRB; 3rd NZRB; 4th NZRB
Pioneers: NZ Pioneer Bn

| 56th Division | 63rd Division (Red motif) | Australian Divisions (appropriate numeral) | 1-4 Canadian Divs. (red, blue, black, green) | NZ Division |

APPENDIX THREE
German Infantry present on the Somme, 1916

3rd GUARD DIVISION: Guard Fusiliers; Lehr Regiment; Grenadier Regt No 9

4th GUARD DIVISION: 5th Foot Guards; 5th Guard Grenadiers; Reserve Regiment No 93

5th DIVISION: Grenadier Regts Nos 8, 12; Regt No 52

6th DIVISION: Regts Nos 20, 24, 64

7th DIVISION: Regts Nos 26, 27, 165

8th DIVISION: Regts Nos 72, 93, 153

12th DIVISION: Regts Nos 23, 62, 63

16th DIVISION: Regts Nos 28, 29, 68, 69

24th DIVISION: Regts Nos 133, 139, 179

26th DIVISION: Grenadier Regt No 119; Regts Nos 121, 125

27th DIVISION: Regt No 120; Grenadier Regt No 123; Regts Nos 124, 127

38th DIVISION: Regts Nos 94, 95, 96

40th DIVISION: Regts Nos 104, 134, 181

52nd DIVISION: Regts Nos 66, 161, 170

56th DIVISION: Fusilier Regt No 35; Regts Nos 88, 118

58th DIVISION: Regts Nos 106, 107; Reserve Regt No 120

111th DIVISION: Fusilier Regt No 73; Regts Nos 76, 164

117th DIVISION: Regt No 157; Reserve Regts No 11, 22

183rd DIVISION: Regts Nos 183, 184; Reserve Regt No 122

185th DIVISION: Regts Nos 185, 186, 190

208th DIVISION: Regts Nos 25, 185; Reserve Regt No 65

222nd DIVISION: Regts Nos 193, 397; Reserve Regt No 81

223rd DIVISION: Regts Nos 144, 173; Ersatz Regt No 29

1st GUARDS RESERVE DIVISION: Guard Reserve Regts Nos 1, 2; Reserve Regt No 64

2nd RESERVE DIVISION: Reserve Regts Nos 15, 55, 77, 91

7th RESERVE DIVISION: Reserve Regts Nos 36, 66, 72

12th RESERVE DIVISION: Reserve Regts Nos 23, 38, 51

17th RESERVE DIVISION: Regts Nos 162, 163; Reserve Regts Nos 75, 76

18TH RESERVE DIVISION: Reserve Regts Nos 31, 84, 86

19th RESERVE DIVISION: Reserve Regts Nos 73, 78, 79, 92

23rd RESERVE DIVISION: Reserve Grenadier Regt No 101; Reserve Regts Nos 101, 102; Regt No 392

24th RESERVE DIVISION: Reserve Regts Nos 101, 107, 133

26th RESERVE DIVISION: Reserve Regts Nos 99, 119, 121; Regt No 180

28th RESERVE DIVISION: Reserve Regts Nos 109, 110, 111

45th RESERVE DIVISION: Reserve Regts Nos 210, 211, 212

50th RESERVE DIVISION: Reserve Regts Nos 229, 230, 231

51st RESERVE DIVISION: Reserve Regts Nos 233, 234, 235, 236

52nd RESERVE DIVISION: Reserve Regts Nos 238, 239, 240

4th ERSATZ DIVISION: Regts Nos 359, 360, 361, 362

5th ERSATZ DIVISION: Landwehr Regts Nos 73, 74; Reserve Ersatz Regt No 3

2nd BAVARIAN DIVISION: Bavarian Regts Nos 12, 15, 20

3rd BAVARIAN DIVISION: Bavarian Regts Nos 17, 18, 23

4th BAVARIAN DIVISION: Bavarian Regts Nos 5, 9; Bavarian Reserve Regt No 5

5th BAVARIAN DIVISION: Bavarian Regts Nos 7, 14, 19, 21

6th BAVARIAN DIVISION: Bavarian Regts Nos 6, 10, 11, 13

10th BAVARIAN DIVISION: Bavarian Regt No 16; Bavarian Reserve Regts Nos 6, 8

6th BAVARIAN RESERVE DIVISION: Bavarian Reserve Regts Nos 16*, 17, 20, 21

BAVARIAN ERSATZ DIVISION: Bavarian Reserve Regts Nos 14, 15; Ersatz Regt No 28

89th RESERVE BRIGADE: Reserve Regts Nos 209, 213

MARINE BRIGADE: Marine Regts Nos 1, 2 3

(*In which Adolf Hitler served as a runner.)

APPENDIX FOUR
British Artillery Weapons

Equipment	Calibre	Weight	Max Range
13pdr RHA	3 inch 76mm	0.34 ton 345kg	5900 yds 5395 mtrs
18pdr Field 1	3.3 inch 84mm	0.44 ton 447kg	6525 yds 5966 mtrs
18pdr Field 4	3.3 inch 84mm	0.42 ton 427kg	9300 yds 8504 mtrs
4.5in How	4.5 inch 114mm	0.42 ton 426kg	7300 yds 6675 mtrs
60pdr Mk 1	5 inch 127mm	2 ton 2032kg	12300 yds 11247 mtrs
6in 26cwt How	6 inch 152mm	1.25 ton 1270kg	11400 yds 10424 mtrs
8in How Mks 1-5	8 inch 203mm	5.3 ton 5384kg	10500 yds 9601 mtrs
9.2in How Mk 1	9.2 inch 233mm	3 ton 3048kg	10060 yds 9198 mtrs
12in How 1	12 inch 305mm	8.8 ton 8940kg	11132 yds 10179 mtrs
12in Gun 9	12 inch 305mm	50 ton 50800kg	32700 yds 29895 mtrs
15in How	15 inch 381mm	10.7 ton 10871kg	10795 yds 9871 mtrs

British Artillery Ammunition

Equipment	Weight	Type	Weight of filling (No.of balls in shell/no.to 1lb. weight)	Fuse
13pdr Field	12.5lbs 5.67kg	Shrapnel	(234/41)	Time
18pdr Field	18.5lbs 8.39kg	Shrapnel	(375/41)	Time
18pdr Field	18.5lbs 8.39kg	HE	13oz 368g	100
4.5in How	35lbs 15.87kg	HE	4lbs 10oz 2.09kg	100

Gun	Weight	Type	Charge	
60pdr Gun	60lbs 27.2kg	Shrapnel	(990/35)	Time
6in 26cwt BL How	100lbs 45.4kg	Shrapnel	(905/27)	Time
8in BL Mk 1-5 How	200lbs 90.7kg	HE	20lbs 9.07kg	100
9.2in BL Mk I Siege How	290lbs 131kg	HE	34lbs 15.4kg	100
12in BL Mk I Railway How	750lbs 340kg	HE	83lbs 3oz 37.67kg	100
12in BL Mk9 Railway Gun	850lbs 385kg	HE	94lbs 42.58kg	100
15in BL Seige How	1400lbs 635kg	HE	200lbs 90.94kg	100

SELECT BIBLIOGRAPHY

Principal works consulted in the preparation of this book were:

Atkinson, C.T., *The Seventh Division 1914-18* (John Murray, 1927)

Atteridge, A.H., *History of the 17th (Northern) Division* (Robt.Maclehose & Co, 1929)

Bean, C.E.W., *Official History of Australia in the War of 1914-1918* (Angus & Robertson Ltd, Sydney, 1923)

Bewster, Maj.F.W., *The History of the 51st (Highland) Division 1914-1918* (Blackwood & Son, 1921)

Bidwell, Shelford, *Gunners at War* (Arms & Armour Press, 1970)

Bidwell, Shelford & Graham, Dominick, *Fire-Power* (George Allen & Unwin, 1982)

Boraston, Lt.Col.J.H., & Bax, Capt.C.E.O., *The Eighth Division in the War 1914-1918* (Medici Society Ltd, 1926)

Buchan, J., *The South African Forces in France* (Maskew & Millar, 1921)

Carrington, Charles E., *Soldier from the Wars Returning* (Hutchinson, 1965)

Coop, Rev.J.O., *The Story of the 55th (W.Lancs) Division* (Daily Post Printers, Liverpool, 1919)

Coppard, George, *With a Machine Gun to Cambrai* (HMSO, 1969)

Dawson, H.H., *History of the 35th Division in the Great War* (Sifton Pread Ltd, 1926)

Dudley Ward, Maj.D.H., *The 56th Division – 1st London Territorial Division* (John Murray, 1921)

Dunn, J.C., *The War the Infantry Knew* (1938; Janes, 1987)

"Edmonds, Charles" (Charles E.Carrington), *A Subaltern's War* (Davies, 1929)

Edmonds, Brig.Sir James E., *Official History of the Great War* (Reprint, Shearer Publications, 1986)

Ewing, J., *The History of the Ninth (Scottish) Division* (John Murray, 1921)

Falls, C., *The History of the 36th (Ulster) Division* (McCaw Stevenson & Orr, Belfast, 1922)

Frey, J.W., & McMillan, T., *The Complete History of the Royal Naval Division* (Privately published, Alnwick, 1919)

Gillon, Capt.Stair, *The Story of the 29th Division* (Thomas Nelson & Sons Ltd, 1925)

Graves, Robert, *Goodbye to All That* (Jonathan Cape, 1929)

Haythornthwaite, Philip J., *The World War One Source Book* (Arms & Armour Press, 1992)

Hogg, I.V., & Thurston, L.F., *British Artillery Weapons & Ammunitions 1914-1918* (Ian Allan Ltd, 1972)

Hutchinson, Lt.Col.G.S., *The 33rd Division in France and Flanders 1915-1919* (Vacher & Son, 1921)

Hutchinson, Lt.Col.G., *Machine Guns, their History and Tactical Employment* (McMillan, 1938)

Hussey, Brig.Gen.A.H., & Inman, Maj.D.S., *The Fifth Division in the Great War* (Nisbet & Co, 1921)

Inglefield, Capt.V.E., *The History of the 20th (Light) Division* (Nisbet & Co, 1921)

Kincaid-Smith, Lt.Col.M., *The 25th Division in France and Flanders* (Harrison & Son, 1918)

Kitchen, Martin, *A Military History of Germany* (Weidenfeld & Nicolson, 1975)

Marden, Maj.Gen.T.O., *A Short History of the Sixth Division 1914-1919* (Hugh Rees Ltd, 1920)

Maude, A.H. ed., *With the 47th London Division 1914-1919* (Amalgamated Press, 1922)

McNish, Robin, *Iron Division: The History of the Third Division* (Ian Allan, 1978)

"Men of the 37th Div. BEF", *The Golden Horseshoe: The Journal of the 37th* (Cassell & Co, 1919)

Miles, Capt.Wilfred, *History of the Grest War, 1916* (Reprint, The Imperial War Museum in association with The Battery Press, 1992)

Mumby, Lt.Col.J.E., *History of the 38th (Welsh) Division* (Hugh Rees, 1920)

Nichols, Capt.G.H.F., *The 18th Division in the Great War* (William Blackwood, 1922)

Nicholson, Col.G.W.L.,CD, *Canadian Expeditionary Force 1914-1919* (Queen's Printer, Ottawa, 1962)

Priestley, R.E., *Breaking the Hindenburg Line: The Story of the 46th (North Midland) Division* (Fisher Unwin, 1919)

Richards, Frank, *Old Soldiers Never Die* (1933; Phillip Austen, 1994)

Sandlands, Lt.Col.H.R., *The 23rd Division 1914-1919* (Wm Blackwood & Son, 1925)

Sassoon, Siegfried, *Diaries 1915-1918* (Faber & Faber, 1983)

Sassoon, Siegfried, *Memoirs of an Infantry Officer* (1930; Faber & Faber, 1965)

Scott, Sir A.B., & Brunwell, P.M. ed., *History of the 12th (Eastern) Division in the Great War* (Nisbet & Co, 1923)

Shakespear, Lt.Col.J., *The 34th Division 1915-1919* (Witherby, 1921)

Shephard, E. ed.Bruce Rossor, *A Sergeant-Major's War* (Crowood, 1987)

Simkins, Peter, *Kitchener's Army* (Manchester University Press, 1988)

Stern, Sir A.G., *Tanks 1914-1918: The Log-book of a Pioneer* (Hodder & Stoughton, 192?)

Stewart, Col.H., *The New Zealand Division 1916-1919* (1921)

Stewart, Lt.Col.J., & Buchan, J., *The 15th (Scottish) Division 1914-1919* (Wm Blackwood & Son, 1926)

Thornton, L.H., & Fraser, P., *The Congreves* (John Murray, 1930)

Turner, William, *Pals – The 11th (Service) Battalion (Accrington), East Lancashire Regiment* (Wharncliffe Publishing Ltd)

Wade, A., *The War of the Guns: The Western Front 1917-1918* (Batsford, 1936)

Wyrall, E., *The History of the Second Division 1914-1918* (Thomas Nelson & Sons Ltd, 1921-22)

Wyrall, E., *The History of the 19th Division 1914-1918* (Edward Arnold & Humphries & Co, 1932)

Wyrall, E., *The History of the 50th Division* (Percy Lund, Humphries & Co, 1939)